The Hiker's Guide
to *Montana's*
CONTINENTAL
DIVIDE TRAIL

Tad Brooks
and
Sherry Jones

FALCON PRESS

ACKNOWLEGMENTS

Our thanks to Jackie Baran, Alicia Delashmutt and Rich Robeson, Dave, Dawn and Pat Maki, Ralph, three Blackfeet from Two Medicine, Al and his dog Bird, Quinn Jacobsen and his two sheepdogs, the future doctor from Duke and his two biker pals, the bow hunter from Salmon, Idaho, the Seattle couple with the VW Microbus, George Ochenski and his snow lion, Gordon Gray and Chuck Neal of the Helena National Forest, Jack Potter of Glacier National Park, the Bear Management staff at Yellowstone National Park and Kraft Deluxe Macaroni and Cheese.

Recreation Guides from Falcon Press

The Angler's Guide to Montana
The Hiker's Guide to Colorado
The Beartooth Fishing Guide
The Hiker's Guide to Idaho
The Floater's Guide to Colorado
The Hiker's Guide to Montana
The Floater's Guide to Montana
The Hiker's Guide to Utah
The Hiker's Guide to Arizona
The Hiker's Guide to Washington
The Hiker's Guide to California
The Hunter's Guide to Montana
The Rockhound's Guide to Montana
The Hiker's Guide to Montana's Continental Divide Trail
The Hiker's Guide to Hot Springs in the Pacific Northwest

Falcon Press is continually expanding its list of recreational guidebooks using the same general format as this book. All books include detailed descriptions, accurate maps, and all information necessary for enjoyable trips. You can order extra copies of this book and get information and prices for the books listed above by writing Falcon Press, P.O. Box 1718, Helena, MT 59624. Also, please ask for a free copy of our current catalog listing all Falcon Press books.

Cover photo by Mike Sample, of Warren Peak, from Continental Divide Trail in Anaconda-Pintler Wilderness.
Book photos by Tad Brooks.

Library of Congress Catalog Card Number 90-080039

ISBN 0-937959-95-2

CONTENTS

FOREWORD

The Continental Divide National Scenic Trail follows the Rocky Mountains from Canada to Mexico.

Congress recognized the 3,100-mile trail in 1968 as part of the National Scenic Trails Act. Only that portion in Montana and parts of Idaho has been completed, signed and dedicated. It is an accomplishment we in the Forest Service's Northern Region take great pride in.

Montana's portion of the Continental Divide Trail travels through an inspiring landscape: glacier-scoured valleys; high mountain meadows; clear, alpine lakes; and vast forests with a wide variety of wildlife. The 961-mile trail links seven of the Northern Region's National Forests. Only a small portion of the trail is outside these National Forests. The trail takes you through four wildernesses within these National Forests.

Your National Forests are many things to many people: timber for the logger; forage for the rancher and cattleman; minerals for the miner; water for industry, agriculture, and for domestic use; game and fish for the hunter and angler; and America's playgrounds, providing outdoor recreation ranging from scenic drives to mountain climbing.

The National Forests of the Northern Region are serving growing numbers as the nation's population and it interest in outdoor recreation grow. In 1989, recreationists spent 13.3 million visitor days in the Northern Region's 13 National Forests in Montana, northern Idaho and portions of the Dakotas.

The Forest Service is dedicated to balanced management. This scenic trail is another step in providing a variety of quality outdoor recreational experiences for National Forest visitors.

Tad Brooks and Sherry Jones, authors of the *Hiker's Guide to Montana's Continental Divide Trail*, hiked the 961 mile trail during the summer of 1989. This comprehensive guide is a product of that hike. You will find this readable guide—with photos, maps and elevation graphs—helpful in planning and enjoying your travel along the Continental Divide Trail. If you have questions, contact our people at our Forest Service Ranger Stations or National Forest headquarters near the Continental Divide.

Welcome to the Northern Rockies and the Continental Divide Trail. Enjoy your travel along the backbone of America.

John W. Mumma
Regional Forester, Northern Region
USDA Forest Service
Missoula, Montana

ON BEARS, BLIZZARDS AND BACTERIA

Words of experience for the backcountry traveler

Its imposing sheer cliffs, glacier-carved peaks, timbered ridges and rolling hills make the Contintental Divide as diverse as the people who travel it. Some on foot, others on horseback or all-terrain vehicle and, in the winter, skiers and snowmobilers, all see the nation's backbone in a different way.

For a few each summer the divide, extending from Glacier National Park through Yellowstone National Park, is a challenge to be met, a dragon to be slain, a 961-mile obstacle course that provides the ultimate test to man's (and woman's) endurance and ingenuity. Others see it in a more friendly light, familiarizing themselves slowly with the stunning vistas along the Chinese Wall, alpine lakes and streams in the high peaks above the Big Hole Valley, and the wildlife and wildflowers that lend uniqueness to each segment.

For most the divide is a source of intimidation. The fear its sometimes aloof demeanor inspires is healthy, for those who venture recklessly into its bosom may emerge shattered. But with the right amount of preparation and planning, anyone can walk or ride any portion of the Continental Divide National Scenic Trail in Montana, Idaho and northern Wyoming—and have fun while doing it!

The key word is "preparation". You cannot be too prepared for the Continental Divide. The more you know about what you'll see, the more you'll enjoy the sights. The more you learn about first aid, outdoor survival, orienteering and grizzly bears, the better you'll be able to deal with adversity if it comes along.

On top of the world, often far away from civilization, you live by your wits. And Mother Nature has enough tricks up her sleeve to drive even the most experienced backcountry traveler to wits' end at times.

History

Congress officially recognized the need for the Continental Divide National Scenic Trail when it passed the National Trails System Act of 1968.

It mandated a study of a proposed 3,100-mile-long path that eventually will wind along the nation's spine from Canada to Mexico. Montana and Idaho were the first states to locate and declare an official route, and other states soon are expected to follow.

While 57 miles of trail had yet to be built, Montana and Idaho officials dedicated their trail on June 21, 1989, at a ceremony at Chief Joseph Pass.

The route follows existing trails through some of the best of the last remaining wilderness in the lower 48 states, a trek from Glacier to Yellowstone National Park that by our measurements tallies 961 miles.

Official alternate routes, described in this guide, skirt those sections where final trail construction is incomplete.

Some of the most splendid hikes are within the 10 national forests the trail traverses—wildlands that include the Bob Marshall and Anaconda-Pintler

The authors at hike's start. All photos, unless otherwise noted, are by Tad Brooks.

wildernesses, as well as proposed wilderness areas in the Italian Peaks, West Big Hole and Nevada-Black Mountain regions.

More than 90 percent of the trail is within five miles of the divide, and much of it is on the crest itself. The trail is almost entirely on public property, and the farthest it wanders from the divide is eight miles. Some 160 miles of the route is along roads.

An official route had yet to be declared for Yellowstone National Park when we hiked in 1989, but we followed the trail that at the time was being considered the preferred route for the National Scenic Trail.

Weather

Snowstorms in mid-July? Not unheard of up here, where some snowbanks never melt and mild temperatures prevail. Warm clothes are a must any time of year, for even at the lowest spots on the divide the mercury can drop to below freezing at night.

Weather is the single greatest factor that will determine where you can hike and when. Parts of the trail where elevation is highest often are snow-packed and impassable until early July. Snow comes early in the Rockies, with some parts of the trail possibly becoming blanketed by mid-October.

Hiking the entire trail in one season requires a lot of planning and a little help from Mother Nature. Travelers may choose to divide the trail into

Be prepared for all forms of precipitation. Summertime clouds like these piling up over the divide near Red Ridge (right) and Pyramid Peak (center) in the Helena National Forest can drop gentle rain or golf ball-size hail.

Bears, be they black, like the one in the photo, or grizzly, don't like surprises. Make enough noise on the trail to let the bruins know you're coming. We saw four bears on our hike: two black and two griz. Chris Cauble photo.

segments and hike lower elevations starting in June, then take to higher altitudes as the snowline recedes.

Rain is more likely than snow, though. Mid-afternoon thunderstorms are a given during late spring and early summer and often bring hail. Good rain gear is a must, especially on longer trips. Wrapping clothes bags, tent, sleeping bags and air mattresses in plastic garbage bags helps keep them dry in the most violent downpours.

These mountains make their own weather, and the wise hiker will prepare for the worst of everything, even if it means carrying a little extra weight.

Glacier Park gets much snow, and more than 100 inches of rain per year in some places. By contrast, the high valleys of the Beaverhead Mountains are very dry and finding drinking water is more of a problem than rain.

Low lying clouds, though, are one of the biggest frustrations. When they roll in to rest on the mountaintops, they can stay there for hours, or days, obstructing scenic vistas and, more important, views of landmarks needed for trail-finding.

We learned early not to try and hike blindly through the mist, after veering off the divide and onto a spur ridge and winding up about 15 miles off the trail. From then on, one of our mottos was, "When the clouds are low, we don't go."

We recommend that you don't, either. Snuggle up in that sleeping bag and go back to sleep until the clouds part.

Water

Once was a time, not too long ago, when mountain streams were considered synonymous with purity. Giardia has changed all that.

The microscopic cyst is spreading so rapidly that, theoretically, at least, no water anywhere is guaranteed safe to drink.

Fish, birds, and mammals—notably beavers and muskrats and the omnipresent steer—all carry the giardiasis parasite. Most suffer no adverse effects from its presence in their intestinal tracts. For humans, though, ingesting the cysts can bring illness that is certainly miserable and potentially chronic.

Giardia symptoms include abdominal bloating, cramping, flatulence and diarrhea, all happening seven to 10 days after exposure. Nausea, vomiting, loss of appetite, headaches and a low-grade fever also may occur.

Symptoms can last seven to 12 days and may relapse, although the body usually eradicates the cyst eventually. Doctors can prescribe medicine that will give quick, permanent relief.

When you're in the middle of the woods, though, chances are a doctor isn't close at hand. Avoid giardia altogether by treating every drop of water before drinking it.

Several water treatment methods are available. The simplest and least expensive, but most fuel-intensive, is boiling. Differing opinions place the minimum time water should be boiled at anywhere from one to 10 minutes.

Purification tablets sold in sporting goods stores kill giardia when dissolved in water, but many people dislike the off-taste they impart.

We prefer a water filter. Sold for about $50, these gizmos are light, durable, very effective and easy to use. A hand-held pump simply sucks water in through a plastic tube and pushes it through the filter. Even lake water, when filtered this way, emerges clear and clean of all offending bacteria.

No one really knows how giardia got into the woods, but it is known to be easily transmitted. We humans can do our part to keep it in check by digging holes for our body waste at least six inches down, away from streams and lakes and above the water table, then covering the evidence thoroughly and firmly. Don't take the chance of animals coming in contact with your germs, or of a big storm washing them into the nearest stream.

While water quality is a big concern in the backcountry, so is water quantity. In the late spring and early summer, heavy runoff can make stream fording tricky if not downright dangerous. Check ahead with rangers to be sure streams are low enough for safe crossing and that high mountain passes aren't blocked with snow.

On the other end of the spectrum, dry stretches along the trail can leave the traveler without fresh water for many rigorous miles. To avoid having to wander off-trail in search of liquid replenishment, carry an extra water bottle or two through dry areas. You'll need it not only for drinking, but for cooking and first-aid, too.

Maps

Maps and a compass are a must, but what kind of map you need depends upon where you are.

The trails in Glacier and Yellowstone national parks are well-traveled and marked. You don't need to buy USGS quadrangle maps to complete these hikes, although the added detail is nice for learning the nuances of the terrain.

Water, even when it comes from remote alpine lakes, should be considered contaminated. Hikers who don't boil or filter drinking water run the risk of contracting Giardia, an illness that is certainly miserable and potentially chronic. Pitamakin Lake in Glacier National Park.

The same holds true for the Bob Marshall and Anaconda-Pintler wildernesses. Forest Service maps of these areas serve as adequate guides.

But USGS maps are a must for most other sections of the trail, particularly those with cross-country hikes. While the Continental Divide National Scenic Trail mostly follows existing paths, the way is not always well marked.

Bears

Encountering bears is a possibility almost anywhere along the trail. Grizzlies make their homes in the north and south parts of the state, in Glacier and Yellowstone parks, and the nearby Bob Marshall and Scapegoat wildernesses, as well as in the Henrys Lake and Centennial mountains.

The omnivorous, enormous grizzly doesn't like to be surprised, and if suddenly met on the trail may become aggressive. This is doubly true if you're standing between a sow and her cubs. And if you haven't packed your food wisely, the bear may mistake you for its next meal.

Taking the necessary precautions can greatly lessen your chances of coming face-to-face with a bear of any kind. Making lots of noise while hiking lets the bear know you're coming. The human voice carries so well the bear usually has time to disappear before you arrive.

Keeping a clean camp and hanging the food bag from a high tree at night are good ways to avoid confrontations. Never keep food inside the tent. Cook well away from where you intend to sleep, and change from the clothes that you cooked in before bedding down.

Carrying freeze-dried foods that are sealed air-tight also will help keep you free of enticing food odors.

Rangers in the national parks and national forests are wise to the ways of the bear and can give valuable information on how to avoid them—as well as what to do if you can't.

Other animals

Ground squirrels are the most common critter seen on the northern section of the hike. Deer are everywhere: whitetail, whose tail looks as if it has been dipped in white paint, and mule deer, with the large ears that gave the species its name.

Elk, resembling deer but darker-colored and much larger and more muscular, also are abundant, especially in the Anaconda-Pintler Wilderness, the Southern Bitterroots and the Beaverhead Range. Social creatures, elk usually are seen in groups; during the "rut," late summer to early fall, their high-pitched "bugling" sounds across the hills as the bulls challenge prospective rivals.

Agile mountain goats with their white shaggy coats may be seen on the high cliffs of Glacier and the Bob. Normally shy, the goats are more bold in Glacier Park where, presumably, they are used to seeing humans. Sure-footed and graceful, these creatures nevertheless suffer many falls which often are fatal. Harsh winters also take their toll, killing up to 50 percent of yearling kids annually. Mountain goats usually are seen alone or in small family groups.

Also preferring the high country is the bighorn sheep, most likely to be seen in the Beaverhead Mountains. Both males and females have horns. Rams' horns are much larger, however—up to 30 percent of their body weight—and curl around their ears somewhat like the hair of the Swiss Miss girl. Think about it.

Found in the lowlands is the moose, a large, homely-faced mammal who frequents marshy areas and shallow ponds. While neither gender is friendly, the female is said to be more belligerent toward humans. The big animals occasionally roam to high mountain valleys, especially in the Centennial and Henrys Lake mountains.

Antelope are lords of the sagebrush flats along the southern part of the hike between Bannock Pass and Red Rock Pass in the Beaverhead and Centennial mountains. Porcupines also are common on the trail, with their coats of sharp quills, as are squirrels, whose chirps warn others of your approach; tiny chipmunks, with a stripe down their backs; little, short-tailed pikas, and fat, salt-crazed marmots, who will nibble holes in your gear as fast as you turn away from it.

Mountain lions, foxes, wolverines, weasels and wolves also make their home on the Continental Divide but are elusive enough usually to avoid being seen. Coyotes are a rare sight, too, but their poignant howls can be heard echoing through the evening air.

A myriad of birds also is encountered, from dainty hummingbirds to dumbfounded spruce grouse to flashy pileated woodpeckers to golden eagles.

Special Rules for National Parks

While travelers in Montana's national forests generally are free to camp and build fires anywhere they please, national parks have their own, more restrictive, backcountry rules.

Because national parks draw visitors from all over the world, they must regulate the amount of use campsites get—and forbid fires in the most fragile areas. Both Yellowstone and Glacier park rangers allocate campsite permits on a first-come, first-served basis to a limited number of people. Camping is forbidden anywhere but at these designated sites.

There is a special campsite in Glacier Park for the exclusive use of people hiking the divide from north to south in a continuous trip.

Park rangers also could bar you from traveling certain segments of trail where bear activity is high. Designated alternate routes have been selected in Yellowstone National Park specifically to accommodate the bruins' behavior.

In national parks, unlike in national forests, the carrying of firearms is illegal.

How We Did It

People who learn we hiked the Continental Divide Scenic Trail often are more interested in how we did it than what we saw. Having met several hikers on the trail who were walking from Canada to Mexico or vice versa, hiking Montana seems less impressive to us; especially since, having the whole summer to do it, we could take our time.

Well, sort of. Because we decided to walk the trail in late May and needed to begin in mid-June, we had less than a month to get ready for the trip-physically, technologically, mentally, and gastronomically. We were in marginal shape those first days. Sore feet, tired hearts, stiff muscles all seemed to conspire to keep us going at a slug's pace. After a week or two, though, we toughened up and started making tracks.

Food was a sore point too. Getting creative and drying our own was out of the question in such a short time, so we opted for instant oatmeal, trail mix and assorted dried pasta and rice dishes. We also took multi-vitamins every day. At first it was difficult getting used to eating food in quantities much smaller than the heaping platefuls we normally stuff ourselves with. Once again though, our bodies adjusted.

Sometimes we gave in to the temptation to under-do it, packing less food than we should have for the sake of light packs. We suffered for that error too. After constant thoughts and dreams of food, one of us became ill on the trail and had to go home to recuperate. The moral of this tale: Don't skimp on nourishment.

Since we live in Montana, it was fairly easy to resupply. We just hopped in the car at the end of each segment and drove to a grocery store. We also cheated and went home between hikes, or checked into a motel for the night. Wimpy, to be sure, but those hot showers and cheeseburgers sure were a treat. Just thinking about getting clean and fed motivated us to walk a little faster near the end of each segment.

Having only one car posed some problems for us, but thanks to our good, good friends in Helena, we were able to arrange car shuttles. Wanting and needing the flexibility to finish each segment in more or less time than planned, we had friends follow us to the end of the upcoming hike. There we'd drop off our car and hop in with our companion who would drive us to the trailhead. When we came out, the Subaru would be waiting to whisk us to civilization.

Our leisurely pace came to a halt for two weeks while we welcomed friends and relatives to our wedding. Hitting the trail again after all that revelry and relaxation was almost as difficult as starting up the first time.

We walked the trail through October, finishing just in time to beat Old Man Winter. The final weeks were worrisome, though. Getting stuck in the middle of nowhere in the snow, unable to see the trail, was a real possibility to the end. That's why we always let friends know where we were hiking and approximately when we'd finish each segment.

We plan to do many things differently next time around. We'll have better raingear. We'll dehydrate our own food, for variety's sake. We'll start preparing physically long before we set foot on the trail. And, hopefully, we can do it over the course of several summers so we don't have to quit our jobs.

The key phrase here is "next time." Yes, we plan to do it again. And again. Hiking across Montana was the most exhilirating experience of our lives, and it made us certain that this is where, in all the world, we want to live as long as we live.

MAP LEGEND

Continental Divide Scenic Trail and Trailhead		Interstate	**00**
Continental Divide		U.S. Highway	(00)
Trail when it follows the road		State or Other Principal Road	(000)
Trail when it follows the Continental Divide		Forest Road	0000
		Paved Road	
Trail when it follows the road and the Continental Divide		Dirt Road	
Alternate Trail		STATE BOUNDARY	
Peak	Camp site △	Directional arrow	
Pass or Saddle	Building ■	and scale	0 1.75 3.5
Ranger Station	Viewpoint ⊗		Miles

GLACIER
NATIONAL
PARK

Continental Divide
Scenic Trail

Kalispell O

O Great Falls

M O N T A

O Missoula

O Helena

Butte O

O Bozeman

O Wisdom

YELLOWST(
NATIONAL
PARK

I D A H O

W Y O M I N G

GLACIER NATIONAL PARK

Waterton to Swiftcurrent — 38 miles

Introduction: Like gems in the rough, the ice-capped peaks of Glacier National Park are a jumble of knife-sharp edges and points and glimmering hollows where remnants of the glaciers that scoured the landscape blink white, or, where they've melted down to alpine lakes, reflect a deep, timeless blue.

Difficult though it may be to imagine today, Glacier Park once was a flat sea bottom, later a desert, then still later the foundation for great expanses of grinding ice that filed the mountains and valleys with their shifting, groaning weight, carrying water and earth and rock with them across the face of the Earth.

Evidence of the past is everywhere in Glacier Park: In the colorful, striated cliffs showing layers of history as tell-tale as the rings of a tree; in the waters made murky by glacial till, sediment created by glacier activity; and, in high valleys such as Fifty Mountain, in the boulders as big as houses sitting in the middle of rolling, grassy meadows, moved by glaciers and dropped there in the melting about 10,000 years ago.

Some of the loveliest views from a campsite are at Fifty Mountain, a lush green carpet strewn with fragrant flowers and wrapped in a snow-capped panorama of mountain peaks. The nearby Sue Lake Overlook and the Highline Trail leading south from the campground continue the show of splendor, taking the traveler high above timberline for unforgettable, far-reaching vistas.

The hike's first portion, although not as spectacular, has its charm. Occasional glimpses of nine-mile-long Waterton Lake treat the traveler headed south along its western shore, as do views of the high, rugged mountains looming over it. Especially impressive is Mount Cleveland, tallest in the park, whose 5,500-foot vertical rise on the north is the highest in the U.S.

Worth visiting are the pretty Kootenai lakes, whose shallow waters and fertile bottom make them a popular feeding place for moose. We counted five during our overnight stay there.

Side trips abound on the stretch: a short jaunt to Ahern Pass off the Highline Trail finds a bird's-eye view of the lovely Belly River Valley; a visit to the Granite Park Chalets could reward with bear sightings via a Park ranger's telescope; a steep climb to the top of Swiftcurrent Mountain inspires with loveliness as far as the eye can see.

Difficulty level: Moderate, with two crossings of the Continental Divide between long, level stretches.

Scenery: Excellent, of vast seas of summits and lovely alpine lakes from the Highline Trail and Swiftcurrent Pass.

Water availability: Excellent.

Maps: USFS—U.S. Park Service Glacier National Park map. USGS (7.5 minute series)—Porcupine Ridge, Mount Geduhn, Ahern Pass, Many Glacier.

Supply points: Granite Park Chalets, at about 30 miles, sells soup, sandwiches

Waterton to Swiftcurrent

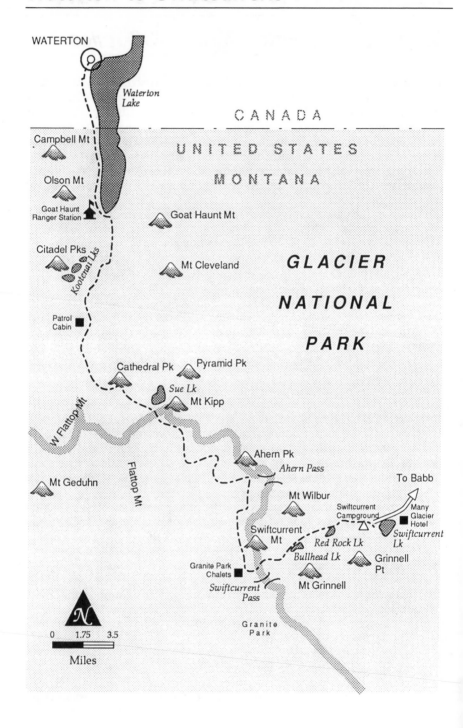

WATERTON

Waterton Lake

C A N A D A

U N I T E D   S T A T E S

M O N T A N A

Campbell Mt

Olson Mt

Goat Haunt
Ranger Station

Goat Haunt Mt

Citadel Pks

Kootenai Lks

Mt Cleveland

GLACIER

NATIONAL

PARK

Patrol
Cabin

Cathedral Pk

Pyramid Pk

Sue Lk

Mt Kipp

W Flattop Mt

Flattop Mt

Ahern Pk

Ahern Pass

To Babb

Mt Geduhn

Mt Wilbur

Swiftcurrent
Campground

Many
Glacier
Hotel

Swiftcurrent
Mt

Red Rock Lk

Bullhead Lk

Swiftcurrent Lk

Grinnell
Pt

Granite Park
Chalets

Swiftcurrent Pass

Mt Grinnell

Granite
Park

0   1.75   3.5

Miles

and the like from 11 a.m. to 5 p.m. Swiftcurrent Inn, at hike's end, has a cafe and motel.

Finding the trailhead: The trailhead is on the west edge of the town of Waterton, Canada, at Cameron Falls Bridge. Or, hikers wanting a fast and easy start can take a one-way boat ride across the lake to the Goat Haunt campsite and ranger station (which doubles as a customs inspection station) on the lake's south tip. Buy a ticket at the boat dock on the lake's north end.

Trail description: Follow the signed trail south from the bridge, walking at first on road and then on a path, toward the International Boundary. The trail skirts Waterton Lake along its west shore, mostly ascending to cross several creeks along the way, and at 4.2 miles, the wide swath cut across the continent at the U.S.-Canada border. Camping is allowed here, with a permit.

From here the trail is mostly forested and offers few views of the lake. At the lake's south tip, at 7.7 miles, the trail swings east to the Goat Haunt campsite and ranger station, 8.7 miles.

Follow the wide, well-maintained trail toward Kootenai Lake, passing a horse corral with, of course, a basketball hoop. The level path enters lush forest, but majestic peaks still are visible. In the southwest rise the Citadel Peaks, a series of high-spired summits (formerly called 'Sawtooths' because of their jagged tops) peaking at 7,750 feet. Mount Cleveland, at 10,466 feet— the highest peak in the Park—looms on the southeast.

Cross several small creeks on footbridges, still remaining level, to an intersection with the Kootenai Lake trail at 11.1 miles. The lake is a short distance to the right (west), and offers some fine campsites.

Continue on the main trail, a gentle, rolling path through thick forest, to the intersection with the Stoney Indian Pass Trail, coming in from the east at 13.5 miles. Continue south, soon crossing Pass Creek on a bridge. A log patrol cabin lies just to the west.

Now begins a long ascent, at first along the fast Waterton River. The white water can be seen carving a canyon through red shale below, in the shadow of 8,542-foot Kootenai Peak.

Cross a creek on a bridge at 14.4 miles, where a high waterfall comes into view in the mountains to the west. Fill water bottles here and veer away from the river, angling up a high ridge in open country. The Citadel Peaks are visible to the northwest; snow-capped Porcupine Ridge and Kootenai Peak are to the west.

After climbing about one mile, find a small waterfall spilling from the rocks and splashing across the trail. Soon another, smaller flow also emerges from the rocks.

Continue climbing, steeply at times, for an increasingly far-reaching view of surrounding peaks: to the southwest rise West Flattop Mountain, 7,702-foot Trapper Peak and Nahsukin Mountain, 8,194 feet, overlooking Nahsukin Lake at the head of the Waterton River. Soon distant Mount Geduhn, 8,375 feet, rears its snowy head, also to the southwest. And high above, just to the west, tower the high stone cliffs of Cathedral Peak, 9,041 feet.

The vista reaches its climax after a climb up a grassy hill at 18.8 miles and,

Waterton to Swiftcurrent
Elevation Chart

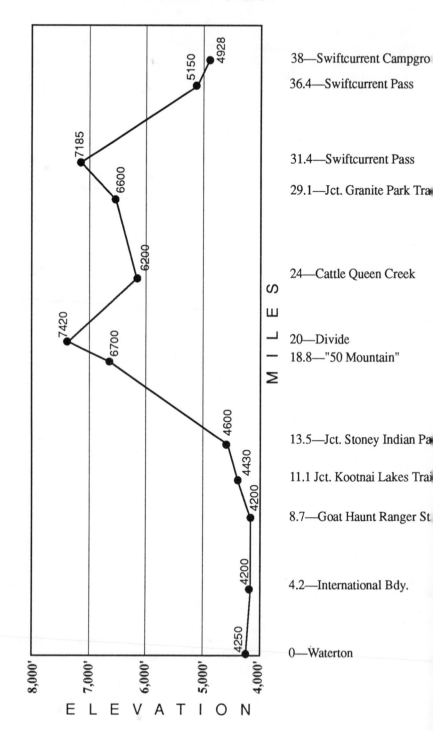

38—Swiftcurrent Campgro

36.4—Swiftcurrent Pass

31.4—Swiftcurrent Pass

29.1—Jct. Granite Park Tra

24—Cattle Queen Creek

20—Divide
18.8—"50 Mountain"

13.5—Jct. Stoney Indian Pa

11.1 Jct. Kootnai Lakes Trai

8.7—Goat Haunt Ranger St

4.2—International Bdy.

0—Waterton

M I L E S

E L E V A T I O N

8,000' 7,000' 6,000' 5,000' 4,000'

4928
5150
7185
6600
6200
7420
6700
4600
4430
4200
4200
4250

then, a small rise in a lush alpine meadow. The panorama unveils snow-topped peaks, rugged, rocky cliffs and distant, purple ranges. (See view map) With this array of summits in view, it's easy to see why the name Fifty Mountain graces this area.

Drop a bit now, into a rolling meadow with streams and ponds and vibrant green grass that is dotted with large boulders dropped by the glaciers that carved this area millions of years ago. The brilliant medley of colors shower the eyes with beauty: snow-capped peaks ahead, dark pines in the foreground, orange, green and gray talus spilling from the base of the cliffs to the east and, underfoot, a bounty of yellow alpine buttercups and bright pink Indian paintbrush.

From here Mount Geduhn dominates the view to the southwest and Heavens Peak, 8,987 feet, stands out on the south.

Continue southeast past the Fifty Mountain campground, 19 miles, where snow is as likely in mid-July as at any other time of the year. Cross another flower-filled meadow and begin climbing, switchbacking up the side of Cathedral Peak to cross the Continental Divide for the first time, at 20 miles.

Just before the notch that marks the divide, a trail strikes off to the west to continue up Cathedral Peak to the Sue Lake Overlook. The side trip is well worth taking as it offers splendid views of the surrounding countryside and the Sue Lake basin, a pristine alpine cirque harboring a deep blue lake and several glaciers. Mountain goats likely will be your neighbors here.

The next 10 miles provide breathtaking views of the Continental Divide and outlying peaks. Heavens Peak still dominates but has a close rival in 8,952-foot Mount Cannon, another pyramidal summit farther to the left, etched with a crazy-quilt pattern of snow.

This section of trail, fittingly named the Highline Trail, wanders through open country most of the way, with occasional forays downward into forest. Water is abundant and so are flowers, including yellow daisies, Indian paintbrush and fluffy beargrass covering the hills like a plantation of cotton.

After crossing Cattle Queen Creek, at 24 miles, the trail climbs above treeline again. Iceberg Peak is directly ahead to the east; Iceberg Notch is on its left and farther left is Ahern Pass, 7,100 feet, all on the Continental Divide.

At 26.4 miles the grassy banks of Ahern Creek make a fine picnic spot. It's also the last available water for a while.

Another beautiful side trip follows the trail here to Ahern Pass, .3 mile away. From the pass the Belly River valley comes into view, with Elizabeth and Helen lakes glimmering far below and Ahern Glacier slashing the rocks to the north with white.

From Ahern Creek the main trail gradually climbs several miles more, contouring along the Continental Divide mostly above treeline. At 29.1 miles round Swiftcurrent Mountain, 8,436 feet, and intersect with a side path that leads to the Granite Park campground.

Continue south toward the Granite Park Chalet, built in the early 1900s as part of a $1.5 million tourism promotion project by the Great Northern Railroad Co. The charming chalets are privately operated now, and reservations are necessary for lodging and meals. Sandwiches and other concessions are available from 11 a.m. - 5 p.m. however.

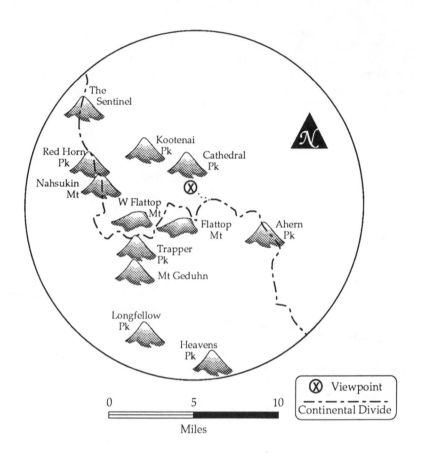

Waterton to Swiftcurrent View Map

Views from the Fifty Mountain area in Glacier National Park: To the southwest, the Livingston Range, including West Flattop Mountain, 7,702-foot Trapper Peak and 8,194-foot Nahsukin Mountain, overlooking Nahsukin Lake at the head of the Waterton River. Distant Mount Geduhn (not shown), 8,375 feet, rears its snowy head also to the southwest. High above, just to the north, tower the high stone cliffs of Cathedral Peak, 9,041 feet. To the south Heavens Peak, 8,987 feet, dominates the view with its pyramidical, snow-streaked summit. A multitude of purple peaks and snow-drizzled mountains extend for many miles, hence the name "Fifty Mountain."

Cathedral Peak rises sharply above its skirt of scree in the Fifty Mountain region of Glacier National Park. The high alpine meadow at its base offers stunning panoramic views of more than fifty mountains and is home to marmots and grizzly bears.

At the chalets ask the ranger, a bear specialist, for a view through the telescope into Bear Valley, a forested bowl at the base of the divide that is roadless and trailless and home to a number of grizzly and black bears.

The main trail turns left (east) from the junction with the chalet's cutoff trail and climbs gradually for .9 mile through rocky alpine terrain and past a smattering of glaciers and snowfields to Swiftcurrent Pass, on the Continental Divide, at 31.4 miles. Swiftcurrent Mountain juts upward to the west as you ascend; look on your way for the 1.2-mile trail to its top and the Swiftcurrent Lookout, 8,436 feet. The views from the lookout are said to be spectacular. Water is not available at the top, though.

Nice vistas also are enjoyed from the pass at 7,298 feet: To the northeast 9,321-foot Mount Wilbur looks over Swiftcurrent Mountain's shoulder and, farther back, is pointed Mount Henkel, 8,770 feet; Mount Grinnell, 8,851 feet, is to the southeast with Grinnell Point at its head. Swiftcurrent Glacier carves its white niche in the rocky slopes to the east.

Glaciers abound at the pass, where fragile grasses and stunted pines spring bravely from the chalky soil. Water is available in the headwaters of Swiftcurrent Creek, here but a trickle flowing beneath Swiftcurrent Mountain.

During the sometimes steep descent along switchbacks, the lakes of the Swiftcurrent Valley pop one by one into view: Windmaker Lake, nearest the

Mountain goats make their sure-footed way to lofty perches high on the divide above the Sue Lake Overlook, a must-see side trip in northern Glacier National Park.

base; then Bullhead, Redrock, Fishercap and Swiftcurrent lakes. Water flows across the trail in several places as the trail swings around the head of the Swiftcurrent Creek canyon. Waterfalls streaming down the cliffs create echoes with their liquid whispers.

After losing nearly 2,000 feet in just three miles, the trail levels somewhat to follow Swiftcurrent Creek past its chain of pretty lakes and waterfalls. At 36.4 miles, hiking mostly in buggy forest, skirt around Redrocks Lake to view Fishercap Lake to the east and the sprawling Many Glacier Hotel complex.

Reenter forest, first of aspen and then pine, and pass a hiker's registration box. Cross a footbridge at 38 miles, pass the Swiftcurrent Campground and enter the parking lot of the Swiftcurrent Inn, a motel and cafe.

A bull moose munches aquatic plants in shallow Kootenai Lake in Glacier National Park. The big animals, normally shy of humans, appear acclimated to hikers at this popular camping spot.

The Rocky Mountains in the United States loom high above Canada's Waterton Lake as the trail begins its 961-mile-long course in Glacier National Park. A tour boat offers better views than the wooded lakeshore trail and drops hikers at the Goat Haunt Ranger Station on the international border.

Swiftcurrent to Two Medicine Campground — 51.8 Miles

Introduction: An initially level stroll through forest along the shore of two lakes becomes an alpine experience with open rocky meadows, glaciers and stunning views along the climb and descent.

Piegan Pass, the gap between 9,190-foot Pollock Mountain, on the Continental Divide to the west, and Cataract Mountain, rising on the east, is the climax of the trip's early portion both in elevation and scenic beauty. The mountains at the pass frame a window with a southward view of Piegan Mountain, awesome Jackson Glacier, 10,104-foot Mount Siyeh and numerous other peaks. Northbound, views open up of the Bishops Cap Glacier, 8,851-foot Mount Grinnell, Mount Gould and the Angel Wing.

Approaching and then leaving St. Mary Lake the trail winds mostly through forest, with glimpses of waterfalls and brilliantly hued lakes keeping things interesting.

From Red Eagle Lake, a favored camping spot, the hike becomes more strenuous, gaining 2,000 feet in the last three miles before crossing Triple Divide Pass, where the hiker will want to pause for more breathtaking views. Another descent into the Cut Bank Creek basin takes the hiker past more waterfalls and lakes before rising again steeply to Pitamakin Pass, the last in the trio. The climb is well worth the effort: an overlook here provides the most spectacular panorama of the entire Glacier Park section.

The name "Pitamakin" comes from a female Blackfeet warrior who wore male dress and led raids in the Flathead country. She also reportedly was a great horse thief, who claimed she'd only marry the man who could steal more horses in a night than she. She died, husbandless, in 1850.

Hike's end is at the Two Medicine Lakes, once the location of two sacred Indian medicine lodges. Boat rides are scheduled daily on the lake, in conjunction with guided walks to nearby Upper Two Medicine Lake.

Difficulty level: Moderate to Red Eagle Lake, with gradual climbs and easy descents; then more difficult to cross two steeper mountain passes.
Scenery: Excellent, with many waterfalls and splendid vistas from Piegan, Triple Divide and Pitamakin passes.
Water availability: Excellent.
Maps: U.S. Park Service—Glacier National Park map. USGS (7.5 minute series)—Many Glacier, Logan Pass, Rising Sun, Mount Stimson, Cut Bank Pass, Squaw Mountain.
Supply Points: Two Medicine Campground, at the end of the hike, contains a store, cafe, restrooms, water, phone and full-service campground.

Finding the trailhead: The trailhead is in a picnic area just east of the Many Glacier Ranger Station, on the south side of Glacier Route 3.

Trail description: Strike out to the south, on the west side of Swiftcurrent Lake, and soon find a sign pointing the way to Lake Josephine (.6 mile).

Cross Swiftcurrent Creek on a wide bridge. At .2 mile emerald-green Swiftcurrent Lake comes into view, adorned on its far shore by unnamed peaks and cliffs. Grinnell Point looms over the trail on the northwest. The point and several other park features immortalize the name of George Bird Grinnell, an early naturalist and writer who proved pivotal in winning the area's designation as a national park.

At an intersection with a paved segment of trail, bear east, staying on the dirt path. Pass a sign pointing to the Many Glacier Hotel and picnic area, both nearby. Continue through cool forest along the south shore of the lake, catching glimpses of the water through the trees.

At .8 mile cross the head of Swiftcurrent Lake and continue to an intersection. Take the right (southwest) path along the southeast shore of Stump Lake and Lake Josephine.

Continue straight at the next intersection, passing a registration box marking the Lake Josephine trailhead.

At the next intersection a sign points the way east to the Piegan Pass Trail, .6 mile. The official trail continues southwest along the lake to join the Piegan

Swiftcurrent to Triple Divide Pass

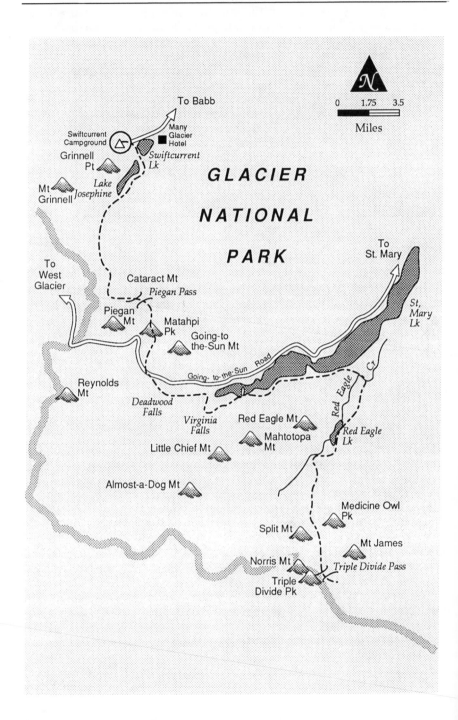

Triple Divide Pass to Two Medicine Campground

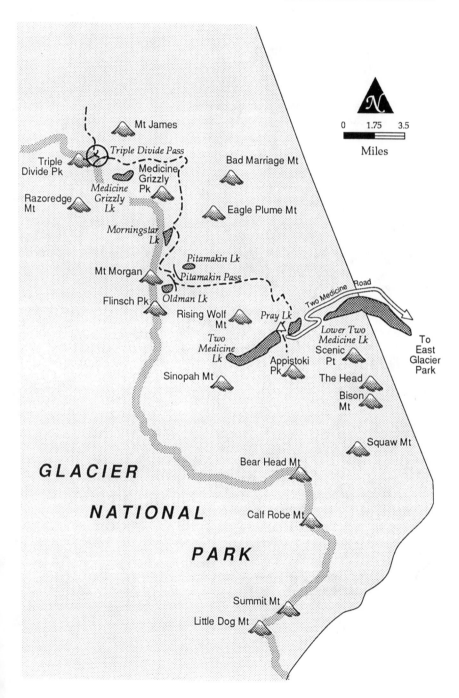

Mt James
Triple Divide Pass
Triple Divide Pk
Medicine Grizzly Pk
Medicine Grizzly Lk
Razoredge Mt
Bad Marriage Mt
Eagle Plume Mt
Morningstar Lk
Pitamakin Lk
Mt Morgan
Pitamakin Pass
Flinsch Pk
Oldman Lk
Rising Wolf Mt
Pray Lk
Two Medicine Lk
Lower Two Medicine Lk
Scenic Pt
Appistoki Pk
Sinopah Mt
The Head
Bison Mt
Squaw Mt
Bear Head Mt
Calf Robe Mt
Summit Mt
Little Dog Mt
Two Medicine Road
To East Glacier Park

GLACIER

NATIONAL

PARK

0   1.75   3.5
Miles

Virginia Falls, one of many waterfalls along the trail in Glacier National Park, is a series of cascades. Its waters flow into St. Mary Lake.

Pass route later; however, heavy use of this trail by horses may make detouring now a good idea.

Continuing on the official route, reach another intersection at 2.4 miles. The right, or west, path leads to the log-and-stone Oastler Shelter, pit toilets and a boat dock on Lake Josephine. Across the lake, the glacier and falls augment the beauty of the mountain whose name they share, Grinnell, 8,851 feet high.

The left (east) trail leads in .3 mile to the Piegan Pass Trail, where another path joins from the right (north). Ascend through forest along a route overgrown with weeds and wildflowers. At about 2.8 miles pass a yellow marker on a tree, then a wooden, arrow-shaped sign with a large "6" and a small "o," also fastened high to a tree.

Climb gently and emerge from the trees to gain views of the Garden Wall, a ridge on the Continental Divide that includes Grinnell Glacier and Angel Wing, whose bare summit does fan out like a wing.

Cross a series of small creeks as you walk through a lovely large meadow whose west edge is lined with peaks and cliffs: Mount Gould, whose summit is fluted like the pipes of a majestic organ; Pollack Mountain, 9,190 feet, cradling Bishops Cap Glacier. Cataract Mountain is ahead and to the east; Piegan Pass is just on its left.

Enter forest again for a brief time, following signs through an intersection to Morning Eagle Falls, 1.2 miles, and Piegan Pass, 4.4 miles.

Bend along the edge of Cataract Creek, a good water source, then cross the creek on a log bridge. Climb to see Morning Eagle Falls cascading gracefully from a high ledge that is hundreds of feet high, and cross the creek on a bridge again near the falls' base, at 4.4 miles.

The trail switchbacks up alongside the falls on open slopes with good views through stunted trees of the Bishops Cap, from here an immense glacier with deep, translucent crevasses.

Cross a clear-running tributary of Cataract Creek and climb beneath pyramid-shaped Cataract Mountain, crossing the creek again and passing a small waterfall to enter a delicate alpine meadow. The trail disappears momentarily in the grass, but stone markers denote the way.

Switchback again across the scree base of Cataract Mountain to Piegan Pass, at 9.1 miles. Views here from 7,045 feet are splendid on both sides of the pass and include 10,104-foot Mount Siyeh to the northeast and (left to right) Matahapi Peak, 9,365 feet, and Going-to-the-Sun Mountain, 9,642 feet. Piegan Mountain is on the right, or south, of the pass.

The trail contours above timberline at the base of Cataract Mountain, heading gradually downward on a wide path. Resist the urge to descend too quickly here—this is bear country, and surprising a grizzly or black bear could be unlucky.

On the descent more distant peaks of Glacier Park cut the sky with their sharp-edged summits, and far-off Jackson Glacier provides a stunning study in white. Piegan Glacier paints its own white streak through an amphitheater near Piegan Mountain's summit, and Piegan Falls cuts a silver swath down the mountain's south side.

Wildflowers bloom promiscuously on the open slopes, including Indian paintbrush, shrubby cinquefoil, bluebells, yellow daisies and beargrass.

After passing beneath the furrowed brow of Mount Siyeh, the trail at 10.1

Swiftcurrent to Two Medicine Campground
Elevation Chart

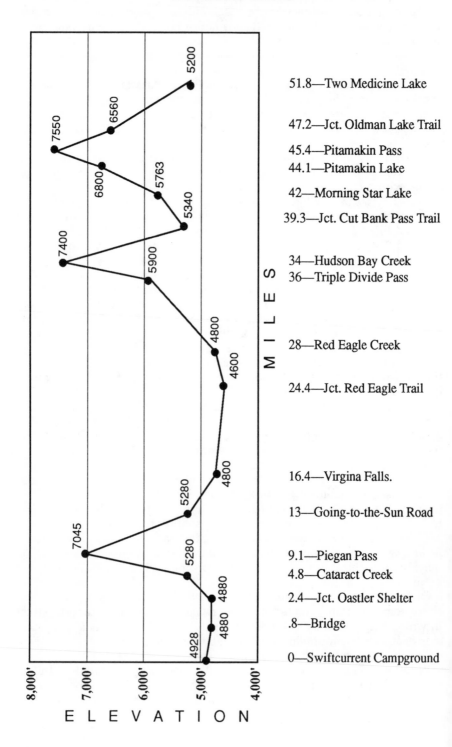

51.8—Two Medicine Lake

47.2—Jct. Oldman Lake Trail

45.4—Pitamakin Pass
44.1—Pitamakin Lake

42—Morning Star Lake

39.3—Jct. Cut Bank Pass Trail

34—Hudson Bay Creek
36—Triple Divide Pass

28—Red Eagle Creek

24.4—Jct. Red Eagle Trail

16.4—Virgina Falls.

13—Going-to-the-Sun Road

9.1—Piegan Pass
4.8—Cataract Creek

2.4—Jct. Oastler Shelter

.8—Bridge

0—Swiftcurrent Campground

miles reaches the junction with the Siyeh Pass Trail, another good side trip. Siyeh (Mad Wolf) was a Blackfeet Indian warrior who, according to lore, led an attack on a band of Kootenai Indians who were trying to cross Cut Bank Pass. The aggressive Blackfeet reportedly killed every Kootenai except one old woman.

Continue through forest toward the Gunsight Pass trailhead, your destination.

More wildflowers thrive in Preston Park, entered before crossing a fork of Siyeh Creek at 10.4 miles. Continue through forest, munching huckleberries along the way, crossing another little creek and by-passing the Siyeh Cut-Off Trail at 11.6 miles. Reach Going-to-the-Sun Road at the Gunsight Pass trailhead at 13 miles.

Blasted through mountains for more than 10 years and costing more than $3 million, the Going-to-the-Sun Road is considered one of man's greatest engineering feats. The 50-mile road was conceived and constructed under the direction of Major William R. Logan, Glacier Park's first superintendent, and was dedicated in 1933.

Because there are no campsites along the Piegan Pass segment, the Park Service has established a special camp near Deadwood Falls, 1.1 miles south

Triple Divide Peak (left) and Split Mountain (right) guard the flanks of Triple Divide Pass in Glacier National Park. Water from Triple Divide Peak drains to three oceans.

of this point, especially for those hiking the Continental Divide Trail. Ask a park ranger for more details.

Head south on the trail, following signs toward Gunsight Lake. Descend through forest about .2 mile, then continue fairly level to 14.1 miles, where lovely Deadwood Falls rushes through a red shale gorge, forming deep aquamarine pools along its course. Soon reach the junction with the Gunsight Pass Trail, which heads southwest to Gunsight Lake. Follow the northeast fork, remaining on the Piegan Pass Trail toward Red Eagle Lake, 12.7 miles away.

The trail rolls gently along Reynolds Creek to meet the St. Mary River, offering a nice look at 9,125-foot Reynolds Mountain to the west, whose slopes harbor patches of snow year-round.

At 15.4 miles the trail meets the St. Mary Lake Trail; head south, remaining on the Piegan Pass Trail toward Red Eagle Lake. Reach two-tiered St. Mary Falls on a bridge at 13.7 miles, glimpsing the deep green waters of the St. Mary River along the way. Ascend, still in forest, past several other pretty falls to high Virginia Falls, marked with a sign at 16.4 miles.

Cross Virginia Falls on a bridge and head toward Red Eagle Lake, north at first and then swinging with the trail to the southeast. Look to the north, through the trees, for views of Going-to-the-Sun Mountain, rising 9,642 feet on the opposite shore of crystalline blue St. Mary Lake.

The mostly-forested trail is overgrown on this stretch and appears to get little use.

Look for waterfalls above as you pass a couple of small creeks. At 20.8 miles, the trees give way to a nice view of the mountain trio that will dominate the scenery for the next several miles: Little Chief Mountain, 9,541 feet; broad Mahtotopa Mountain; and Red Eagle Mountain, 8,881 feet. The Big Three rise behind you, to the south.

Across the lake, to the northwest, loom the familiar pyramid of Reynolds Mountain and, from the left, Heavy Runner Mountain, 8,016 feet; Mount Oberlin, casting its shadow on Logan Pass; and Piegan Mountain.

Directly across the lake, to the north, Dead Horse Point juts out beside Going-to-the-Sun Mountain.

Reenter woods, passing a rock engraved with the words, 'Eagle Scout Trail 1930'. Soon another clearing reveals the Narrows, where rocky beaches slip into St. Mary Lake. The trail crosses talus at the foot of a rockslide, then plunges into forest again to by-pass the point and Silver Dollar Beach.

The trail turns to the east at 22.8, climbs for about one-half mile, then descends gradually for a half-mile more. It then swings to the north again to follow Red Eagle Creek, passing an old, blocked-off trail that leads to a flooded-out bridge.

Climb along the creek for about .5 mile, enjoying views to the west of the Big Three. Pass a horse ford sign and reach a signed intersection pointing the way to Red Eagle Lake.

A suspended plank bridge spans rushing Red Eagle Creek; it is safe for only one hiker at a time. On the other side head southwest, upstream on the creek's east bank, ascending slightly and then descending through forests and tall-grassed meadows. At 26 miles the trail makes a final, steeper ascent to place the glimmering Red Eagle Lake at your feet.

From the lower campground here by the lake, the twin summits of Split

Morning Eagle Falls adds to the picturesque beauty of the Piegan Pass Trail in Glacier National Park. Its clear waters are fed by the Bishops Cap Glacier nestled in a cirque on the divide.

Mountain rise to 8,792 feet on the south. Logan Glacier reflects the sun in white to the southwest, while Mount James, 9,375 feet, peeks shyly from the southeast; and Medicine Owl Peak and Kakitos Mountain, 7,841 feet, loom more closely. Red Eagle Mountain, just across the lake, commands the most attention as Mahtotopa crowds its left shoulder. Little Chief and Almost-A-Dog mountains lag behind.

The trail continues through trees along the lake's east shore, passing a campground at the head at 27 miles and immediately striking off uphill. It drops to cross Red Eagle Creek, flowing along the base of Red Eagle Mountain, by veering west at the intersection with a horse ford and taking you over another suspension bridge.

Three-quarters of a mile later cross the creek again on a log bridge with a handrail. The trail then heads west and continues ascending.

Another blocked-off trail soon joins from the right, and huckleberries may tempt you with their tart purple fruit on bushes along the way.

At about 32 miles the forest clears to present magnificent Split Mountain, a high, rugged cliff whose great cirque is host to several small glaciers; a stream tumbling over its high ledge makes a sheer drop into Hudsons Bay Creek.

Cross the creek flowing from the falls and continue through lovely country on a badly overgrown trail. Approach in open forest the cliffs of Norris Mountain, along whose base numerous waterfalls tumble and in whose crags glaciers rest. On Norris' left are Mount James and Triple Divide Peak, whence trickles of water flow indirectly into the Pacific Ocean, the Hudsons Bay and the Gulf of Mexico.

Boulder-hop across Hudsons Bay Creek at 34 miles, fill water bottles (there are no more reliable sources for miles on the other side of the pass) and enter a scene from a fairy tale: a waterfall cascades into the creek; tender green moss covers the rocks; grass and plants are the lushest hues and Indian paintbrush, daisies and other flowers, including the rare Jones columbine, add splashes of orange, yellow and pink.

Now the climb begins in earnest, crossing a small creek flowing from Triple Divide Peak as it switchbacks upward in a long trek to the pass. The hike is not overly steep but it can be tiring. One more small flow may be coming from the rocks just before the final ascent.

From the pass, at 36 miles, views are spectacular to the southeast and northeast of rugged, wind-and-ice-carved summits, bluish-white glaciers and sweet little lakes tucked in stone cirques.

Look just to the south for Razoredge Mountain, with a summit of jagged teeth; pretty, unnamed mountains rise farther east, then Medicine Grizzly Peak, with a tiny, deep blue lake at its base. Just behind Medicine Grizzly Peak, to the northeast, are Red Mountain, Eagle Plume Mountain, whose 8,724-foot-high summit can just be seen behind Medicine Grizzly Peak and Bad Marriage Mountain, a green-gray set of cliffs.

From the southwest heading northwest, the view encompasses Triple Divide Peak, Norris Mountain, Split Mountain, Almost-A-Dog, Little Chief and Mahtotopa mountains, 8,356-foot East Flattop Mountain, far beyond and, just to the northeast, Mount James.

Watch for bold, salt-hungry marmots on the pass; they work in twos and threes, diverting your attention while another gnaws on your gear.

The descent is easy along the rocky, but stable, slopes on the east side of the pass. Medicine-Grizzly Lake comes into sight below, under the smaller lake that could be seen from the pass. Keep a high eye to the hillsides on the north for bighorn sheep.

At 38.7 miles reach the intersection with the Medicine Grizzly Trail. Continue .3 mile to the Atlantic Creek campground, a good water source. The trail in this area shows lots of horse use.

In forest again and still looking for huckleberries, reach the junction at 39.3 miles with the Cut Bank Pass Trail, which also leads to Pitamakin Pass. Heading south on the trail, see Atlantic Falls shimmying down like a Slinky over a set of rock cliffs. Cross a bridge over Atlantic Creek and continue through lush forest that ends abruptly where the trail spans an open hillside; views are lovely here of surrounding peaks to the east.

At 42 miles greet Morning Star Lake, as pretty as its name but chilly, at 5,800 feet. Camping is permitted here and just over the pass at Oldman Lake.

From the lake the trail begins its uphill journey in forest, climbing rather steeply past a small waterfall, and along the North Fork of Cut Bank Creek, which cascades down a series of large red rocks. Here and there vibrant pink Indian paintbrush and fluffy beargrass bloom alongside thick blue spruces and huckleberry bushes. Asters, yellow daisies and cow parsnip add to the cornucopia of beauty.

Cross a small creek at 43.3 miles and continue climbing to see Katoya Creek below. The trail levels out in about .5 mile and passes through an open forest to Pitamakin Lake, nestled in a wall of high cliffs dotted with snow.

Cross the stream flowing from the lake's north shore and begin switchbacking, steeply at times, up the base of the Continental Divide to Pitamakin Pass, 45.4 miles, on a spur ridge leading east from the divide.

Atop the barren, windswept pass, a sign points the way west to the Pitamakin Overlook, 8,248 feet high—the highest point on the trail in Glacier Park. The short climb to the overlook is a must: it provides the most far-reaching panorama of cragged summits and timeless glaciers in the Glacier Park section of this hike. To the west rises Mt. Stimson, at 10,142 feet the park's second highest peak; just south of it, Mt. Pinchot is 9,310 feet. To the north, Mt. Siyeh peeks around the shoulder of Triple Divide Peak; Red Mountain on the northeast. Cut Bank Pass can be seen below, to the northwest, in the shadow of McClintock Peak, 9,285 feet. (See view map.)

The views from Pitamakin Pass are not bad either. Oldman Lake sends up his deep blue twinkle on the southwest; to the east, through the majestic ridges nearby, the Two Medicine Lakes and the flat plains beyond all are in sight.

Descend steeply from the pass on the bare hillside, enjoying sapphire glimpses of Oldman all the way down. At 47.2 miles a sign notes the junction with the Oldman Lake trail where, .3 mile away, water awaits in the lake.

On the main trail cross a rushing creek on a log bridge at 50.6 miles to reach a washed-out, rock-strewn area scattered with wildflowers. From here, at the junction with the Dry Fork trail, a sign points the way to the Two Medicine entrance station; take the southeast fork to the Two Medicine Campground.

A bridge crosses Dry Creek at 50.8 miles, which in the late season indeed may be dry. Descend gradually through light forest for another mile to cross a bridge at 51.8 between Two Medicine Lake, on the west, and tiny Pray Lake, on the east. The Two Medicine campground, picnic area and store/cafe all are in the vicinity.

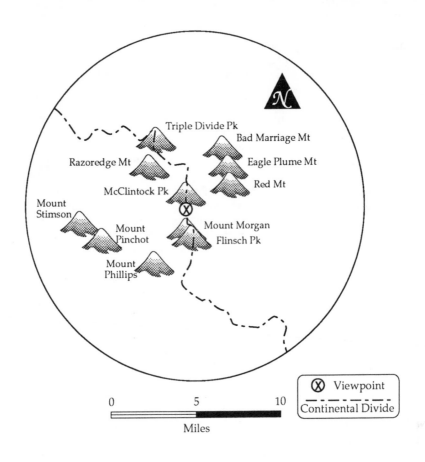

Triple Divide Pk
Bad Marriage Mt
Razoredge Mt
Eagle Plume Mt
Red Mt
McClintock Pk
Mount
Stimson
Mount
Pinchot
Mount Morgan
Flinsch Pk
Mount
Phillips

⊗ Viewpoint
— · — · — ·
Continental Divide

0   5   10

Miles

Swiftcurrent to Two Medicine Camp View Map

Views are magnificent from the Pitamakin Overlook, at 8,050 feet the highest point reached on this hike in Glacier Park: Razoredge Mountain and Triple Divide Peak rise on the northeast side of the divide, with 10,142-foot Mount Stimson, second highest in the park, to the west. Mount Pinchot is just south of Stimson, seemingly dwarfed at 9,310 feet; Mount Phillips is next in line. Just to the north towers McClintock Peak, 9,285 feet; on the south-hand side are Mount Morgan and Flinsch Peak.

A look to the east reveals a totally different picture: views include the vast plains far-off as well as (north to south) Bad Marriage Mountain, Eagle Plume Mountain and, nearby, brick-colored Red Mountain, 9,377 feet.

Two Medicine to Marias Pass — 19.7 miles

Introduction: The spectacular peaks, alpine glaciers and jewel-like lakes of earlier segments give way in this walk to gentle, lowland terrain, lush forest and along streams. The initial climb up Appistoki Peak offers beautiful views of nearby mountain ranges in Glacier Park and the Bob Marshall Wilderness. Below lie the Two Medicine lakes and the vast plains to the east past the town of East Glacier.

From here, the trail contours beneath the Continental Divide on an easy, rolling path until, on the divide, it swings southeast to Marias Pass. At 5,215 feet Marias Pass is the lowest point on the Continental Divide in the United States. Meriwether Lewis of the Lewis and Clark expedition named the pass for his cousin, Maria Wood, but locals pronounce the word "Mar-eye-as," not "Mar-ee-as."

Difficulty level: Easy, with gradual switchbacks up the face of Appistoki Peak, a fast descent to East Glacier and a flat walk to Marias Pass.
Scenery: Fair, with good views of surrounding peaks and plains from Scenic Point.
Water availability: Fair, with some creeks that may be dry.
Maps: U.S. Park Service—Glacier National Park visitors' map. USGS (7.5 minute series)—Squaw Mountain, East Glacier, Summit.
Supply Points: Two Medicine Campground, at the beginning of the hike, offers food and some groceries in a store/cafe. East Glacier, midway through the segment, is a full-service town with phones, motels, restaurants and grocery stores. A Forest Service campground is at Marias Pass, and U.S. Rt. 2 is a major highway leading to East Glacier to the east, and the town of Essex to the west.

Finding the trailhead: From the Two Medicine campground, follow the Two Medicine Road .3 mile west, where a sign on the left (south) denotes the Scenic Point trailhead. Immediately upon entering the parking area see the trail coming in from the left, where a sign for the Mount Henry Trail points the way to Appistoki Falls, .6 mile, Scenic Point, 3.1 miles and the East Glacier Ranger Station, 11.8 miles.

Trail description: The trail is wide and well-maintained as it heads into forest, following level terrain to a path to Appistoki Falls, .5 mile. A short walk off trail leads to a glittering waterfall cascading down a narrow gorge between two sheer cliffs.

From the junction the trail begins ascending, at first in forest, passing a trickle of water seeping from the mountainside at 1.5 miles. Continue uphill on long switchbacks to open terrain, where shrubby cinquefoil, asters and Indian paintbrush cling to the rocky slopes. Below, the blue waters of Two Medicine Lake and the nearby campground can be seen, and as you climb, more and more peaks jut into view.

The final switchback takes you up and across a rocky ridge, past a couple of stone cairns, and swings over to cross the saddle at 3.9 miles between

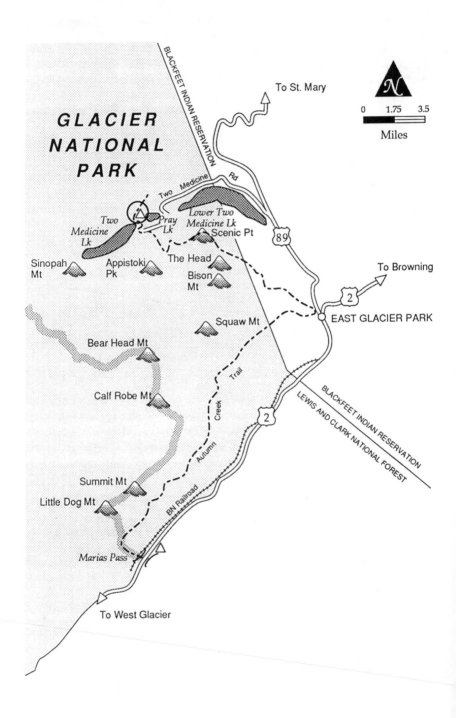

GLACIER
NATIONAL
PARK

To St. Mary

N

0   1.75   3.5

Miles

BLACKFEET INDIAN RESERVATION

Two Medicine Rd

Two Medicine Lk

Pray Lk

Lower Two Medicine Lk

Scenic Pt

89

Sinopah Mt

Appistoki Pk

The Head

Bison Mt

To Browning

2

EAST GLACIER PARK

Squaw Mt

Bear Head Mt

Trail

Calf Robe Mt

Creek

Autumn

BLACKFEET INDIAN RESERVATION

LEWIS AND CLARK NATIONAL FOREST

2

Summit Mt

Little Dog Mt

BN Railroad

Marias Pass

To West Glacier

Appistoki Peak, 8,164 feet, and Scenic Point, 7,522 feet. The view on the saddle, high above treeline, is spectacular: Mount Henry to the south, 8,847 feet, and Two Medicine Ridge; to the north, Spot Mountain, 7,831 feet; Mad Wolf Mountain beyond, 8,341 feet, and Rising Wolf Mountain, 9,513 feet, hovering on the northwest over Two Medicine Lake.

Continue east on the ridge to Scenic Point, 4.4 miles, which affords a look at East Glacier to the south, the town of Browning on the Blackfeet Indian Reservation, and to the southeast, and, farther east, the mountains of the Bob Marshall Wilderness.

Now descend steeply through bluebells and big, red-centered blanketflowers. Snowfields dot the nearby mountains year-round.

The trail becomes a narrow, rocky trench as it descends in bushes to Forty Mile Creek, at 6.2 miles, where water flows from glaciers above. The trail skirts the stream before entering a clearing where a sign names the creek; cross on a log bridge after filling water bottles.

Now begin a steep but short climb to round the Head, a high, rocky buttress that, with a little imagination, could be said to resemble a person's head. Next enter an alpine valley, then at 6.7 miles begin the long, gradual downhill journey to East Glacier. Footing can be tricky here, where the trail becomes an eroded gully overgrown at times with weeds. Asters, bluebells, wild roses and Indian paintbrush send their sweet fragrance to soothe the soul frustrated by poor trail maintenance.

At 7.3 miles cross fortyone Mile Creek, another good water source. The land is used for cattle grazing, though, so treat the water before drinking.

Soon walk through a large meadow dominated by a 5,064-foot hill to the south, and climb gradually to Bald Hill. From the hilltop see East Glacier and the green-roofed buildings of the Glacier Park Lodge.

Descend on the hillside through open woods and begin following a jeep track where it merges with the trail. Continue on the track, ignoring trails coming in from the right (south). The track becomes a road for a short time, then becomes a jeep rut again to pass a series of large beaver ponds and marshes on the right (southeast) at 9.8 miles.

Soon hear a creek running on the right, or south. At the trail junction follow the signs to the East Glacier Ranger Station; continue descending, soon on pack trail again. At the next junction take the right-hand, most heavily-traveled route, looking down at Midvale Creek spinning a silver thread along the road. Pass a picnic area to see the Glacier Park Lodge, on the northeast.

At the bottom of the descent, follow the signs to the trailhead of the Mount Henry Trail and a dirt road at 11.3. Head east on the road, following a fence. At the road junction stay to the right (south,) to meet another dirt road. A log house is on the left at this intersection.

Continue southwest on this winding road to a bridge spanning Midvale Creek. Cross the bridge and meet a fork in the road where a barn stands. Take the left (south) fork for .1 mile to a place with a trail, jeep road and tree with an orange marker, at 12.0. Follow the road, which merges with the trail, about 1,000 feet to a fork. Again bear left (west), using the orange markers as guides.

The jeep road follows gently rolling, forested terrain to pass a marshy area at 13.2 miles, where the path becomes a poorly-maintained pack trail. From here the trail heads gradually uphill along the base of the divide, crossing

Two Medicine to Marias Pass
Elevation Chart

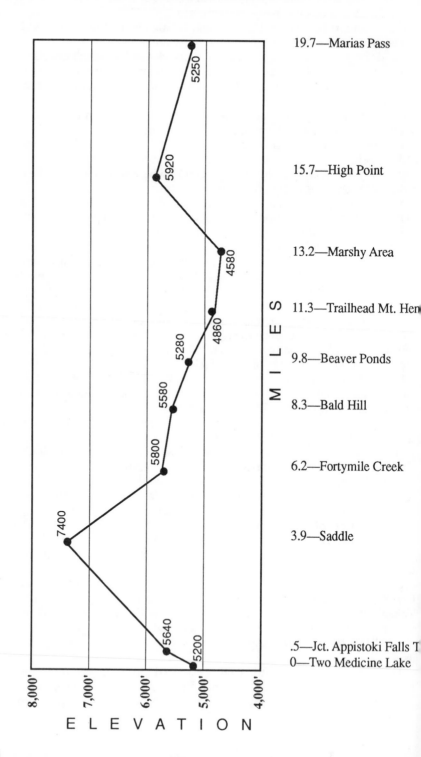

19.7—Marias Pass

5250

15.7—High Point

5920

13.2—Marshy Area

4580

11.3—Trailhead Mt. Hen

4860

9.8—Beaver Ponds

5280

8.3—Bald Hill

5580

6.2—Fortymile Creek

5800

3.9—Saddle

7400

.5—Jct. Appistoki Falls T
0—Two Medicine Lake

5640

5200

M I L E S

8,000' 7,000' 6,000' 5,000' 4,000'

E L E V A T I O N

numerous small creeks. Summit Mountain, 8,770 feet, looms on the northeast.

At 15.7 miles the trail begins a slow downhill trek, swinging to the south with the divide at 18.6 miles and passing the south end of Three Bears Lake at 19.1 miles. The trail crosses railroad tracks and ends at Marias Pass, 19.7, across U.S. Rt. 2 from the U.S. Forest Service's Summit Campground.

Giant boulders lay where melting glaciers dropped them after centuries of grinding Glacier National Park into ranges of sharp-edged summits. Heavens Peak, snow-capped year 'round, rises beyond an alpine pool near Fifty Mountain and the Continental Divide.

GLACIER
NATIONAL
PARK

Continental Divide
Scenic Trail

Kalispell O

*BOB MARSHALL
WILDERNESS*

O Great Falls

O Missoula

M O N T A N

O Helena

Butte O

O Bozeman

O Wisdom

YELLOWSTO
NATIONAL
PARK

I D A H O

W Y O M I N G

BOB MARSHALL WILDERNESS

Marias Pass to Benchmark — 97.2 miles

Introduction: Leave the grand high peaks of Glacier National Park and begin a good deal of valley travel as the trail follows stream beds to thrust and parry with the divide, crossed five times along the segment.

But the hike is not lacking in alpine splendor. Massive Goat and Big Lodge mountains are but a prelude to the sheer high cliffs near Hahn Peak, and the unforgettable vertical face of the Chinese Wall beyond.

Water and wildlife abound, and, except for a 12-mile section of yet-unconstructed trail near Marias Pass, the path is well traveled and easily followed.

There are no convenient resupply points along the 10-to-14-day trek, but hikers carrying fishing rods can augment packed-in food with native cutthroat trout that live in the larger streams and, reportedly, in glacial Lake Levale.

There is fishing in the South Fork of the Two Medicine River, Strawberry Creek, and the main tributaries feeding the South Fork of the Sun River. The best fishing is off-trail a bit in the Middle Fork of the Flathead River, a designated wild river, where Dolly Varden trout are added to the fare.

Stream-side travel is easy but occasionally mucky on trails well-trodden by pack trains, and, in the northern section, by grazing cattle. The larger streams must be forded in early season.

The trees thin and views become spectacular by mid-hike, when the trail climbs out of Open Creek to skirt the divide's sheer limestone cliffs—your backdrop for the next 15 miles.

The Lewis Overthrust—the cataclysmic force that helped form the divide in Glacier National Park—also was at work here in the Bob Marshall Wilderness, a 2,400-square-mile wonderland named after an early giant of the conservation movement.

Once above treeline the trail's occasional marshiness gives way to fragile alpine meadows, permanent snowbanks, cold clear water and jewel-like lakes.

Wildlife abounds in this section: ground squirrels and pikas squeak and scurry at your approach, marmots are non-plussed, and mountain goats are kings of the crags.

The mule deer are especially friendly at My Lake, a popular camping spot for horse parties.

Moose are less congenial. A huge bull grazing near our camp in the early morning was so startled by our presence that he crashed crazily through the trees and into frigid My Lake. Once on the opposite shore, shaking the water off his antlers, he returned our slack-jawed stares with a look of downright hostility.

Bears are common here, too. The Bob Marshall, Great Bear and Scapegoat wildernesses are home to the largest non-park population of grizzly bears in the lower 48 states.

And insects are omnipresent; bring plenty of bug repellent.

Marias Pass to Benchmark

The high country trails are easily followed, with only a few steep stretches that are mercifully short.

The walking can be difficult, however, in areas burned by the 59,850-acre Gates Park Fire, ignited by lightning on July 11, 1988 near the Gates Park Guard Station. Fire-weakened trees topple easily during storms, and deadfall will be a problem for some time to come.

A watchful eye for weather is helpful as you enter the burn: a hailstorm caught us by surprise and, with nowhere to turn for shelter, we could only pull our hoods and hope the pellets didn't get any bigger.

And the blackened, ashy layer underfoot quickly turns to slippery gumbo as hail turns to rain.

The hike's highlight comes near its end, as the trail for 5.5 miles skirts the base of the breathtaking, 13-mile-long Chinese Wall. Its towering cliffs stretch south as far as the eye can see and rise straight up a thousand feet from trailside.

Difficulty level: Easy, mostly along river drainages, with some moderate climbs to low passes on the divide.
Scenery: Excellent, highlighted by the sheer cliffs of the 13-mile Chinese Wall.
Water availability: Excellent, with numerous streams and lakes convenient to the entire length of the trail.
Maps: USFS—Lewis and Clark National Forest visitors map. USGS (7.5 minute series)—Summit, Hyde Creek, Crescent Cliff, Morningstar Mt., Gooseberry Park, Pentagon Mt., Porphyry Reef, Three Sisters, Gates Park, Slategoat Mt., Amphitheater Mt., Prairie Reef, Pretty Prairie, Benchmark.
Supply Points: There are no convenient resupply points between Marias Pass and Benchmark. For supplies at hike's end, mail and food packages may be sent to the Benchmark Wilderness Ranch (406-562-3336), or Ford Creek Ranch (406-562-3672) guest ranches, where lodging is available. Phone to make arrangements ahead of time.

Finding the trailhead: Marias Pass is 10.75 miles south of East Glacier on U.S. Rt. 2.

Trail description: This section contains 12 miles of trail near Glacier National Park that are scheduled to be built from south to north along the divide in the next two years at an estimated cost of $260,000.

One segment will carry an existing trail from Elkcalf Mountain southward over Running Crane Mountain before dropping along Lee Creek near Bullshoe Mountain to join already-built Trail 103, the North Badger Creek Trail.

The other is a .6-mile-long path just south of U.S. Route 2 that will connect the Forest Service campground at Marias Pass with the Pike Creek Road and remove hikers from the busy highway's shoulder.

In the interim, hikers must follow an alternate route to reach the divide's lofty heights and the Bob Marshall Wilderness.

The official alternate route is in poor condition and hasn't been maintained in years. But there are two other paths hikers can follow with confidence to regain the official trail.

The shortest and easiest alternate follows Trail 133 as it climbs from the campground at Marias Pass, then drops to follow Trail 137 for a short distance

Marias Pass to Benchmark
Elevation Chart

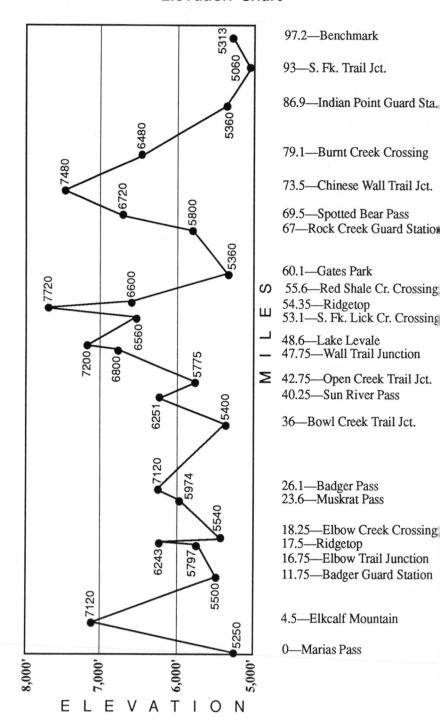

97.2—Benchmark

93—S. Fk. Trail Jct.

86.9—Indian Point Guard Sta.

79.1—Burnt Creek Crossing

73.5—Chinese Wall Trail Jct.

69.5—Spotted Bear Pass
67—Rock Creek Guard Station

60.1—Gates Park
55.6—Red Shale Cr. Crossing
54.35—Ridgetop
53.1—S. Fk. Lick Cr. Crossing

48.6—Lake Levale
47.75—Wall Trail Junction

42.75—Open Creek Trail Jct.
40.25—Sun River Pass

36—Bowl Creek Trail Jct.

26.1—Badger Pass
23.6—Muskrat Pass

18.25—Elbow Creek Crossing
17.5—Ridgetop
16.75—Elbow Trail Junction
11.75—Badger Guard Station

4.5—Elkcalf Mountain

0—Marias Pass

8,000'   7,000'   6,000'   5,000'

E L E V A T I O N

M I L E S

before joining Trail 101, the Two Medicine-Elk Calf Trail.

The route is blazed, well-signed and popular with pack trains. Trail 101 is a jeep track that parallels the South Fork of the Two Medicine River, passing numerous riverside campsites before it reaches the Badger Guard Station, 11 miles from the trailhead.

The second alternate—11.75 miles to Badger Guard station but poorly signed and with steeper ups and downs—more closely follows the official alternate route and is the path we took.

Head south from the Marias Pass campground along U.S. Route 2 for .6 mile. Turn left (northeast) onto Forest Service Road 83, the Pike Creek Road, passable by car, and stay on the main route for two miles as it climbs steadily through forest toward burned and logged Elkcalf Mountain, 7,607 feet.

Take the seventh left, leaving the main road for a jeep road that leads to the northeast while descending slightly through lodgepole pine. Flattop Mountain can be seen to the south from this intersection, Elkcalf Mountain to the east, Marias Pass below and to the west, and the sheer faces of Calf Robe and Red Crow mountains to the northwest.

The jeep road forks in about 200 yards at the edge of a regrowing clear-cut. Splashes of bright red Indian paintbrush and purple mountain asters can be seen among the young pines.

Continue to head straight (southeast), avoiding the less traveled route to the right (southwest). Soon swing to the north as the jeep road becomes a faint jeep track that vanishes altogether in the thick grasses.

The trail continues into the trees ahead along a true compass bearing of 20 degrees. Pick up the overgrown but traveled footpath soon after entering the forest.

Descend to cross Pike Creek, then climb gradually through lush lodgepole and spruce forest thick with undergrowth. Strike an unsigned "T" intersection at 3.6 miles with Trail 137, and bear right (southeast), beginning a moderate climb through lush open forest.

Pass through some parks at the base of Elkcalf Mountain, looming to the south, and follow as the trail swings eastward and crosses a willow-filled boggy area.

There are good views here to the north of tree-covered Two Medicine Ridge, rising up to 6,600 feet beyond the South Fork of the Two Medicine River.

Continue contouring eastward, crossing several side creeks and meadows filled with cow parsnip, before reaching an unsigned intersection at 4.25 miles.

Head north along the main trail, avoiding the side route that climbs to the east, blocked by logs, and the faint track to the south, which leads to the Dodge Creek Road.

Soon reach another unsigned intersection. An overgrown blazed trail, blocked by deadfall, leads to the east. The heavier-traveled route, Trail 137, begins a switchbacking descent.

Follow Trail 137 as it drops into heavy forest and circles the head of Townsend Creek before intersecting with Trail 136, the official alternate route, at five miles.

Trail 137, leading to the South Fork of the Two Medicine River via Benson and Lost Shirt creeks, was poorly blazed and littered with deadfall but may have been reopened since.

We opted to descend gradually through lodgepole along Trail 136, joining

Trail 101 at 6.25 miles and heading upstream.

There is good camping in the numerous riverside parks, and the hiking is easy along the gradual ascent.

At 11.5 miles strike the intersection with Trail 102 in a small meadow. Here are good views to the southeast of 8,191-foot Goat Mountain, its multi-tiered crown of snow-coated cliffs rising gray and craggy above the tree tops, and of 7,836-foot Running Owl Mountain to the south.

Badger Creek Guard Station, a log cabin and barn complex, is reached at 11.75 miles, where the trail bends south and enters the North Badger Creek basin on Trail 103.

This is a jeep track, which at first climbs gradually through beautiful meadows graced with limber stands of aspens.

Bullshoe Mountain, 8,006 feet, comes into view to the northwest over Running Owl's shoulder as elevation is gained, and to the northeast rises 8,091-foot Half Dome Crag, topped with a radio tower, one of the largest peaks in the Sawtooth Range.

There is good camping in a meadow just before Lee Creek is crossed at 12.75 miles and in another meadow a quarter-mile beyond where the trail swings along the bank of North Badger Creek. The grasses in these lovely parks cradle wild strawberries, yellow cinquefoil, tender pink Indian paintbrush and mariposa lilies.

The canyon narrows as the trail continues its gradual climb in forest at the foot of the steep-faced mountains. Keep a sharp eye out for a cairn to the left of the trail at 13.75 miles; it marks a side route that drops to a pretty, multi-stepped waterfall cascading into steep pools at the base of Goat Mountain.

The second and more muscular of the Bruin Peaks comes into view to the southeast through the trees as the trail nears Kip Creek, 15.75 miles. Wildflowers offer a riot of color amid the lush trailside greenery.

A mile later the trail breaks into a meadow, with the peaks and cliffs of the divide towering ahead, dominated by 7,657-foot Big Lodge Mountain.

Head east here along North Badger-Elbow Creek Trail 145, a well-defined pack trail that drops to ford North Badger Creek (fill water bottles here) before climbing gradually out of the basin on switchbacks.

At mid-ascent the view opens to the northwest, exposing Crescent Cliff, a fluted peak flanked by wall-like cliffs dotted with snow. At trailside find pretty purple vetch, a vine.

Crest the ridge and begin descending through open lodgepole and lush parks filled with beargrass, a stark contrast to the dead trees littering the rocky slopes of the Bruin Peaks to the north.

Later the trail ascends to near timberline, and the ridge of the divide can be seen to the south across the valley.

The trail soon descends to a meadow overlook with a spectacular view of the Muskrat Creek basin, and the divide crossing beyond as it bends in a reverse "S."

Elbow Peak, 7,131 feet, dominates to the northeast, while Family Peak, 8,086 feet, lies to the east beyond Muskrat Pass.

Descend along switchbacks and reenter forest, boulder-hopping Elbow Creek at 19.25 miles. There is good camping in a shaded flat at the crossing, and on a small bench on the opposite side of Muskrat Creek.

Pick up Trail 147 and ascend through lush forest along a series of switch-

The North Fork of Badger Creek flows clear and crisp below the jagged face of Goat Mountain in the Lewis and Clark National Forest. The stream harbors native cutthroat trout and waterfalls that rush and echo in the canyon.

backs to gain the shoulder of Elbow Mountain. Views of the divide open up to the west after the trail passes an old landslide and crosses a series of small parks; wildflowers on the open slopes include bluebells and pink spiraea.

Climb slightly, then drop steadily to the basin floor and cross a willow-lined branch of Muskrat Creek. Blue Lake lies some 100 feet below and to the right of the trail at 21.75 miles, its shores marshy and unsuited for camping.

Climb gradually along Muskrat Creek through semi-open country to 5,974-foot Muskrat Pass, which, with a boggy area near its head, is one of the lowest passes on the divide. This wide, open pass reputedly is a favorite gathering spot for elk.

Here enter the Bob Marshall Wilderness along level trail that passes some good meadow campsites. There also is good camping—and a good place to see the sunset—on the northeastern shore of shallow Beaver Lake, lying in a cirque at the base of the divide at 23.5 miles. The lake's waters aren't suitable for drinking, but a creek flows out of rocks and across the trail, just to the northeast.

The trail climbs to the northeast toward the unnamed pass ahead, before leaving the Bob Marshall Wilderness near the top. Here the trail levels out in a section of large lodgepole pine and spruce trees, which allow glimpses of the divide to the north and of craggy, unnamed peaks to the east.

Reach tree-covered Badger Pass, 6,278 feet, at 26.1 miles, and head south back into "The Bob" on Strawberry Creek Trail 191, a level path that soon emerges into a big meadow covered with wild strawberry plants and red Indian paintbrush. Unnamed peaks loom above treeline on the basin's east side here, dominated by a pyramidal summit streaked with snow and scree.

Stay on the main trail on the gradual descent, avoiding side routes to the left that disappear into boggy areas dammed by beavers. Tree-covered Cap Mountain, 7,512 feet, lies to the west of the trail, and the Winter Points later come into view along the descent.

Boulder-hop Strawberry Creek at 30 miles, where there is sheltered camping at stream-side. The creek must be forded at 33 miles, just above its confluence with Gateway Creek.

Continue downstream through an unsigned intersection just above the Grimsley Creek crossing and descend through lodgepole and spruce onto the broadening valley floor.

The trail has been rerouted near the bottom of the descent and climbs to contour above mucky spots along the creek. The intersection with Bowl Creek Trail 324, 36 miles, and a second ford of Strawberry Creek also have been moved and are about 200 yards downstream from their location on the USGS map.

The beautiful Middle Fork of the Flathead River, a designated Wild and Scenic River with excellent cutthroat trout fishing, lies a short distance downstream from the trail junction and is a worthy side trip.

The Bowl Creek Trail also has been newly reconstructed, and is easily followed as it climbs steadily from the ford past some rocky outcrops enroute to the divide.

There is good camping in the open, cinquefoil-laden meadows of Grizzly Park, 38.6 miles, and in a flat at the Bowl Creek ford, at 39.25 miles. The

Rugged cliffs mark the beginning of the Bob Marshall Wilderness' spectacular Chinese Wall formation at the head of Open Creek near Switchback Pass. Beautiful wildflowers and lingering snowbanks lie at the base of the formidable cliffs that rise a thousand vertical feet from the trail.

trail climbs steadily for the next mile to tree-covered Sun River Pass, 6,251 feet—named by sun-worshipping Indians because of brilliant sunlight reflecting from nearby cliff walls—then drops gradually through forest to intersect Open Creek Trail 116.

Here head west to cross shallow Fool's Creek and enter Round Park, an excellent campsite. The next camping opportunity is about four miles ahead, in a small stream-side meadow.

From Round Park begins a 5-mile-long ascent to the divide and your first encounter with the sheer cliffs and rugged high country for which the Bob Marshall Wilderness is famous.

Signal Mountain, 8,259 feet, becomes visible across the valley to the south as the trail climbs steadily; views are intermittent of Open Creek below. Farther south are the snow-dotted peaks of the divide, some with crests of cliffs and others with jagged buttresses. A red rock outcropping protrudes above treeline to the north below the 7,975-foot summit of Angle Point.

Cross Open Creek at the base of the divide, passing a possible campsite before joining Wall Trail 175 at the bottom of scree slopes streaming from the fluted cliffs ahead.

Turn left (southeast) and contour below the sheer, solid face of the divide, with snow melt cascading down crevices exposed to the sun. The music of

Striated rocks, vertical and horizontal, bespeak the cataclysmic forces that gave rise to the Chinese Wall, a continuous cliff rock face winding through the heart of the Bob Marshall Wilderness.

The 13-mile-long Chinese Wall looms over verdant alpine meadows resplendent with wildflowers in the Bob Marshall Wilderness. The well-marked trail skirts the base of the wall in one of the most delightful hikes along the entire divide.

the waterfalls and the creek's headwaters enhances the beauty of this landscape, with its colorful alpine flowers, tender green plants, boulder-strewn slopes and wide sweeps of snow at the base of spectacular cliffs.

Signal Mountain and the Open Creek basin spread below to the east, while a look backward reveals 8,412-foot Kevan Mountain guarding the notch for Switchback Pass.

Patches of lingering snow likely are to be encountered as the trail dips and climbs eastward. At 48.6 miles, pass a good campsite and a short spur trail leading to glacial Lake Levale.

Nestled in a beautiful cirque with its milky blue waters half-surrounded by pipe-organed cliffs, and clusters of purple mountain penstemon adorning its rocky shore, Lake Levale is truly one of the highlights of the entire segment. Look for mountain goats.

The trail continues eastward, ascending through forest and small meadows strewn with dogtooth violets. Crest the rocky point ahead to see the world suddenly unfold in a breathtaking panorama of rugged mountains and sheer cliffs. Drop and enter a long stretch of beautiful high meadows rolling from the base of the divide's sheer and snow-streaked face.

Red-topped Moonlight Peak, 8,102 feet, lies to the east of the trail, which drops to cross the head of the South Fork of Open Creek before climbing to again level off along the base of the cliffs.

Water is plentiful in the high meadow and in the north and south forks of Lick Creek, which embrace tree-covered Lick Mountain to the east.

Climb steeply from the North Fork of Lick Creek for a rewarding view to the south of massive Hahn Peak, 8,310 feet, with its banded layers of snowy cliffs topped with a rocky crown.

Later, as the trail climbs to a saddle abreast of Hahn Peak, enter a section burned in the Gates Park Fire; blackened trees and ashen earth covers much of the South Fork Lick Creek basin and the ridge to the east.

The skyline beyond is a procession of jagged high summits, including the rock cone of 8,416-foot Teton Peak. Slategoat Mountain, 8,887 feet, dominates the view ahead to the south.

Switchback down from the saddle and ascend through burned forest to the 7,220-foot ridgetop to the south, which offers impressive views overlooking the burned basin of Red Shale Creek.

Drop into the basin and enter fringe areas of the burn after crossing the head of Red Shale Creek. The trail soon bends sharply east and recrosses the creek at a heavily-used meadow campsite, 55.6 miles, before beginning a steady descent along its left bank.

Lookout Mountain, tree-covered except for a red cliff on its northern face, lies to the south across the valley and can be seen through the trees along the descent.

Cross the creek on a wooden bridge and reenter the burn area as the trail passes beneath Lookout Mountain; the remainder of the hike is mostly through charred forest until just before the lush bottomland of Gates Park is reached at 60.1 miles.

Gates Park is a beautiful meadow—and a good camping spot—with rolling grassy hills and a Forest Service guard station that originally was a homesteader's cabin. The line of four peaks bulging above the meadow from north to northeast are Teton Peak, Old Baldy, Rocky Mountain and Beartop, 8,094 feet. Sulphur, Horse and Mule hills lie further to the east.

Follow the edge of the park and swing to the southeast to reach the junction of Rock Creek Trail 111. Turn right (southwest) and climb gradually, reentering the burn area before dropping to ford Red Shale Creek.

The trail climbs steeply from the creek, then levels off on the ridge top ahead, passing through two fringe areas of the burn before entering lush living forest.

Ascend gradually and boulder-hop Hoxsey and Miners creeks, then descend gradually into the Rock Creek basin, skirting the edges of mucky spots in the path. A camp can be made on the grassy bench above the stream.

Ford Baldy Bear Creek and continue the gradual ascent through forest, with the three summits of Moose Ridge looming to the southwest and a ridge of red rock rising to the right.

Rock Creek Guard Station, a small log cabin with a porch, is reached at 67 miles. Boulder-hop a side creek and pass a developed campsite to the left of the trail just beyond the guard station.

The climb becomes steeper as the trail passes the 7,785-foot mountain that divides Rock Creek into branches, its northeastern face bearing exposed green and red rock.

Spotted Bear Pass, a tree-covered cut offering limited views, is reached at 69.5 miles. The pass reportedly was named by three adventurers, who around 1861 saw a black bear in the vicinity that had an unusual amount of white on its chest and underbelly.

Turn west from the pass along Wall Trail 175 and continue the ascent, with good views of the basin below. To the southwest see pretty, tree-covered mountains against a dramatic backdrop: a distant high, rocky peak whose summit curves to a point like a cresting ocean wave.

Deciduous western larch trees, with their lacy light green leaves resembling pine needles, are growing on the ridge tops here, and along the shoreline of shallow My Lake, one mile ahead.

My Lake is another alpine gem, lying at the base of the divide amid a fragile carpet of moss pink that forms a rosy ring around the clear green waters. There is good camping along the western shore; eastshore sites are closed due to overuse. Drinking water flows in a small trickle to the west across a small park frequented by deer.

The well-worn trail continues level from the lake before descending gradually past ship-shaped Larch Hill to a triangular trail junction at the base of Larch Hill Pass, at 73.25 miles. The grand spectacle of the Chinese Wall can be glimpsed ahead through the trees along the approach.

The Wall's full impact is felt upon emerging into the meadow along its boulder-strewn base: continuous layers of fluted, multi-hued limestone cliffs rise vertically more than a thousand feet in places, crested with a cornice of snow and skirted with scree.

Water and campsites are plentiful in the high meadows, especially at a shallow lake at the head of Moose Creek, at 77 miles.

And the well-trodden trail dips and rises above treeline, with excellent eastward views overlooking creek basins below and peaks beyond. After all, though the cliffs loom high above, you're at 7,000 feet.

Watch for mountain goats on the sheer cliffs and, in the meadow, pikas and ground squirrels.

A short, steep climb takes you to a saddle near 8,576-foot Cliff Mountain,

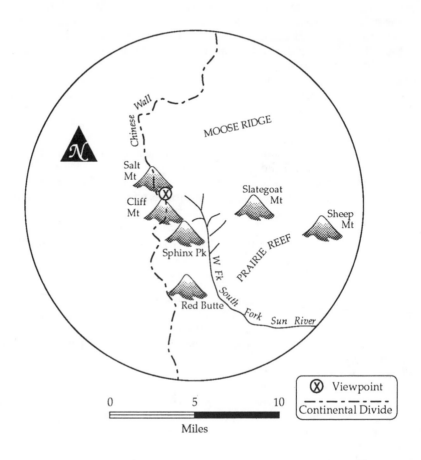

0   5   10

Miles

⊗ Viewpoint
Continental Divide

Marias Pass to Benchmark View Map

Views eastward from the Chinese Wall are among the most impressive in the Bob Marshall segment, but the scene from a saddle near 8,576-foot Cliff Mountain is especially sweet. The expanse of peaks from southeast to northeast includes Red Butte, Prairie Reef, Sheep Mountain and Slategoat Mountain. The Wall itself can be seen from its origins at Larch Hill Pass to well beyond the Burnt Creek basin to the south. Evidence of the geologic overthrusting that formed these mountains is ample, with the west-facing slopes resembling hump-backed waves that break eastward in a line of sheer cliffs.

the formation's high spot. The view from the top, though, is among the best in the Bob. (See view map.)

The trail drops from the saddle, paralleling the wall before dropping to cross Burnt Creek at 79.1 miles. Here the trail turns sharply to the east, leaving the wall on a descent at first through open forest and parks, then later through young stands of lodgepole.

Ford the west fork of the South Fork of the Sun River and descend along its left bank on mucky trail. A trio of peaks, with 8,590-foot Red Butte its centerpiece, is visible through forest to the west where the trail passes the mouth of a canyon beyond No Name Gulch.

Later, crescent-shaped Prairie Reef comes into view ahead as the trail continues descending to ford the river four times.

A popular campsite is at 86.1 miles, the junction with Indian Creek Trail 211, and there are numerous campsites in the grassy stream-side parks near the Indian Creek Guard Station.

The walking is easy as the heavily used trail swings to the southeast and begins descending gradually along the west fork of the South Fork of the Sun River. Cross small parks filled with wildflowers and stands of aspen in the upper river valley.

Tree-covered Deadman Hill, high above the confluence of the Sun's forks, is seen to the southeast from large parks reached later in the descent.

Cross the West Fork on the pack bridge at 92 miles for a short cut to Trail 202, the South Fork Sun River Trail. The official route continues downstream for another mile, crossing the West Fork at West Fork Licks before climbing through forest to join Trail 202 at 93.5 miles.

Here the trail veers away from the South Fork, climbing steadily through small parks and then lodgepole forest before contouring above the river along the ridge.

The trail is very mucky in spots, especially near side creeks that can be boulder-hopped easily. The path improves along the gradual descent to the river, reached at a wooden pack bridge at 96.7 miles.

Cross the bridge and climb gradually through forest to reach the Forest Service's South Fork Campground and Benchmark Work Station, a trail resupply point.

SCAPEGOAT WILDERNESS

Benchmark to Rogers Pass — 57.5 miles

Introduction: A pleasant six-day hike that combines easy walking through glaciated valleys with 15 miles of divide ridge-running.

Water is plentiful most of the way, as the trail winds along five main drainages and drops to two alpine lakes. It becomes more scarce as the trail leads south from Caribou Peak into dry rocky country.

The trail first meanders along the pretty Sun River, named by Indians as "Natae-osueti." French trappers translated the words to mean "medicine" or "sun" river.

Lewis and Clark named it the "Dearborn" after then-Secretary of War Henry Dearborn; this name eventually went to the river to the south followed later in the hike.

Fording is necessary at the many stream crossings into early summer when streams are swollen by still-melting snow. Extra caution is a must when crossing the Sun's deep waters at Hoadley Creek.

At mid-hike the trail traverses part of the 240,600-acre Canyon Creek Fire, a lightning-caused blaze that blew out of control on Sept. 6, 1988, burning entire drainages in the Scapegoat Wilderness and threatening the town of Augusta.

The Forest Service allowed the fire, ignited June 25, to burn in accordance with its wilderness fire management plan. But high winds and an unprecedented drought fueled the flames for three months across an area eight times larger than predicted.

Clues to the dynamics of wildfire are apparent throughout the upper Straight Creek basin, where wind and weather combined to burn a hot fire in some areas and a "cooler" fire in others. Some trees were unscathed by the inferno that reduced their immediate neighbors to charred skeletons.

But the forest is healing: Lodgepole pine seedlings are pushing through the soil along with a myriad of wildflowers. And a delectable windfall from the fires—wild morel mushrooms— awaits the fungi-savvy hiker who enters the burned area in early spring. They're especially tasty sauteed in olive oil, garlic and Butter Buds.

Be sure you know they're morels before eating, though. Some look-alikes are poisonous.

Campsites are numerous in streamside parks strewn with wildflowers. Cutthroat trout inhabit the major creeks and bright blue Bighorn Lake, nestled high in a snow-dotted cirque.

The view from the top is outstanding, with the major peaks of the Scapegoat Wilderness and the high mountains of the Bob Marshall Wilderness to the north, and glimpses of the plains beyond.

Part of the trail crosses an historic route Indians followed on their buffalo hunting treks to the east. Captain Meriwether Lewis and party camped along the trail in 1806 near Lewis and Clark Pass, and part of the path bisects the historic mining camp of Alice Creek.

Benchmark to Rogers Pass

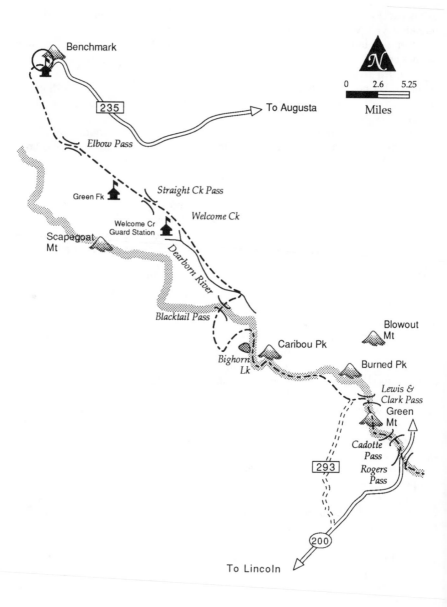

Benchmark

235

To Augusta

N

0   2.6   5.25

Miles

Elbow Pass

Green Fk

Straight Ck Pass

Welcome Ck

Welcome Cr
Guard Station

Scapegoat
Mt

Dearborn River

Blacktail Pass

Bighorn
Lk

Caribou Pk

Blowout
Mt

Burned Pk

Lewis &
Clark Pass

Green
Mt

Cadotte
Pass

Rogers
Pass

293

200

To Lincoln

Difficulty level: Moderate, with some strenuous stretches.

Scenery: Excellent, of high peaks and narrow valleys.

Water availability: Good, but more scarce to the south.

Maps: USFS—Lewis and Clark National Forest visitors map. USGS (7.5 min. series)—Benchmark; Wood Lake; Scapegoat Mountain; Jakie Creek; Steamboat Mountain; Heart Lake; Caribou Peak; Blowout Mountain; Cadotte Creek; Rogers Pass.

Supply Points: There are no convenient supply points between Benchmark and Rogers Pass.

However, Elk Pass Road #196 ends seven miles from the trail at 20.1 miles and could serve as a supply point if prior arrangements can be made. The Diamond Bar X guest ranch (406-562-3524) is just nine miles from the junction of the Dearborn River and Blacktail Creek trails, 24.8 miles, and the Alice Creek Road is convenient to Highway 200 near the end of the hike. At hike's end, Rogers Pass is 18 miles east of Lincoln, a full-service town with campgrounds, stores, restaurants and a post office (ZIP 59639).

Finding the trailhead: Take Forest Service Road 435 west from Augusta, bearing left where the road forks at 14.4 miles. Stay on the main track where the road again forks at 27.6 miles. Pass the entrance to the Benchmark Campground on the left at 29.5 miles and continue straight past the Forest Service's Benchmark work station. The South Fork Campground is dead ahead; bear right at the next fork to reach the trailhead parking area at 30.4 miles.

Trail description: The hike begins at the trailhead at the South Fork Campground, a popular departing point for hikes and horseback trips into the Bob Marshall and Scapegoat wildernesses.

Hike north a short distance on well-marked trail and cross the packer's bridge over the South Fork of the Sun River, noted for its excellent cutthroat trout fishing.

Turn left (south) at the intersection beyond the bridge onto trail 202 and head upstream along the South Fork of the Sun River Trail. Sunny balsamroot flowers line the path and, later, carpet hillsides on the right.

At 1.75 miles intersect Trail 255, a cutoff trail that returns to the Benchmark work station area. Continue straight to a hiker's registration box and at two miles enter the Scapegoat Wilderness.

The trail is well-marked and rutted by pack trains as it continues upstream through a sun-streaked lodgepole pine forest, offering intermittent views of the Sun River. Streamside parks strewn with blue pasqueflowers, yellow Wyeth biscuitroot and purple larkspur offer ideal camping sites.

Along the way a phalanx of cliffs, dimpled with pockets of snow, looms to the west, and to the east rises the jutting buttress of Patrol Mountain, 8,015 feet.

At four miles intersect the Hoadley Creek Trail 226, which continues to the Continental Divide five miles beyond. Ford the South Fork of the Sun River and continue along trail 202 as it heads upstream through some pretty parks containing obvious elk sign.

Crossing the river here in early season can be a tricky business; the chilling waters are deceptively deep and powerful. There are no suitable alternate crossing points immediately downstream of the ford, but the river may be

Benchmark to Rogers Pass
Elevation Chart

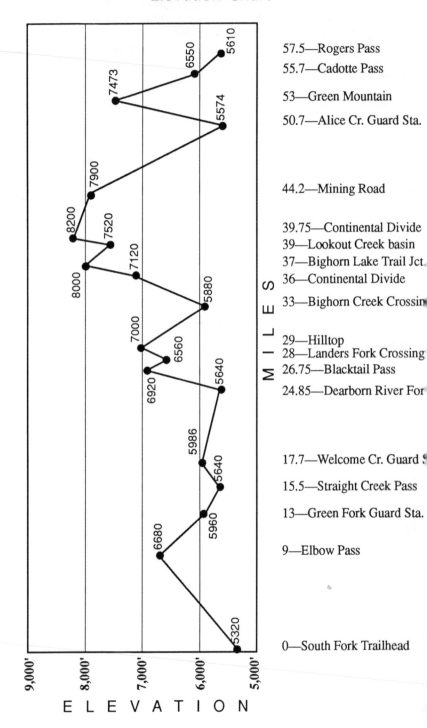

57.5—Rogers Pass
55.7—Cadotte Pass

53—Green Mountain

50.7—Alice Cr. Guard Sta.

44.2—Mining Road

39.75—Continental Divide
39—Lookout Creek basin
37—Bighorn Lake Trail Jct.
36—Continental Divide

33—Bighorn Creek Crossin

29—Hilltop
28—Landers Fork Crossing
26.75—Blacktail Pass

24.85—Dearborn River For

17.7—Welcome Cr. Guard S

15.5—Straight Creek Pass

13—Green Fork Guard Sta.

9—Elbow Pass

0—South Fork Trailhead

MILES

ELEVATION

9,000' 8,000' 7,000' 6,000' 5,000'

crossed after bushwhacking to more shallow waters upstream of its confluence with Hoadley Creek.

At five miles intersect Ellis Creek Trail 227, which is not shown on the USGS map. Bear left (east) onto Elbow Creek Trail 248 at eight miles, and begin a gradual but steady ascent toward Elbow Pass. This trail has been reconstructed recently by the Forest Service, which installed much-needed switchbacks on both sides of the 6,680-foot pass.

As you climb, look to the right for 8,698-foot Sugarloaf Mountain, whose snow-sprinkled, craggy summit dominates the view.

Once over the pass, the trail crosses numerous streams as it descends into Straight Creek Basin and blooms in a profusion of beargrass, forget-me-nots and lavender clematis. There are good camping sites at the Straight Creek ford at 10 miles, but the afternoon sun leaves this narrow section of valley early.

Cross the creek and bear right (south) on Straight Creek Trail 212, which climbs gradually as it heads upstream past a landslide. Cross Straight Creek six times in the next two miles, fording or boulder-hopping as the water level allows.

Crown Mountain, 8,041 feet, is the dominant peak to the east, and Bunyan Point and Cigarette Rock, 8,252 feet, rise to the west as the trail continues on to the intersection with Green Fork Trail at 12.75 miles. A short side trip here finds the Forest Service's Green Fork Guard Station nestled in a pretty meadow at the base of Red Slide Mountain and Half Moon Peak, 8,178 feet.

Fill water bottles at the creek before continuing the gradual ascent toward 5,640-foot Straight Creek Pass and enter the first of several areas burned in the Canyon Creek Fire.

One of the wilderness' highest peaks, 9,204-foot Scapegoat Mountain, becomes visible through the stark, burned forest as the trail climbs to the pass at 15.5 miles.

The view from the top reveals the dimensions of the Canyon Creek Fire. Burned-over hillsides extend from Steamboat Mountain to the southeast to the upper Dearborn River Valley far below.

The trail descends gradually, crossing Welcome Creek several times before entering a very pretty meadow (and a perfect campsite) at about 16.9 miles. Here intersect Jakie Creek Trail 214, and the Dearborn River Trail 206.

The Dearborn Trail crosses to the west side of Welcome Creek and heads downstream through more fire-charred terrain and past the Welcome Creek Guard Station at 17.7 miles.

Ford the Dearborn and pass the guard station on your right (northwest), to head upstream for a short stretch. The trail soon forks, with the right branch leading toward Scapegoat Mountain. Take the left fork to head east, gain the bluffs, and begin contouring downstream into the Dearborn River Valley. Soon pass a nice meadow on the left that is closed to camping due to over-use.

Cross Lost Cabin Creek on the log at 19.4 miles and ford the Dearborn River a short distance beyond. Shaded areas on the valley floor harbor pretty fuschia shooting stars and larkspur. At 20.1 miles intersect Elk Pass Trail 205, which leads to a trailhead on the Elk Pass Road seven miles away.

Here the west side of the Dearborn Valley is unscathed by fire, while the east side has been scorched up and over the brim. The trail is well-trodden by pack trains and easy to follow. The valley broadens at 23 miles, giving good views of the Continental Divide and the upper Dearborn River Valley.

Go right (west) on Blacktail Creek Trail 207 at 24.8 miles and descend into the river bottom. Ford the Dearborn and rise to a trail junction in an open meadow. There is good camping at streamside and in the meadow.

Go right (southwest) and head upstream above the Dearborn a short distance; the trail fades out in the meadow here but is marked by a blaze ahead and on the right. Soon cross Blacktail Creek, fill water bottles for the climb ahead, and bear left on the steeply ascending trail through a vacant hunting camp toward Blacktail Pass and the Continental Divide.

The trail soon veers from the creek and heads arrow-straight uphill for a strenuous hike that gains 1,280 feet in just 1.3 miles.

Bear left at an unsigned intersection on the mountain's shoulder, continuing upwards toward the 6,920-foot-high pass at 26.75 miles. A good, ice-cold stream—the headwaters of Blacktail Creek—may be flowing through the rocks on top of the wildflower-strewn pass.

Camping is possible here, where alpine buttercups bloom and some trees offer shelter. Views of surrounding peaks are stunning.

But a better, grassy campsite and a reliable water supply lie just over the pass, at the headwaters of the Landers Fork.

The path leaves the Scapegoat Wilderness at the pass and enters the Helena

An overview of the Upper Bighorn basin shows the extent of the damage caused by the 1988 Canyon Creek Fire in the Scapegoat Wilderness.

National Forest as Trail 479, descending gradually from the divide along the Landers Fork.

Many of the trees here have brown needles, presumably victims of winter burn caused by a sudden 30-degree drop in temperature during the winter of 1988-89, one of the most severe in Montana's history. Much of the area has been burned by fire as well (the summer of 1988 set records for fires and drought), and the basin is framed by hillsides spiked with charred trees.

At 27.75 miles reach a large meadow overrun with ground squirrels. Here reach a three-way intersection with trails 433 and 438. Bear left (southeast) on Trail 438, cross the Landers Fork twice and begin ascending.

The official trail climbs steeply from an unsigned intersection and becomes overgrown near the hilltop ahead. Traveling is easier on the spur trail to the right (southwest), which contours around the 7,202-foot-high knob and rejoins the official route.

The official trail may be difficult to follow here; it peters out in a clearing but can be regained by heading up the hill on the left (east).

Both routes converge on a level hilltop at 29 miles for a view of burned-over hills and snow-capped Red Ridge and 8,688-foot Pyramid Peak. The trail skirts the rim of the Landers Fork basin before striking an unsigned, four-way intersection. The route to the southeast bearing 150 degrees is the correct path, dropping in a four-mile long, circuitous descent into burned-out Bighorn Creek basin.

The trail passes a sheer cliff and a lovely, three-tiered waterfall as it approaches the valley bottom, intersecting with Bighorn Creek Trail 441 at 33 miles.

Follow Trail 441 (referred to as Sheep Creek Trail on the Forest Service sign) as it winds through a narrow canyon; some bushwhacking and boulder-hopping is needed to cross Bighorn Creek more than a dozen times along the trek upstream. Find many good campsites in the creek basin, which is recovering nicely from the fire. Fill water bottles as you approach the head of the drainage; water won't be available again for 3.5 miles.

Bighorn Creek flows through an impressive canyon below as the trail skirts the upper basin and forks at about 35 miles.

Bear left (northeast) on the more heavily traveled path and continue the moderate climb to a high alpine meadow, inhabited by a colony of ground squirrels that whistle at passersby.

The trail forks again as it nears the divide; bear right (east) and skirt the foot of 7,994-foot Monitor Mountain. Continue climbing to strike Trail 440, the Continental Divide Trail, at about 36 miles. Go right (south) to follow the trail.

The views here are spectacular, revealing waves of distant ranges to the west and wide slices of the plains to the northeast.

The trail follows the ridge of the divide, circling to reveal 8,755-foot Caribou Peak, snow-capped well into the summer.

Snowdrifts may linger across the trail on northern slopes into late June, but these can be circumvented easily.

Approaching Caribou Peak, reach the intersection with Trail 442, a nearly mile-long path to the right (southwest) that drops to Bighorn Lake, lying in a cirque nearly 1,000 feet below. There is good camping and reliable water

Fire-charred hillsides in the Scapegoat Wilderness offer an advantage: unobstructed views of distant peaks. Here Red Ridge (center) and Pyramid Peak (left) rise into view on the Landers Fork Trail.

here, plus a healthy population of cutthroat trout.

Adventurous hikers may choose to stay on the divide by climbing the spur ridge and crossing the saddle below to crest Caribou Peak. But the official route skirts Caribou Peak and descends through woods into lovely Lookout Creek Basin, with two emerald green lakes and a silver ribbon of stream.

The basin escaped the fires and is alive with wildlife, a refreshing change from the stark forests along Bighorn Creek.

Good water and campsites are available throughout the basin, especially at the shallow lake at 39 miles. Fill water bottles here, as the next 6.5 miles of trail are dry.

The trail circles the lake's shoreline counter-clockwise before bending southeast to begin a sharp climb to the divide, gaining nearly 700 feet in .7 mile.

On top, the trail continues along a grassy crest in open country, sometimes petering out in the meadows; keep an eye out for cairns and note the spine of the divide as it curves over three minor summits ahead.

Mining test pits are alongside the trail as it follows the rim of the Alice Creek basin along a rugged and narrow ridge before strking an old mining road at 44.2 miles. Descend along the road for 4.5 miles as it switchbacks into the basin, reaching water on the third switchback and good camping on the valley floor.

Water bottles should be filled before leaving the creek; the next reliable source is 7.5 miles away.

Hike two miles on the old road along Alice Creek before intersecting with

The open rolling divide in the Helena National Forest offers easy hiking and spectacular views, as seen from this vantage at 6,050-foot Cadotte Pass.

the Alice Creek Road, a good gravel road that extends about 12 miles to Highway 200.

Bear left at the fork, taking the more heavily traveled route as the forest gives way to open sagebrush country in the basin proper. The foundation of the old Alice Creek Ranger Station lies to the left of the trail just before the next road junction is reached.

Turn left (northeast) at the intersection, cross the gate at the trailhead and ascend along the jeep track through open country toward Lewis and Clark Pass.

Follow the jeep track that cuts to the right midway up the mountain, to a sign just below the pass. The sign notes that a former trail on the ridge was used heavily by Indians enroute to buffalo hunting grounds, and was traveled by Captain Meriwether Lewis.

The trail peters out at 52.5 miles in a large open meadow at the base of 7,453-foot Green Mountain, towering on the left.

Climb steeply to gain its summit, and circle counter-clockwise at the top until a small concrete platform near a stone pyramid marker is reached.

The views here are splendid: Lewis and Clark Pass lies below and to the northeast; Red Mountain is on the west; Silver King Mountain, topped with a tower, lies to the southwest, and the Big Belt Mountains beyond Helena mark the eastern skyline. (See view map.)

The trail continues along the ridge in a southeasterly direction in a lazy reverse "S" toward Rogers Pass, named for Major A.B. Rogers, an engineer who surveyed it in 1887 while seeking a divide crossing for the Great Northern Railroad.

Descend Green Mountain through open woods south-southeast toward the 6,973-foot hill ahead that is scarred by two road cuts traversing from left to right.

Be careful along the descent to avoid the spur ridges to the west unless you want a long and frustrating hike back into the Alice Creek Basin.

Strike a jeep track three-quarters of the way down, bear left and cross an open saddle leading to the road-scarred hill's base, 54.2 miles.

Ascend along the uppermost road, contouring to the right before switching back to the summit. A cairn points the way eastward to Cadotte Pass, 6,050 feet, the narrow ridge below that is bisected by a power line.

Descend to strike a faint jeep track. Follow as it forks to the left before dropping to Cadotte Pass, at 55.7 miles, and tops the hill ahead.

Formerly named Blackfoot Pass, this ancient Indian crossing was renamed for French-Canadian guide Pierre Cadotte, a member Northern Pacific Railroad Survey of 1853.

Highway 200 can be seen in the valley below. Sunset Mountain, 6,412 feet, lies to the northeast, topped by a microwave tower.

Follow as the divide turns to the south, ascending the high point at 6,499 feet. Be careful to avoid the ridge to the southeast that forms part of the Cadotte Creek Basin.

The divide bends sharply to the east just above Rogers Pass, 5,610 feet, ending at 57.5 miles with a steep descent to the parking area. Don't try to scramble down; a small drainage to the right (south) offers an easier route to the road, the first asphalt crossed since leaving U.S. Route 2 at Marias Pass some 155 miles to the north.

Water likely can be found .5 mile south on the west side of Hwy. 200, in Pass Creek.

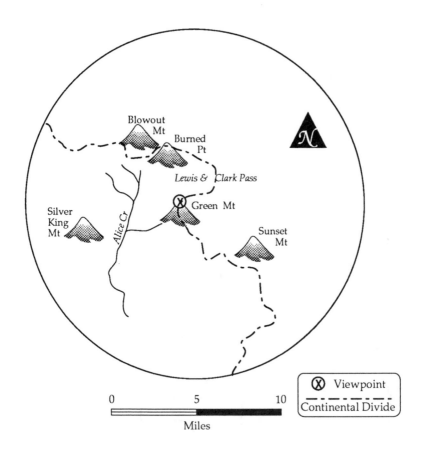

Scapegoat Wilderness View Map

The view from the summit of 7,453-foot Green Mountain is one of the best in the Scapegoat Wilderness segment, with a sea of high peaks trailing to the northwest into the Bob Marshall Wilderness, and wide slices of the Great Plains, last seen from Glacier National Park, rolling to the northeast. To the west rises lookout-topped Silver King Mountain, with the snow-capped Garnet Range well beyond. The eastern horizon belongs to the Big Belt Mountains, north of Helena, while Sunset Mountain, topped with a radio tower, commands the view closer at hand.

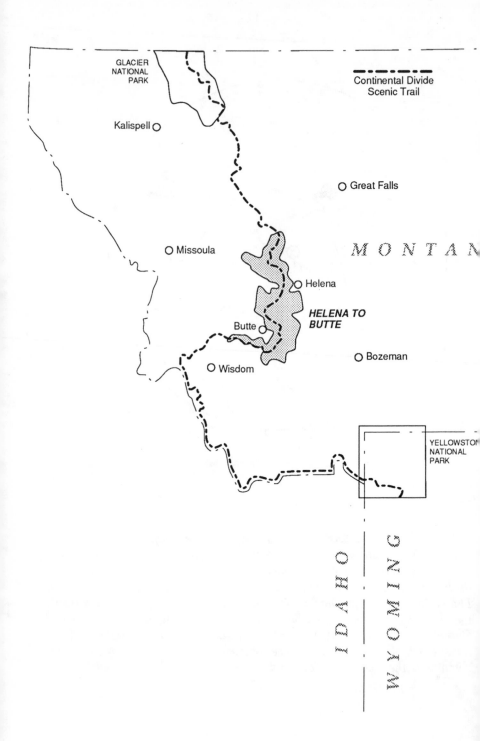

GLACIER
NATIONAL
PARK

Continental Divide
Scenic Trail

Kalispell ○

○ Great Falls

○ Missoula

M O N T A N

Helena ○

*HELENA TO
BUTTE*

Butte ○

○ Bozeman

○ Wisdom

YELLOWSTO
NATIONAL
PARK

I D A H O

W Y O M I N G

HELENA TO BUTTE

Rogers Pass to Flesher Pass — 11.5 miles

Introduction: Breathtaking views make up the segment's first seven miles as the trail rolls along the backbone of the divide, mostly above timberline, from Rogers Pass, north of Lincoln, Montana.

Wildflowers fleck the grassy ridges with color, while the rock in the divide's craggy east slope affords a muted contrast in reds and browns.

The trail, cross-country save for a few game trails and jeep tracks, is easy to follow but arduous to walk, with steep ascents and descents. The going gets rougher in the forest, starting at 6.9, miles, when the trail disappears, leaving the hiker to use compass bearings and game trails to remain on the divide.

History abounds even on this relatively short day hike, starting with Rogers Pass. Hard as it may be to imagine in the sweltering, dry days of summer, a mining camp near this pass recorded the coldest official temperature ever in the continental United States. The mercury dipped to a chilly minus 70 degrees on Jan. 20, 1954.

Mines abounded in the mountains between Lincoln and Rogers Pass. The Mike Horse Mine, seen from on high at about four miles, was the most productive, yielding about $10 million worth of gold, silver and lead before its closing in the first half of this century. Rich copper deposits reportedly have been discovered since, but the mine remains closed.

Rogers Pass was named for Major A.D. Rogers, who surveyed it in 1887 while looking for a low crossing on the divide for the Great Northern Railroad.

Difficulty level: More difficult, with steep ups and downs on the crest of the divide and some cross-country travel through dense forest.

Scenery: Excellent in the first half, as open ridges provide nice views of distant Caribou Peak, Red Mountain, nearby Sunset Mountain and the Blackfoot River Valley.

Water availability: Poor. There is no water convenient to the trail; however, a small stream may be found about one-half mile east of Flesher Pass, in a culvert under Hwy. 279.

Maps: USFS—Helena National Forest Visitors Map. USGS (7.5 minute series)—Rogers Pass, Wilborn.

Supply Points: Resupply is possible at the hike's beginning, Rogers Pass, and at its end, Flesher Pass. Both are serviced by well-traveled highways leading to the nearby town of Lincoln.

Finding the trailhead: Take Hwy. 200 north from Lincoln about 18 miles to Rogers Pass. The trailhead is at a parking area on the east side of the road.

Trail description: Start at a turnout just to the left of a dry creek bed. Climb the grassy slope along the fringe of trees, then traverse diagonally and to the right through open parks to gain the ridgetop.

Rogers Pass to Flesher Pass

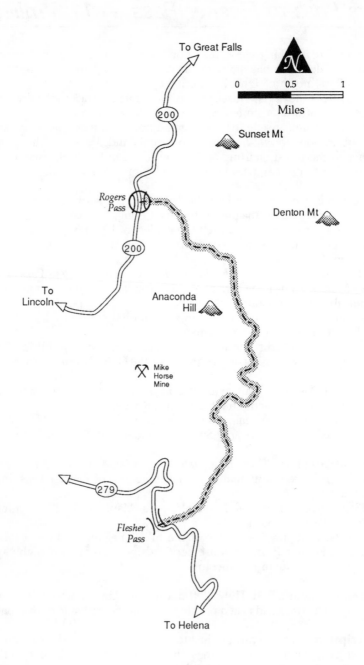

Ascend partially forested Rodgers Mountain, 7,043 feet, along the left edge of the tree line, staying on the open slope to keep the summit in view.

Top the mountain's first ridge and angle to the right, crossing stunted woods before climbing to the top at 1.2 miles for a seemingly endless panoramic view: rust-colored Red Mountain, 7,161 feet, to the northwest; rocky Caribou Peak looming 8,773 feet on its right, and, nearer, Sunset Mountain, topped with a microwave tower, to the northeast.

From this pinnacle, see the ridge of the Continental Divide to the south skirting a precipitous, craggy slope before dropping to a low grassy saddle on the southeast. Already you can see the spur ridge from the divide to the west that you must avoid: It ends with tree-covered Anaconda Hill.

Drop down into the saddle across talus sprinkled with blue alpine forget-me-nots. Pick up a faint trail here that contours to the right of the next peak but fades at the edge of sparse woods. Continue along the ridge in a southeasterly direction and enjoy the views. The trail follows an intermittent footpath along the rest of the hike.

At 2.4 miles turn left (east) with the crest of the divide and drop into another little notch. Snowbanks, a possible source of water, may linger here in the early season. To the north is the valley of the west prong of the Dearborn River's south fork: Shave Gulch, stubbled with trees, is to the south.

After ascending another smaller summit, the trail continues on level terrain for about a mile, approaching a rocky knoll on the left and a high, grassy peak on the right—your next destination.

Two ridges must be topped to gain this 7,217-foot summit: the first, rocky and open; the second, grassy at first, then becoming forested about half-way across. A faint trail leads into the trees but soon peters out. The view from the top at 3.7 miles, of lush green valleys and deep purple, distant peaks, is your reward.

Avoid the spur ridge leading west to Anaconda Hill. Instead, drop steeply into a narrow saddle overlooking the Blackfoot River Valley and the now-defunct Mike Horse Mine to the southwest.

The high peak looming ahead is foreboding, but avoid the climb by contouring to the right of the summit along a prominent game trail that leads to the next low point on the divide, at 5.4 miles.

Two large cairns mark the divide on the open saddle, which is blanketed with purple-velvet larkspur. Camping is a possibility in the grove of pines on the right, but there's no water here. Several small drainages, including Teepee Lodge and Anaconda creeks, flow in the gulches below the divide, about .2 mile to the west.

The trail continues south, rising and then dipping slightly, before joining faint jeep tracks along the climb up the next, 7,220-foot summit. More snowfields may be found in the trees to the east.

From atop the rocky, windswept summit, at 6.3 miles, note how the divide swings to the southwest, and becomes covered with forest.

Follow the game trail that forks to the right along the next descent and contours around the mountain ahead. It leads to a grassy saddle on the divide, at 6.9 miles, and joins another jeep trail. Climb along the jeep track through a narrow band of forest, then a flowery field strewn with larkspur and dainty yellow Wyeth's biscuitroot.

Follow the jeep track downhill into a burned area, the victim of the 208-acre

Rogers Pass to Flesher Pass
Elevation Chart

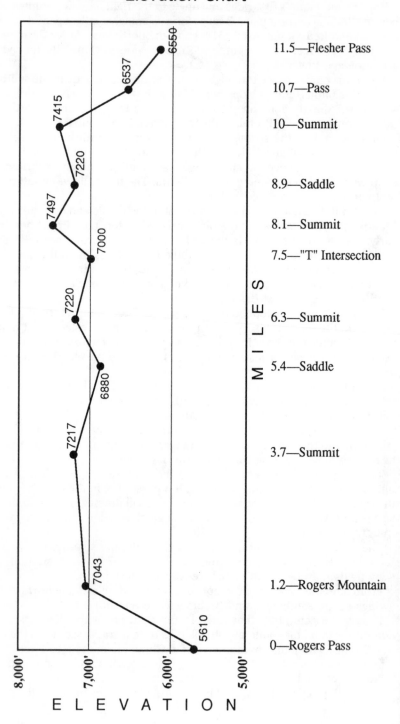

11.5—Flesher Pass

10.7—Pass

10—Summit

8.9—Saddle

8.1—Summit

7.5—"T" Intersection

6.3—Summit

5.4—Saddle

3.7—Summit

1.2—Rogers Mountain

0—Rogers Pass

M I L E S

6550

6537

7415

7220

7497

7000

7220

6880

7217

7043

5610

8,000'   7,000'   6,000'   5,000'

E L E V A T I O N

Canyon Creek blaze of 1979. Older trees are barren and twisted from the heat, but grass and new lodgepole pine seedlings are growing nicely.

The jeep track ends at 7.5 miles at a ''T'' intersection with a road running north-to-south; turn to the left to hike southeast, around the head of Canyon Creek and begin a one-half-mile climb that gains 600 feet in elevation. At the next intersection go left again and ascend, ignoring the jeep road that comes in steeply from the right.

Veer right at the next fork and keep climbing. Near the mountain's top, just ahead, the trees give way to an open, grass-covered meadow. Pause at the high point (still on the Continental Divide) to see Hwy. 279 curving below. Note the ridge to the left that leads to a grass-covered saddle. Leave the jeep track and follow the ridge line, dropping across talus to reach the saddle, at 8.9 miles. A faint trail appears from time to time between this point and Flesher Pass.

Hike a short distance from the saddle on fairly flat terrain and strike a jeep track. Follow the track as it climbs along the edge of open forest, then dips a bit alongside a small, rocky knoll before climbing again.

Leave the trail at its high point and hike cross-country to the right (southeast) through light forest to the hill's peak, 7,415 feet. Try to stay on the open ridge, where hiking is easiest.

Begin descending from the summit through forest, bearing 200 degrees.

The divide rolls high and bare above the Mike Horse Mine in the Helena National Forest, with unobstructed views that let you see where you're going and make cross-country travel a pleasure

Follow the divide as it crosses two jeep roads about one-half mile apart and descends to a grassy, shaded pass thick with fragrant lupines, at about 10.7 miles. Pick up a pack trail that leads west, to the next summit.

Follow the faint trail through an open area and contour along the south slope of the hill, with Hwy. 279 visible to the left. Continue contouring just below the crest of the ridge and reach the next summit, high above Flesher Pass. Descend along the divide, steeply in places, reaching the highway and a parking area at Flesher Pass, 11.5 miles.

Flesher Pass to Stemple Pass — 11.2 Miles

Introduction: A shimmering grove of mature aspens at the edge of a large, flower-filled meadow is the signature of beauty for this pleasant stroll through forest and parks, west of Helena, with only one steep climb.

Popular in the winter with cross-country skiers and snowmobilers, the trail is easy to follow and, except for the lack of water, makes for a perfect one-day family hike.

The last mile of the segment is a direct, no-nonsense descent through forest and some clear-cut areas to Stemple Pass. The proliferation of logging roads criss-crossing the trail keeps the going interesting, however.

Flesher Pass, 6,131 feet, was named after an early settler of the area; Stemple Pass for J.A. Stemple, who located the Stemple Mining District.

Difficulty level: Easy, with gradual ups and downs on well-marked trail and dirt roads.

Scenery: Fair, with forest obscuring most views. A clearing about mid-hike offers a nice look at nearby summits, and a climb above timberline near hike's end presents distant, impressive Caribou Peak.

Water availability: Poor. None convenient to the divide.

Maps: USFS—Helena National Forest Visitor's Map. USGS (7.5 minute series)—Wilborn and Stemple Pass.

Supply Points: There are no supply points convenient to the trail. Stemple Pass, at hike's end, is about 15.5 miles east of Lincoln along Forest Service Road 689, which receives a fair amount of traffic.

Trail description: A jeep road blocked to traffic leads from the parking area along the Helena (southwest) side of the divide. Climb gradually through mostly open terrain that, in the spring, hosts a lush flower garden. Brilliant blue lupines tumble from the gently sloping hills to the right (north) to spill their perfume across the trail; tall puffs of beargrass add white accents.

A sign on a tree at .6 mile points to Continental Divide Trail 440 bearing right (west). Follow the trail gently upward through light forest and parks with more lupines. Camping is possible in these flat, grassy parks, but there is no water close at hand.

The trail continues climbing steadily through forest before leveling out on a ridge at 2.2 miles for a nice view of some unnamed mountains nearby, to the east. To the southwest lies the forested Virginia Creek basin.

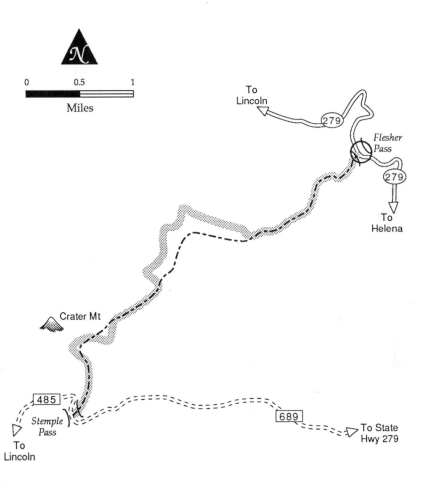

Flesher Pass to Stemple Pass
Elevation Chart

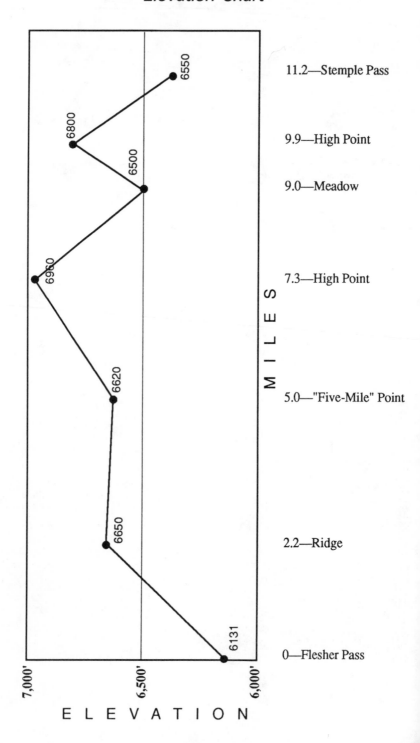

11.2—Stemple Pass

9.9—High Point

9.0—Meadow

7.3—High Point

M I L E S

5.0—"Five-Mile" Point

2.2—Ridge

0—Flesher Pass

6550
6800
6500
6960
6620
6650
6131

7,000'   6,500'   6,000'

E L E V A T I O N

An unmarked trail comes in from the left (south) at 2.4 miles; bypass it and stay on the main path, which drops a bit. A dry camp can be made at the bottom of the descent in a grove of pines.

The trail climbs again to pass another unsigned trail junction at 3.6 miles. Stay on the divide trail and contour around the summit ahead.

On the open hillside the trail fades in grass and wildflowers, but tree blazes make the route easy to follow.

Continue mostly in forest for nearly two miles, with gradual ups and downs, bending with the trail to head southwest. Pass another unsigned junction with a trail striking off to the right (north).

A "5" carved in a tree marks the 5-mile point. A faint trail soon appears on the left (east). Ignore it to ascend through an open stand of young lodgepole pines.

At 7.3 miles the trail begins descending, at first through woods and then into an open area with views of the surrounding tree-covered hills.

At 7.5 miles two large stone cairns mark the trail as it crosses the east side of the open slope. Soon see the prettiest views of the trip so far, featuring rusty Red Mountain, 7,161 feet, in the distance to the north and lovely hills and grassy meadows below on the right (west).

The trail then switchbacks suddenly to the right and continues up along

Route 279 winds its way up a narrow canyon to meet the divide at Flesher Pass, in the Helena National Forest. Flesher Pass marks a transition as the divide leaves open, rolling ridges and enters thickly wooded country.

the open slope to enter a large meadow at nine miles, with another good, but dry, campsite. The path fades in the grass here but is marked with three tall wooden posts and occasional blazes on the larger trees. ATV tracks swing in from the left (east) near the bottom of the descent; continue past them toward the woods at the south end of the grassy slope.

The worn footpath reappears at the meadow's edge, where four tall aspens shimmer in the sun. Enter a cool, dense forest, passing a trail that joins from the right (west). Climb to an opening that offers views of distant summits, including rocky Caribou Peak, to the northwest.

In forest again, begin a very steep climb that crosses an open area, under a power line, and past a jeep road on the right (west). Another jeep road, marked by tree blazes and Continental Divide Trail markers, comes in shortly afterward; follow it to head west.

Continue through forest and several clear-cut areas to climb slowly but steadily in a southwesterly direction along the divide. After a high point at 9.9 miles, begin descending along the road to switchback down the side of a hill. Pass a sign along the descent that points the way to Flesher Pass for south-to-north travelers.

Pick up a series of blue diamonds marking the trail for cross-country skiers, and pass through lightly shaded parks with brilliant blue lupines. Continue descending for another .5 mile to merge with another road. Bear right onto Forest Service Road 1841 at the next, four-way, intersection, reaching 6,376-foot Stemple Pass at 11.2 miles.

Stemple Pass to Dana Spring — 17.6 Miles

Introduction: The rugged twin peaks of Nevada and Black mountains provide an enchanting backdrop to the rolling, open ridges of the Continental Divide in this most beautiful of all hikes in the Helena section.

Walking can be hard at first, with 4.5 miles of tramping on gravel road, but the ascent to the divide is gradual and offers a bird's-eye view of Davis Gulch to the west.

Uphill walking turns to uphill puffing when the trail becomes a primitive jeep road, with views obscured by trees.

The sudden emergence into a picturesque meadow, however, marks the beginning of spectacular countryside along the wind-swept heights of the divide, as the trail rises and dips above treeline. The vista sweeps across a tree-topped sea of hills and valleys to reach towering Nevada Mountain, 8,293 feet, and its partner, Black Mountain, 8,338 feet.

The more closely they loom, the more foreboding they appear, but neither of the peaks is scaled to its summit. The trail almost tops Black Mountain, though: It climbs to 8,180 feet, the highest point of the section, before heading sharply down through forest to pastoral Dana Spring.

Difficulty level: More difficult, with a steep ascent along the base of Nevada Mountain and a climb up the face of 8,338-foot Black Mountain.

Scenery: Excellent, with panoramic views along the open ridge of the divide.
Water availability: None, save for snowbanks in early season, until Dana Spring.
Maps: USFS—Helena National Forest Visitor's Map. USGS (7.5 minute series)—Stemple Pass, Granite Butte, Nevada Mountain; (15 minute series)—Avon, Elliston.
Supply Points: There are no supply points convenient to the trail. Dana Spring is 13 miles from Avon, which has a cafe, general store and post office (ZIP 59713), via Forest Service Road 136 and Hwy. 272.

Finding the trailhead: Stemple Pass is on Forest Service Road 689, off Montana Hwy. 279, about 32 miles west of Helena, and 15.5 miles east of Lincoln off Hwy. 200.

Trail description: Head south along the crest of the divide on Forest Service Road 485 from the Stemple Pass Recreation Area parking lot. The gravel road is passable by auto.

The road climbs gradually through forest for .5 mile, where the view opens up to reveal pretty mountains to the west and Davis Gulch below. Continuing upward and passing some clear-cuts, the road at three miles affords a look at Granite Butte, 7,600 feet, with a lookout tower poking above its tree-covered summit.

Reach a signed intersection and bear right, remaining on Forest Service Road 485. Soon begin descending a bit, through forest again and more clear-cuts.

Reach another four-way intersection at 3.5 miles, with a road descending to Poor Man's Gulch on the right (west). Continue straight on the main road, ascending again. Pass abandoned log cabins on both sides of the road and then, on the right (west), see hillsides strewn with logging debris. The land here is privately owned; Forest Service property begins again at 3.85 miles.

At 4.2 miles a road descends to the right (west). Continue south on the main road, climbing slightly. Leave Forest Service Road 495 at the next intersection and bear right onto a jeep track that crosses a grassy flat before beginning a gradually climb.

The spring shown on the Granite Butte topo map lies .6 mile to the south from this junction, at the head of Marsh Creek.

Pass through a gate and continue climbing, through woods and then into a small park. A dry camp is possible here.

Cross a cattle guard and enter forest to climb steeply, topping out in another park. Staying on the jeep road, drop a bit to a blazed tree at six miles, then climb again to a flat, open area with pretty views of the grassy hillsides below. A Forest Service road closure sign and a small bulletin board nailed to a tree are landmarks.

Keep climbing on the rutted jeep road, ignoring a road coming in from the right at 6.4 miles, where the main trail levels out.

Now descend again and follow the road as it bends sharply to the right; a yellow diamond marker and an arrow on a tree point the way. Continue descending, still in forest, to a large grassy area on the divide between the head of Nevada Creek and the North Fork of Little Prickly Pear Creek.

The meadow is another possible campsite, with water a half-mile away in Nevada Creek. Wildflowers bloom in profusion in the meadow, and pines

Stemple Pass to Dana Spring

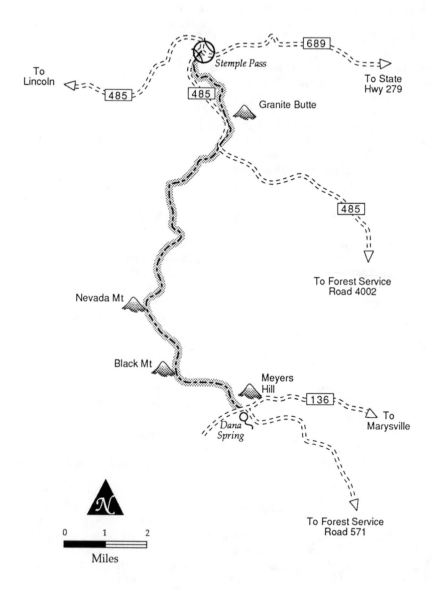

To Lincoln

485

485

Stemple Pass

689

To State
Hwy 279

Granite Butte

485

To Forest Service
Road 4002

Nevada Mt

Black Mt

Meyers
Hill

136

To
Marysville

Dana
Spring

To Forest Service
Road 571

0   1   2
Miles

Stemple Pass to Dana Spring
Elevation Chart

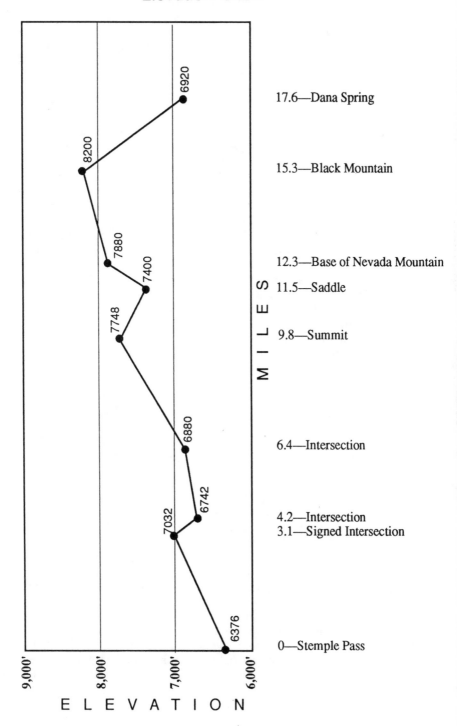

17.6—Dana Spring

15.3—Black Mountain

12.3—Base of Nevada Mountain
11.5—Saddle

9.8—Summit

6.4—Intersection

4.2—Intersection
3.1—Signed Intersection

0—Stemple Pass

M I L E S

6920

8200

7880
7400

7748

6880

6742

7032

6376

9,000'   8,000'   7,000'   6,000'

E L E V A T I O N

and aspens grow along its edges. The grass-topped, 7,600-foot mountain looming over the meadow on its opposite side is your next goal.

Leave the jeep track where it swings right (west) to Nevada Creek, and head cross-country past a shallow mining pit. Ascend through trees, picking up a faint trail, to a small park; follow the trail until it disappears, then simply continue the uphill puff to the summit, gaining nearly 1,000 feet in a mile.

From the pinnacle, the Granite Butte Lookout Tower can be seen to the north and, to the south, the winding ridge of the Continental Divide.

Here the hike at last rewards your effort, with views extending far across the countryside. The trail from here follows the ridge of the divide for several miles.

Continue south, reentering light forest. Head to the right (west) to pick up a faint trail that climbs to the next summit.

From the top the divide again can be seen trailing south. Follow a jeep track through open trees along the ridge's east side, to ascend again. At 9.8 miles, near the top of the peak, the trail disappears; continue upward to the summit.

Here another jeep road appears. Follow as it bears to the right (west), and enjoy the views of Nevada Mountain ahead and, to the left, Black Mountain. A set of jagged cliffs connects the two dark, foreboding peaks; lingering snowbanks, a possible water source, paint a stark white contrast along the ridge.

The route is obvious from here: up and over the next hill, down across the long, grassy saddle, up along the ridge beside Nevada Mountain and then atop the cliffs, to Black Mountain. As close as they may appear, those cliffs are more than three miles away.

Top the next summit and drop down to cross the mile-long saddle. Pick up a trail as you then enter woods to begin the steep ascent up the base of Nevada Mountain. Stay high and to the right, ignoring game trails that contour and descend.

At 13.3 miles make a steep, very rocky, very careful drop to the next low point. A sign here points the way to Black Mountain Trail 337, which continues level for a short time before climbing again.

The next intersection, at 14.7 miles, brings a trail from Dead Man's Creek, to the southeast. Continue on Trail 337, signed again here, which soon becomes very rocky.

Ascending the face of Black Mountain the trail makes two long switchbacks to climb 550 feet in .6 mile, and, ultimately round the mountain's southeast side. Here, at the high point are lovely views of the Helena Valley below and some distant peaks, including summits in the Gates of the Mountains Wilderness and the Big Belt Mountains.

At 8,200 feet, this is the highest point reached on the trail so far since leaving Canada.

Descend on a jeep track through barren trees that apparently were burned long ago. The area is grassy now, and young trees grow as high as 10 feet beside their ancestors' skeletons.

Pass through some clear-cuts before emerging into a grassy, wildflower-strewn meadow at about 17.6 miles. Follow the trail to the top of a small ridge with a rocky outcropping on its right edge, and look south across the vast meadow to pole-fenced Dana Spring, a good source of water and a terrific campsite.

Good views of the rugged Flint Creek Range are seen from the meadow. Watch the rises surrounding the spring for elk silhouetted in the twilight, and keep an eye to the night sky for some of the best star-gazing on the entire Montana divide.

Dana Spring to Mullan Pass — 15.3 Miles

Introduction: History, not scenery, is the fascination here as the trail follows dirt roads and power lines past now-defunct gold mines and near the town of Marysville, site of one of Montana's richest mines.

Thomas Cruse, an Irishman who came to Montana to seek his fortune, found it in these hills in the late 1880s after years of fruitless panning and digging and living in poverty. With the discovery of a wealth of quartz, gold's geological grandparent, Cruse began a long tunneling by hand into the hill he later named Drumlummon, after his parish in Ireland. He struck gold there, and his discovery became known throughout the area.

In contrast to the rugged peaks characterizing the section just to the north, the divide here follows rolling, hill-like terrain through grasslands. The walking is pleasant, especially when the abundant beargrass is blooming. But the trail does pass through a number of logged areas, and power lines are visible during most of the hike.

The walk ends at Mullan Pass, where the first good road across the Continental Divide was built in 1863. Near the pass is another historic site: first meeting place of the Masons in Montana, in 1862.

Difficulty level: Easy, with gentle ups and downs on dirt roads.
Scenery: Fair, as the route winds through forests and logged areas.
Water: None convenient to trail; short side trips yield spring water.
Maps: USFS—Helena National Forest Visitor's Map. USGS (15 min. series)—Elliston.
Supply Points: The trail passes within three miles of Marysville, a ghost town and ski resort with a post office (ZIP 59640) and a restaurant, along Forest Service Road 136.

Finding the trailhead: Dana Spring is on Forest Service Road 136, about 9.5 miles west of the historic mining town of Marysville.

Trail description: Head left (east) on Forest Service Road 136, a smooth dirt road that is perpendicular to the trail running alongside Dana Spring. At the road-trail intersection, a sign points the northbound traveler to Black Mountain Rt. 337.

Strike out uphill to pass through a fence and across a cattle guard. This driveable dirt road is your route for the next four miles, passing through woods and parks brimming with beargrass. Pass a small, fenced-enclosed pond at 1.5 miles; a bit farther, a sign points the way to nearby Charity Gulch, Faith Gulch and Hope Creek.

Dana Spring to Mullan Pass

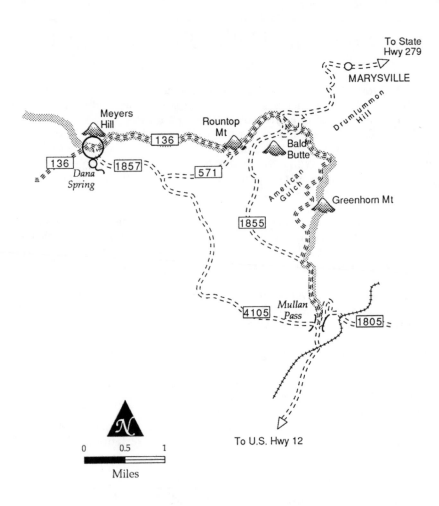

To State
Hwy 279

MARYSVILLE

Meyers
Hill

Rountop
Mt

Bald
Butte

Drumlummon Hill

136

136

1857

Dana
Spring

571

American Gulch

Greenhorn Mt

1855

4105

Mullan
Pass

1805

N

0   0.5   1

Miles

To U.S. Hwy 12

Dana Spring to Mullan Pass
Elevation Chart

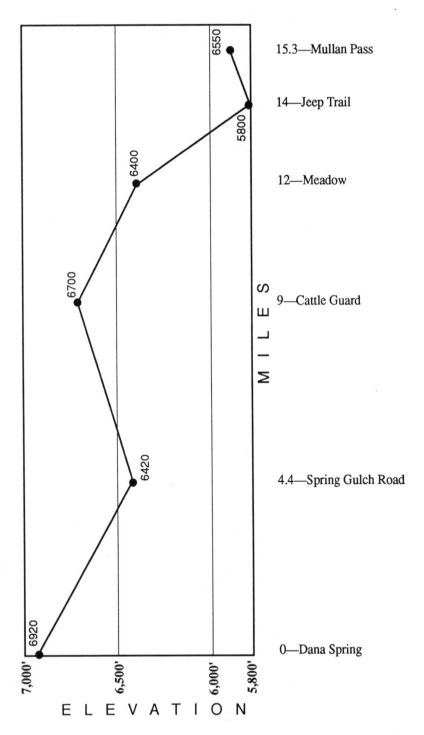

15.3—Mullan Pass

14—Jeep Trail

12—Meadow

9—Cattle Guard

4.4—Spring Gulch Road

0—Dana Spring

Roundtop Mountain, studded with microwave towers, comes into view at three miles as the road bends to the left (south). At 4.4 miles a sign points the way to Spring Gulch; at 4.7 miles take the jeep road that comes in from the right (south), leaving Forest Service Road 136 for a short time to contour along the south edge of Roundtop Mountain.

Forest Service Road 136 could be followed straight ahead here, to pass Roundtop Mountain on its north edge. Although a more straightforward route, it doesn't afford the open views to the south that the official route provides.

Soon another jeep road, badly eroded, intersects the trail. Bear right here and enter a cool, sheltered glade that harbors a small mining test pit. A dry camp could be made here.

Tree-covered Greenhorn Mountain, 7,505 feet, can be seen looming ahead. Pass two roads leading left (northeast) to Woodchopper Gulch and Drumlummon Hill. The partially clear-cut trail swings around and to the right (south); ahead, a faint jeep track comes in from the left. Bear left (northeast) here and ascend through fertile hills rounding the south side of Roundtop Mountain.

Intersect a good dirt road, the Hope Creek Road, and turn left to drop back onto Forest Service Road 136.

Ascend on the road, heading northeast, to the top of a grassy saddle on the Continental Divide, which consists of small, open hills along this stretch. At an unsigned intersection at 6.9 miles, turn right and head uphill, toward the old Neenan Mine.

(Water can be found less than one-half mile off the route by heading straight at this intersection. Look on the right for spring water flowing from a small pipe, near a grove of trees.)

Next descend through open country on a jeep road, to cross under a set of power lines at 7.7 miles. Travel uphill again to see another set of lines crossing north-to-south; head for these and turn southeast with them to drop past the abandoned Neenan Mine. Keep an eye out for hostile cattle.

After crossing a cattle guard at nine miles, the trail begins its easy contour of Greenhorn Mountain. Soon a jeep road ascends steeply to the left; bear right to take the low road. Near the end of the three-mile contour the trail drops through forest and crosses beneath the power lines. It then veers away from the lines to pass through a large, open meadow beginning at 12 miles.

Meet the power lines again at 12.6 miles and continue south beneath them on a dirt road. Less than .5 mile later reach the head of Uncle George Creek, a pretty oasis with grassy, sheltered benches good for camping. Water is minimal in the trickle of a creek, however, and its quality is questionable. Cattle frequently graze this area.

At 14 miles the road intersects a jeep trail. Turn left (southeast) to follow it gradually up a grassy hill toward the power lines and the top of the Continental Divide. On the unimpressive ridge a fork leads left to an historical marker noting the site of the first Masonic meeting in Montana, in 1862.

Bear right (south) at the intersection, heading for the power lines, to drop to Mullan Pass, at 15.3 miles, and Forest Service Road 1805.

Beargrass is omnipresent along the trail in northern Montana, but it blooms profusely only in five-to-seven-year cycles. It can be found in open meadows and clear-cuts in the Helena National Forest. The leaves were dried and bleached and used by Indians to make baskets and clothing.

Mullan Pass to Priest Pass — 2.2 Miles

Introduction: A variety of terrain, including a huge boulder slide, makes for an interesting, challenging hike. With much of the trail overgrown in grasses, flowers and weeds, compass following is essential.

The reward for all this exertion: a huge, colorful, flower-strewn meadow just north of Priest Pass and a nice view of surrounding hills from an opening overlooking the pass.

Difficulty level: Moderately difficult, with steep, rocky ascents and descents—all cross-country.

Scenery: Fair, with no vistas but a riot of wildflowers in grassy parks.

Water availability: Good, at a spring near Mullan Tunnel.

Maps: USFS—Helena National Forest Visitors Map. USGS (15 min. series)—Elliston.

Supply Points: Mullan Pass, 15 miles from Helena on Forest Service Road 1805, and Priest Pass, 12 miles from Helena on Forest Service Road 335. Both are good, driveable dirt roads.

Finding the trailhead: Mullan Pass is 15 miles from Helena, on Forest Service Road 1805.

Trail description: From the pass head south, taking a faint jeep road coming across the grass to the west of the Mullan Pass sign. Descend to the left (east) for a short time until intersecting a set of power lines.

Turn right (southeast) and ascend cross-country along the power lines to another, better, jeep track. Follow the track south to continue climbing, still along the power lines, through forest. We saw a rusting, 1950s-make auto riddled with bullet holes in the trees along the way.

At about .5 mile the jeep track veers to the right (west) and crosses under the power lines. Leave the track here to continue south along the wires, taking a cross-country route that drops steeply down a bumpy, overgrown hillside.

At .8 mile cross another jeep track; below, a set of railroad tracks can be seen running east-to-west and into the Mullan Pass Tunnel, to the west.

Drop down the steep, rocky bank to the tracks. Cross the tracks and drop again, into a gully on their south side. Water seeping from the rocks beside the tunnel, above, and trickling down through the gully may be tempting, but it is dirty and should not be drunk. Clean water awaits at the top of the huge boulder slide before you.

From the gully, climb carefully up the boulder pile. Clear spring water flows at the top from a small pipe. Fill up those water bottles; clean water may not be at hand for eight miles.

At the head of the boulder slide lies an old creek bed, now dry. Take the south-bound path along its left (east) bank, passing a barbed-wire fence. A bit farther down a large rock outcropping looms on the right (west) and two boulder slides come in on the east.

After passing the second, larger rock slide, find a faint trail leading upward to the left (east). Take this route until it fades, then continue climbing at 155

Mullan Pass to MacDonald Pass

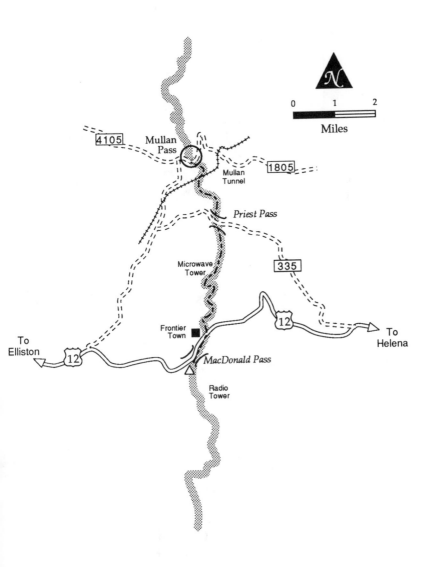

Mullan Pass to MacDonald Pass
Elevation Chart

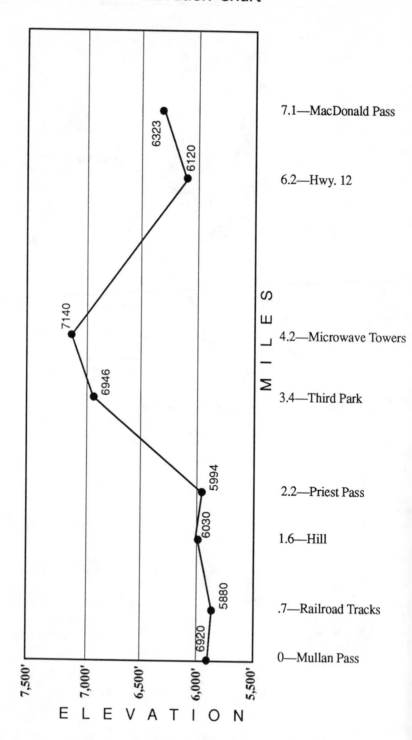

7.1—MacDonald Pass

6.2—Hwy. 12

M I L E S

4.2—Microwave Towers

3.4—Third Park

2.2—Priest Pass

1.6—Hill

.7—Railroad Tracks

0—Mullan Pass

6323
6120
7140
6946
5994
6030
5880
6920

7,500'   7,000'   6,500'   6,000'   5,500'

E L E V A T I O N

degrees through the trees, to the top of the hill. Pass an old pole fence as you go.

At the top of the hill, 1.6 miles, the woods give way to a meadow tall with grass and ablaze with flowers. Slender aspens enhance the area's lush beauty.

Cross the flat meadow at a bearing of 162 degrees, walking one-half mile before climbing, again through trees, to top a small summit on the divide. The views open at the top to reveal Forest Service Road 335 (Priest Pass Road) winding below on the south, through Priest Pass, 2.2 miles.

Priest Pass to MacDonald Pass — 4.5 Miles

Introduction: This well-marked, pleasant trek near Helena climbs 1,000 feet in 1.2 miles from Priest Pass through dense forest interspersed with flower-strewn parks.

The trail then levels a bit before climbing gradually to the 7,215-foot apex with a microwave tower and nice views of surrounding hills, the rugged Flint Creek Range, and MacDonald Pass.

Priest Pass, 5,994 feet, was named after Valentine Priest, a tuberculosis sufferer who moved to here from out East and was cured by the healthful alpine climate. He built the Priest Pass road in 1879, which proved an easier and more popular route across the divide than nearby MacDonald Pass.

The descent to MacDonald Pass along a dirt road is long and full of switchbacks, but is open enough so that the pretty views are enjoyed all the way to the bottom. Here, 15 miles west of Helena, U.S. Hwy. 12 crosses MacDonald Pass, a recreation area complete with campground.

Another campground nearby is named after Cromwell Dixon, an early aviator who, on Sept. 30, 1911, became the first to fly an airplane over the Continental Divide. Dixon, who was then only 19 years old, won a $10,000 cash prize for his effort.

MacDonald Pass, 6,323 feet, is named after Alexander MacDonald, who from 1876 to 1883 managed a toll gate along the road that featured extensive log "corduroying," a bane of stagecoach travel.

Near the pass is Frontier Town, an Old West-style tourist attraction complete with a saloon and restaurant.

Difficulty level: Moderate, with a steep initial ascent that becomes more gradual and a downhill finish on dirt road.

Scenery: Fair, of forested hills, with the best view at two miles atop a 7,215-foot peak studded with radio towers.

Water availability: None until the descent, when water seeps from hillsides along the road.

Maps: USFS—Helena National Forest Visitors Map. USGS (15-min. series)—Elliston.

Finding the trailhead: Priest Pass is on Forest Service Road 335, 12.5 miles west of Helena.

Trail description: Take the jeep track on the south side of Priest Pass and begin climbing through forest. Pass through one park, a possible campsite, then reenter woods for another brief stretch. A fenced spring at the far right corner of the meadow was trampled by cattle and had gone dry when we hiked.

Enter a second park where the trail fades out in the lush grass. Bear right (southwest) across the park to find a tree blaze; enter woods again to continue ascending on a well-worn trail.

The third park, at 1.2 miles, lies atop the Continental Divide and provides open views of surrounding hills. The tree-covered mountain looming on the southwest, studded with microwave towers, is your next goal. Strike out toward the summit on a jeep track.

Enter forest once more near the summit, following tree blazes. Ascend, passing through an opening in a barbed-wire fence as you near the top.

Forest gives way at the top to an open, grassy field sporting a block house and an impressive array of radio communication towers. A sign here denotes Trail 312, the Continental Divide Trail; pause to enjoy the views here that include the rugged sawtooths of the Flint Creek Range to the southwest.

From here the trail follows a dirt road that switchbacks down nearly 1,000 feet in two miles to U.S. Hwy. 12., passing beneath power lines enroute.

Strike the hardtop next to a state Department of Highway maintenance shed and turn right, ascending gradually. Soon pass water pipes with faucets, on either side of the road.

Pass the entrance to Frontier Town on the right just before topping the 6,323-foot pass at 4.5 miles. A recreation road leading to the Cromwell-Dixon picnic area and Vista Point is on the east side of the pass.

MacDonald Pass to I-15 — 58.8 Miles

Introduction: The trail winds along the forested and rugged crest of the divide from MacDonald Pass west of Helena to cross Interstate 15, north of Butte.

It follows a combination of jeep roads, jeep tracks, pack trail and graded Forest Service roads through the varied terrain of the Boulder Mountains.

The trail is generally well marked, but is forced from the divide to follow an alternate route near Bison Mountain. The trail disappears near Thunderbolt Mountain, requiring a short trek cross-country through thick forest.

Water is plentiful in creeks and shallow Cottonwood Lake. Game is abundant, with moose, mule deer, whitetail deer, black bear, and blue and ruffed grouse frequenting the area.

Although much of the hike is through forest, the trees give way periodically to offer fine views of a variety of features: the Big Belt and Elkhorn mountains beyond the broad Helena Valley, the rugged Flint Creek Range and the Clark Fork River basin, and the Highland and snow-capped Tobacco Root mountains south of Butte.

Logging activity is heavy along this segment, and numerous clear cuts are crossed. Parts of the divide also have been mined, with the trail swinging through the abandoned mining camp of Leadville.

Mineral wealth along the divide is wrested from granite that marks the Boulder Batholith, a huge granite mass extending from Helena to Butte.

Geologists believe the area 70 to 75 million years ago was a vast, resurgent volcano that periodically spewed cubic miles of lava, called Elkhorn Mountains rock, onto the surface. But most of the rock crystallized into pale gray granite beneath the surface, which gradually was exposed by steady erosion.

Then about 50 million years ago another period of volcanic activity yielded Lowland Creek volcanic rock, mostly white and brown.

From Champion Pass the trail mostly follows road, dropping to a developed Forest Service campground at Lowland Creek. The trail crosses Burlington Northern Railroad tracks and Interstate 15 just north of 6,374-foot Elk Park Pass, at the head of a high mountain basin that no longer has a stream running through it.

Difficulty level: Easy on mostly well-marked trail that follows pack trail and roads, but with a cross-country hike near Thunderbolt Mountain.
Scenery: Good, mostly of tree-covered peaks.
Water availability: Good, in numerous streams and Cottonwood Lake.
Maps: USFS—Helena National Forest visitors map. USGS (15 min. series)— Elliston, Basin, Deer Lodge, Butte North; (7.5 minute series)—MacDonald Pass, Three Brothers, Bison Mountain, Thunderbolt Creek, Sugarloaf Mountain, Lockhart Meadows, Sheepshead Mountain, Elk Park Pass.
Supply Points: The trail intersects Interstate 15 at the Trask interchange. Butte, a full-service community, lies about 10 miles to the south; Basin, about 16 miles to the north.

Finding the trailhead: MacDonald Pass is 15 miles west of Helena, on U.S. Hwy. 12. Turn left from the pass onto the MacDonald Pass Recreation Road at the entrance to the Cromwell-Dixon picnic area. Continue straight through the first intersection and head onto gravel, with radio towers in view ahead. Bear left at the next fork and reach a parking area and trailhead at Vista Point, with signs for the Continental Divide National Scenic Trail.

Trail description: Descend from the Vista Point parking area along Trail 348, crossing an open meadow before entering forest. Soon pass a good spring to the left of the trail that has been fenced to protect it from cattle. There is good camping here.

Pass some mining test pits as the trail generally descends through forest mixed with small meadows. Climb to a rocky summit with limited views, then drop slightly and climb again to a second summit at 2.25 miles.

The word "VIEW" and a directional arrow have been carved into a tree near the summit. Follow a short side trail to the right and reach a rocky outcrop, with views to the northeast of the Big Belt Mountains in the background with the tree-covered mountains of the divide in the foreground. Rolling, tree-covered hills lie to the east and southeast against the backdrop of the rugged Flint Creek Range. Hills to the south are being clear-cut.

Descend gradually from the overlook through lodgepole pine past an aspen-lined boulder field. Drop to a saddle and begin ascending again through mature lodgepole with grasses and juniper covering the forest floor.

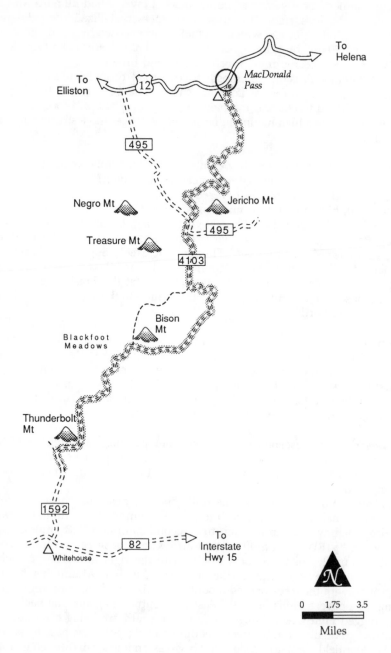

To
Helena

To
Elliston

12

MacDonald
Pass

495

Negro Mt

Jericho Mt

495

Treasure Mt

4103

Bison
Mt

Blackfoot
Meadows

Thunderbolt
Mt

1592

Whitehouse

82

To
Interstate
Hwy 15

N

0   1.75   3.5

Miles

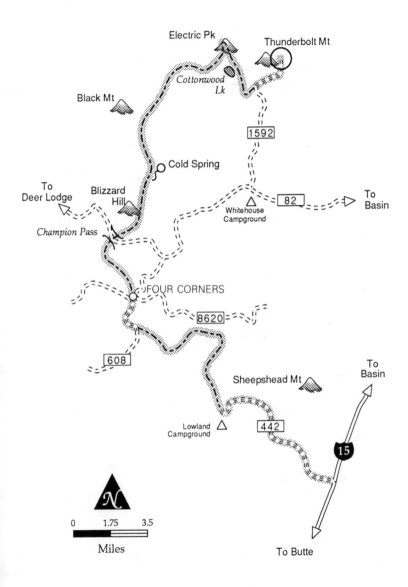

Soon pass through younger stands of lodgepole and enter a willow-lined marshy area, ideal habitat for moose. A good creek and dry campsites are along the fringes of the meadow.

Ascend through a series of meadows, following the stream up past its source. Reach an open hilltop at 3.25 miles with a panoramic view, including MacDonald Pass to the north and the Helena Valley to the northeast.

Intersect the Bear Gulch Jeep Road on the hilltop and turn right (west). Drop along the jeep track and reenter forest, then climb to top the grass-covered hill ahead.

There are good views here of the Flint Creek Range to the distant west, the valley of the Little Blackfoot River with the towns of Elliston and Avon to the northwest, and to the west and southwest of clear-cuts on tree-covered hillsides.

Descend gradually along jeep tracks through open forest and parks to the edge of the clear-cuts below. Intersect a more heavily traveled jeep road at 4.75 miles just before reaching a large clear-cut. Turn left (south) onto the jeep road and cross a good creek flowing through a culvert.

Pass clear-cuts to the right and left of the trail. Reach an intersection with a jeep track entering from the right at the head of another good creek. Bear left (southeast) and pass another clear-cut to the left.

Ascend slightly, passing alternately through three stands of lodgepole and three clear-cuts as the road winds around the head of the Flume Creek basin. Jericho Mountain, 7,378 feet, is the tree-covered summit to the left.

Skirt the base of Jericho Mountain and bend to the north, with good views back to the northeast of MacDonald Pass. Pass several shallow ponds in a large, regrowing clear-cut at 7.6 miles, with rugged cliffs rising to the south and east.

Bear left (south) near the end of the clear-cut onto a jeep road and ascend gradually up the low ridge separating Flume Gulch from the Jericho Creek basin. More clear-cuts come into view from the top. Stay on the jeep road as it contours through another clear-cut, offering good views to the west of the Little Blackfoot River Valley.

Descend across a clear-cut, then climb gradually and contour around the next low ridge. The jeep road dead-ends just before it enters the forest ahead. Pick up a well-signed, newly constructed pack trail that forks to the left and enter the forest.

The trail winds through lodgepole mixed with juniper, occasionally passing small, aspen-lined parks cradling trickling creeks as it descends and contours to join the Jericho Creek Trail, a jeep track, at 9.1 miles.

Turn right (southwest) and descend along the creek, a reliable water supply. Soon intersect Forest Service Road 495, the Telegraph Creek Road, and turn left (east).

Pass several good campsites along Telegraph Creek as the road ascends gradually, reaching an intersection at 10.3 miles. Turn right (southwest) onto Forest Service Road 1859 and climb gradually. Bear left at the next intersection, 11 miles, onto Forest Service Road 495.

Pass in a half-mile a regrowing clear-cut alongside a freshly cut area. Stay on the main road, ignoring numerous side tracks. Continue straight through the intersection with Trail 373, which leads to the Ontario Mine, at 12.5 miles.

Good views to the southwest through the trees here reveal the tree-covered

MacDonald Pass to I-15
Elevation Chart

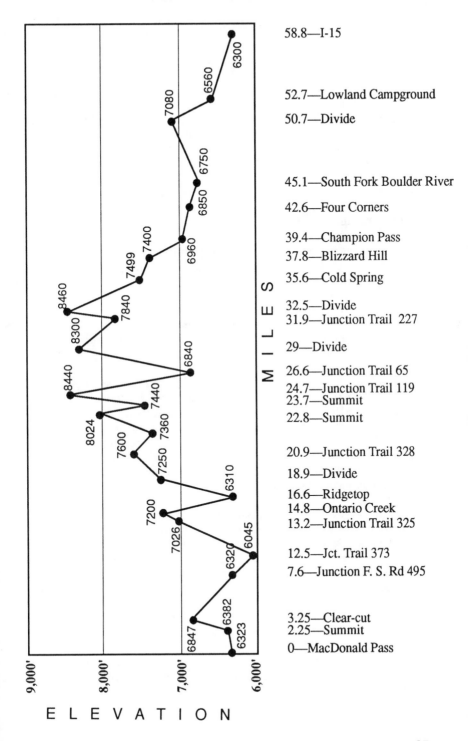

58.8—I-15

52.7—Lowland Campground
50.7—Divide

45.1—South Fork Boulder River
42.6—Four Corners

39.4—Champion Pass
37.8—Blizzard Hill
35.6—Cold Spring

32.5—Divide
31.9—Junction Trail 227

29—Divide

26.6—Junction Trail 65
24.7—Junction Trail 119
23.7—Summit
22.8—Summit

20.9—Junction Trail 328

18.9—Divide

16.6—Ridgetop
14.8—Ontario Creek
13.2—Junction Trail 325

12.5—Jct. Trail 373
7.6—Junction F. S. Rd 495

3.25—Clear-cut
2.25—Summit
0—MacDonald Pass

M I L E S

9,000' 8,000' 7,000' 6,000'

E L E V A T I O N

divide ahead extending to 8,028-foot Bison Mountain, looming beyond the forested basin of Bison Creek. Intersect Trail 325 at 13.2 miles. Turn right onto the rocky jeep road and descend into the forest.

This point marks the beginning of a short alternate route that rejoins the official trail on Bison Mountain. When constructed, the official route will remain along the crest of the divide.

Stay on the jeep track and drop through a small clear-cut before reentering forest on the far side. Trees obstruct views of the divide to the left (east). Cross a tributary of Ontario Creek, a good water source, and continue descending through thick lodgepole pine.

Descend gradually through a clearing at 14.7 miles, passing some mining prospects and the remains of an old log cabin. Bear left at a signed intersection just beyond the meadow onto a jeep track that drops to cross Ontario Creek. Climb from the crossing and soon enter a large clear-cut that is bisected by logging roads.

Turn left at the first intersection and ascend gradually to a second road junction. Turn right here, then in a short distance turn left onto a jeep track that climbs to reenter the forest. Climb, steeply in places, reaching the ridgetop at 16.6 miles. There are good views here to the southeast through the trees of the tree-covered divide. Stay on the jeep track, reaching a junction with a good jeep road, Forest Service Road 123, at 17 miles.

Turn left and pass through a clear-cut. Stay on the main road as it enters forest and ascends gradually toward Bison Mountain. There are good views to the north and northwest overlooking the forested Little Blackfoot River basin, with Negro and Treasure mountains rising above the low, rolling ridges.

Reach a road barricade at 18.4 miles and continue straight, now on jeep track. Bear right at a fork a short distance ahead, remaining on the heavier-traveled track. The trail regains the divide at 18.9 miles in thick lodgepole pine. Stay on the main jeep track, ignoring heavily traveled game trails.

Break into a meadow at 20.5 miles, with good views overlooking the Blackfoot Meadows area to the north and Thunderbolt Mountain, 8,597 feet, rising slightly above treeline on the divide ahead to the southwest.

Descend through the meadow along the jeep track and enter open forest. Reach a signed junction with Trail 328 at 20.9 miles. Bear left and in a short distance reach a good campsite, with water in a small creek nearby. Turn right at the junction to continue the hike, following Trail 328 toward Blackfoot Meadows.

Pass through a small flat meadow, then reenter forest and descend, passing through an opening in a rickety wooden pole fence. Keep a sharp eye out here: A poorly signed intersection lies a short distance ahead.

Bear left at the intersection and head toward the prominent blaze on the tree ahead along a faint footpath. This trail was poorly maintained when we hiked but is fairly well blazed.

The footpath soon peters out, and blazes are the only trail sign. Follow the blazes and descend steadily to cross a side creek, a marshy area and, at the bottom of the descent, a tributary of the Little Blackfoot River, reached at 21.4 miles.

Climb from the creek crossing, keeping a sharp eye out for blazes, and ascend the tree-covered, 7,740-foot ridge ahead. The ascent is quite steep in places, but a footpath is visible along switchbacks near the ridgetop.

Stay with the blazes as the trail levels out on the ridgetop and swings to the south and southeast through more open forest. Axe blazes give way to orange paint blazes as the trail nears the head of the tributary of the Little Blackfoot River. Drop to cross the head of the drainage, then climb steeply up the opposite bank, following the blazes through very dense stands of young lodgepole. Orange blazes give way to blue blazes. Later, the trail reaches a "T" intersection of paint blazes; turn right (southeast) and climb, with the forest becoming more open as elevation is gained.

Break out of the forest at the base of a talus-covered, cone-shaped, 8,024-foot summit on the divide, at 22.8 miles. From the top are good views to the south of Thunderbolt Mountain, its rocky outcrops rising above the forest. The trail disappears, and the Forest Service had yet to construct the connecting link to Thunderbolt Mountain when we hiked.

The divide jogs to the west and flattens out a bit between this summit and Thunderbolt Mountain. Get a compass bearing on the distant peak to help as a guide. Begin a cross-country hike, dropping gradually through forest and angling to the southwest to avoid the steep drop into the head of a tributary of the North Fork of Red Rock Creek.

Reach a low spot on the divide at 23.7 miles between the tributary and the head of a tributary that drops to the west into the Little Blackfoot River. Climb steadily along the divide toward the summit of Thunderbolt Mountain, which can be glimpsed through the trees.

Begin contouring eastward around the peak midway along the ascent to avoid the steep cliffs and outcrops near the summit. Reach blazed Trail 119 at 24.7 miles, with a well-worn footpath angling to the southwest through the forest.

Trail 119 intersects Trail 65, a rocky jeep track, at 26.2 miles. Turn right (northwest) and ascend toward Cottonwood Lake. The trail levels as it passes through several large meadows that cradle Thunderbolt Creek.

Intersect Trail 147 just before reaching shallow Cottonwood Lake and turn left, descending to boulder-hop Thunderbolt Creek just below the lake's earthen dam and wooden spillway.

There are excellent campsites at Cottonwood Lake, with broad, grassy meadows leading to its northwestern shore. Trail 147 has been rerouted, and circles the lake from south to west along a freshly blazed pack trail.

The trail soon leaves the lake and climbs through forest toward the tree-covered ridge to the south and 8,346-foot Electric Peak. The forest becomes more open as altitude is gained, but trees generally obstruct the views.

The trail swings west along the ascent and the climb becomes more steep on switchbacks near the summit on the divide, at 29 miles. The trail levels off on top and heads west through forest, then drops slightly before swinging to the south along the wooded ridgetop.

After a short descent the trail levels off on another wooded ridgetop, then drops again through forest. Reach a meadow with a shallow pond and descend gradually through a series of meadows. There are some mucky spots in the trail in the lower meadows.

Pass a cairn with a wooden post and blue diamond blaze, and continue descending alternately through stands of lodgepole and small parks, each a potential campsite. Reenter continuous forest and soon intersect

Trail 227, a jeep track, at 31.9 miles.

Continue straight (south) and climb gradually, crossing a good side creek, then switching back to cross it again. Pass the remains of several log cabins with numerous mining test pits at trailside.

Enter a small park at the top of the climb, with good views of an impressive line of peaks to the southeast. Note the power line towers to the south; the trail later passes beneath this power line.

Descend slightly, crossing a small meadow with a tiny spring, and follow as the jeep tracks swing to the northwest and climb through a meadow toward the divide. Reenter forest at the top, at 32.5 miles, remaining on the main jeep track as it levels off, then begins a long descent.

Emerge from the forest at the head of Long Park, where the jeep track merges into a heavier-traveled jeep road, an extension of Forest Service Road 5158. High meadows here offer good views to the west overlooking the Clark Fork River Valley, containing the towns of Deer Lodge and, further south, Warm Springs, against a backdrop of the rugged Flint Creek Range.

Stay on the jeep road and head south along the crest of the divide. Pass Cold Spring, fenced for protection from cattle, to the left of the road at 35.6 miles. Cross under the power lines and turn right (south) at the next road junction, remaining on Forest Service Road 5158.

Forest obscures the views here; the next vistas overlooking the Clark Fork River basin are seen from the shoulder of 7,658-foot Blizzard Hill, at 37.8 miles.

Switchback down the hill and enter forest, remaining on the road as it weaves back and forth across the divide to reach tree-covered Champion Pass, 6,960 feet, at 39.4 miles.

The trail continues southward across the pass along Forest Service Road 8496, dipping and rising gradually along the divide to the Four Corners road junction, at 42.6 miles.

Continue south along the forested crest on the main track, now Forest Service Road 608. Leave the divide and main road at 43.9 miles, where the road forks, and follow the jeep road that bears left and descends into the forested upper basin of the South Fork of the Boulder River. Cross on boulders below the jeep ford and begin a gradual climb through forest, regaining the divide at 45.7 miles.

The trail winds along the crest, following the divide as it bends to the east around the head of Alaska Gulch, then jogs sharply to the south. The track becomes heavier-traveled at the head of Olson Gulch. Leave the divide at 50.7 miles and descend along improving road to reach a junction with Forest Service Road 5001, at 51.2 miles.

Pass Lowland Campground, a developed site popular with recreational vehicle users, and continue eastward toward the broad valley floor along Forest Service 9485. Bear right at the next major junction onto Forest Service Road 442, which leads directly to the Trask interchange on I-15, reached at 58.8 miles.

Introduction: The trail heads west from Interstate 15 and climbs through broken, forested country mixed with grassy flats before bending south and west to strike the divide long busy Interstate 90 just east of Butte.

The trail follows a series of pack trails, jeep tracks and graded gravel roads past numerous signs of civilization: cabins, new and old; mines, active and closed; power lines; railroad tracks, and developed campsites on the shores of Whitetail Reservoir and Delmoe Lake.

We hiked this section in a miserable, soaking rainstorm with low clouds that obscured distant views of the Highland and Tobacco Root mountains.

The terrain along this section is a sharp contrast to that of the previous hike. The trail crosses numerous sagebrush flats, marshy meadows and willow-lined streams.

Homestake Pass, 6,356 feet, southeast of the mining town of Butte, got its name in the 1870s from a man who made a mining stake between Miners Gulch and Niles Gulch.

Difficulty level: Easy on generally well-marked trail through rolling forest, meadows and sagebrush flats.
Scenery: Fair.
Water availability: Excellent, in numerous streams and two large lakes.
Maps: USFS—Deerlodge National Forest visitor/travel map. USGS (7.5 minute series)—Elk Park Pass, Whitetail Peak, Delmoe Lake, Homestake.
Supply Points: Homestake Pass, on Interstate 90, is 5.25 miles southeast of the city of Butte, a full-service community.

Find the trailhead: The trailhead is at the Trask interchange on Interstate 15, 10 miles north of Butte and about 16 miles south of Basin.

Trail description: Cross under the overpass and turn right (south) onto the frontage road. Turn left at the next intersection onto gravel Forest Service Road 78154, and head east across the broad valley floor of Elk Park.

Cross Bison Creek and climb gradually toward the forest ahead. Nez Perce Creek is to the left, the outlet for a small, unnamed lake ahead whose shores are dotted with homes and vacation cabins. The lake, reached at two miles, is privately owned, and the official trail skirts to the southeast through forest behind the private homes.

It may be easier to simply remain on the gravel road, following it north and east around the lake and a small pond before continuing east along the banks of Nez Perce Creek.

The trail, now a jeep track, passes beneath a power line and boulder-hops the creek at 2.9 miles miles before breaking out of forest at the head of Bakers Meadows. Continue east, heading upstream along the right bank.

Turn right (south) at 3.8 miles and begin climbing steeply along a pack trail, Forest Service Trail 148, that follows the drainage for a tributary of Nez Perce Creek. Step across a small feeder creek and continue climbing through forest.

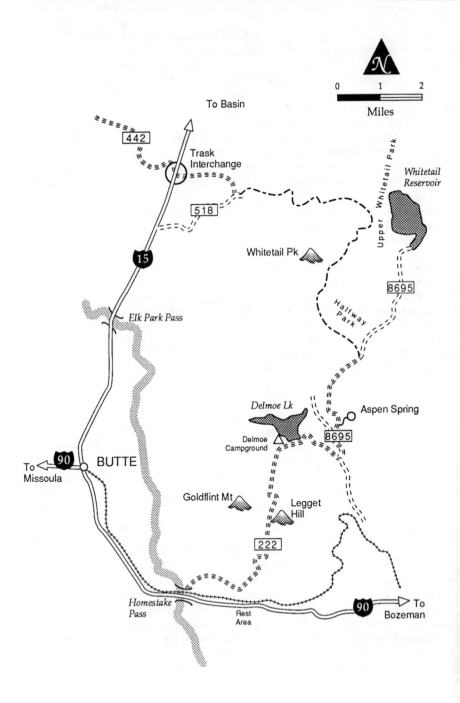

To Basin

442

Trask
Interchange

518

15

Whitetail Pk

Upper Whitetail Park

*Whitetail
Reservoir*

8695

Elk Park Pass

Halfway
Park

Delmoe Lk

Aspen Spring

Delmoe
Campground

8695

To
Missoula

90

BUTTE

Goldflint Mt

Legget
Hill

222

*Homestake
Pass*

Rest
Area

90

To
Bozeman

0   1   2

Miles

I-15 to Homestake Pass
Elevation Chart

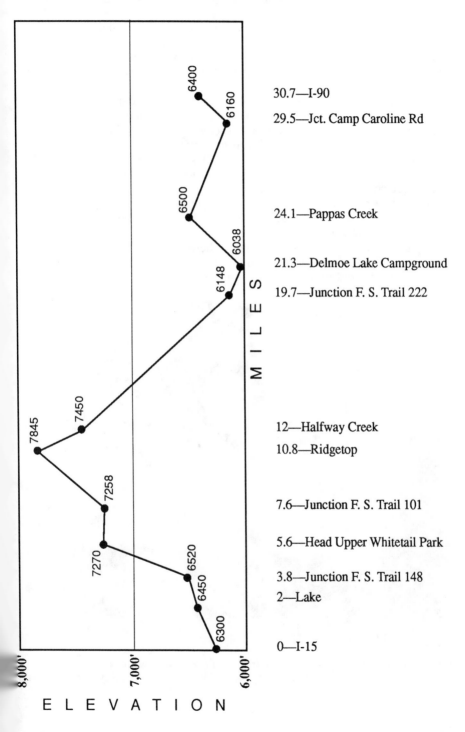

30.7—I-90

29.5—Jct. Camp Caroline Rd

24.1—Pappas Creek

21.3—Delmoe Lake Campground

19.7—Junction F. S. Trail 222

12—Halfway Creek

10.8—Ridgetop

7.6—Junction F. S. Trail 101

5.6—Head Upper Whitetail Park

3.8—Junction F. S. Trail 148

2—Lake

0—I-15

The trail swings east and begins to level out a bit at the head of a series of marshy meadows in Upper Whitetail Park, 5.6 miles. The parks become more broad as the trail nears Whitetail Reservoir, with good campsites along the grassy shoreline.

The fringe areas along the grassy parks are ideal for whitetail deer and ruffed grouse that flush in a heart-stopping thunder of wingbeats.

The trail curves south as it nears the grassy shores of the reservoir and crosses a marshy feeder stream before joining with Forest Service Trail 101, at 7.6 miles.

Climb gradually along the pack trail, recrossing the feeder creek and beginning a steady climb through forest that gains about 525 feet in two miles. Top the low, forested ridge at 10.8 miles that separates Upper Whitetail Park from Halfway Park. The trail is fairly level for a bit, then drops into the head of Halfway Creek, reaching its banks at 12 miles. Break out of the forest at the head of Halfway Park, another series of meadows, and skirt briefly along its southwestern edge.

The trail becomes a jeep track here that traverses the park and reenters forest along Halfway Creek. The track, an extension of Forest Service Road 8695, improves as it swings to the south.

Stay on the main track, bearing right where the road forks at 15.3 miles. Pass Aspen Spring to the right of the trail as the road dips and climbs over rolling hills covered with sagebrush and open forest.

Deer range over the entire length of the trail, with mule deer (like this one) in the higher country and whitetail deer congregating in streamside thickets in the valleys. Photo Chris Cauble.

Turn right (south) at the next road junction, then bear left, at 19.7 miles, onto Forest Service Road 222, the Delmoe Road. Follow as the road heads west, passing Delmoe Cabin and crossing a bridge over Big Pipestone Creek before reaching the entrance to Delmoe Lake Campground, popular with recreational vehicle users.

The road climbs gradually, reaching a high spot in an open sagebrush flat before dropping gradually to cross Pappas Creek, at 24.1 miles. Reenter forest and stay on the main track, crossing a buried pipe line and soon passing twice beneath some power lines.

Cross Homestake Creek, and follow as the road swings west, climbing gradually. Continue straight from the junction with the Camp Caroline Road, at 29.5 miles, and climb over another low, forested ridge.

Go over the Burlington Northern railroad tracks at 30.3 miles. A side road here leads to nearby Homestake Lake, with picnic grounds and a swimming area. Cross above I-90 at the Homestake Interchange, at 30.7 miles. The divide crosses at Homestake Pass, broad and flat, a short distance to the west.

Homestake Pass to
Deer Lodge Pass — 27.1 Miles

Introduction: Mother Nature was not being kind when we hiked this section south of Butte. A driving rainstorm combined with the lack of a marked trail persuaded us to abandon the official route along the rugged and tree-covered divide for easier valley travel along roads.

Perhaps it would be wise for you do the same, unless the trail between Homestake Pass and Pipestone Pass is well-marked and maintained. It wasn't when we hiked in early October, 1989.

It is said there are some fine views from the trail of the Highland and Tobacco Root mountains.

Pipestone Pass, 6,418 feet, got its name from the nearby hot springs, which supplied Indians with pipe-making materials.

The Chicago, Milwaukee and St. Paul Railroad built its line under the sharp, tree-covered pass through a 2,290-foot-long tunnel. Inexpensive electricity from hydroelectric facilities enabled the Milwaukee Road to be electrified all the way through the Rockies.

A short cross-country hike from Pipestone Pass leads to the start of a long stretch of road travel through the Highland Mountains past the mining town of Highland City.

Broad, rolling grasslands are crossed enroute to Deer Lodge Pass, 5,902 feet, and Interstate 15 southwest of Butte.

The flat pass separates the Highland Mountains from the Anaconda Range. Its name is taken from the tipi-shaped mounds of salty minerals formed by hot springs throughout the valley that attracted deer.

Difficulty level: Moderate. An initial cross-country hike over rugged, forested peaks that follows roads and jeep tracks beyond Pipestone Pass.

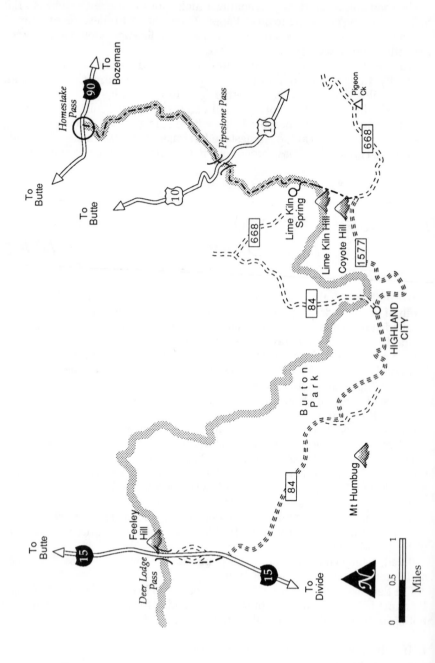

Scenery: Said to be good: rain clouds hid views when we hiked.
Water availability: Poor initially but good beyond Pipestone Pass in numerous creeks.
Maps: USFS—Deerlodge National Forest visitor/travel map. USGS (7.5 min. series)—Homestake, Pipestone Pass; (15 min. series)—Butte South.
Supply Points: Pipestone Pass, at mid-hike, is on Hwy. 10, nine miles southeast of the center of Butte. Deer Lodge Pass, at hike's end, is on Interstate 15, seven miles north of the town of Divide, with a gas station and a bar, and 16 miles southwest of Butte, a full-service community.

Finding the trailhead: The trailhead is at the Homestake interchange on Interstate 90, 5.25 miles southeast of Butte.

Trail description: The first 6.2 miles of trail follows the rugged, forested crest of the divide as it dips and rises from Homestake Pass to Pipestone Pass.

The prospect of a cross-country hike in poor weather prompted us to stick out our thumbs and hitch a ride to Deer Lodge Pass, on I-15, at the end of the segment. We later returned to the area and scouted as much of the trail as was feasible by car.

The trail heads west from Pipestone Pass along the forested crest of the divide in a cross-country hike before intersecting Forest Service Trail 85, at about 8.6 miles.

The trail soon strikes the Limekiln Road, Forest Service Road 668, and begins a gradual descent along Tanner Creek, a reliable water source. Creek-side property here is privately owned.

The gradual climb to the crest of the Highland Mountains begins at the confluence of Tanner and Fish creeks at the base of Coyote Hill, where the trail turns right (west) onto Forest Service Road 1577, at 11.2 miles.

Water is plentiful in this section, as the road crosses two tributaries and the main trunk of Fish Creek for a second time at 12.8 miles. Here begins a gradual but steady climb that gains nearly a thousand feet in 1.1 miles.

Descend steeply from the 7,975-foot high spot and reach a junction with Forest Service Road 8520 at 14.5 miles. There are good views here of Red Mountain, 9,701 feet, its base pockmarked with clear-cuts.

Turn right (north), crossing the upper fingers of Moose Creek before striking the Highland Road, Forest Service Road 84, at 15.6 miles. Bear left (west) and climb gradually through pastures, with Burton Park on the right and Humbug Mountain on the left.

A strange looking rock formation lies to the left of the road. Bear straight at 20.1 miles where one jeep track turns left and another goes straight.

Continue climbing gradually, reaching a high spot at 22.6 miles with good views overlooking the divide at Deer Lodge Pass and the broad valley below. Begin a long descent to the valley floor, remaining on the main track.

Leave the Deerlodge National Forest at 23 miles and soon break out of forest onto the broad grasslands. Fleecer Ridge, dominated by Mount Fleecer, 9,436 feet, lies to the west across the valley. Divide Creek is a reliable water source. The road turns into hardtop as it nears I-15, reaching the highway at 26.6 miles.

The divide and Deer Lodge Pass lie to the north. Cross I-15, bear right (north) onto the frontage road and hike parallel to the interstate and the railroad tracks. Bear left at the next interchange onto Forest Service Road 96. The grassy divide and Deer Lodge Pass lie about a half-mile to the north.

Homestake Pass to Deer Lodge Pass
Elevation Chart

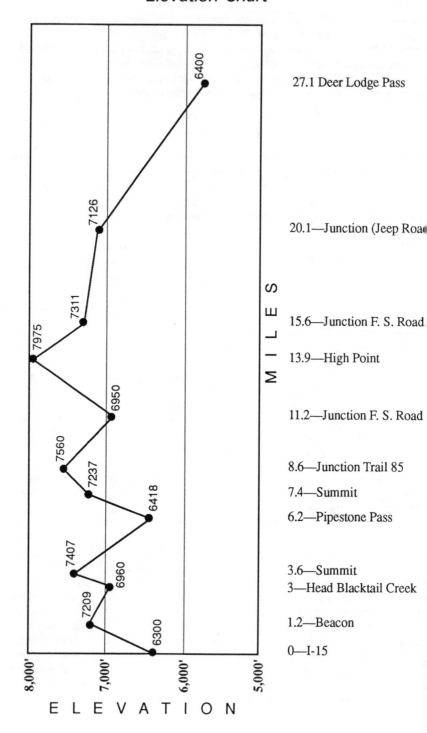

27.1 Deer Lodge Pass

20.1—Junction (Jeep Road)

15.6—Junction F. S. Road

13.9—High Point

11.2—Junction F. S. Road

8.6—Junction Trail 85

7.4—Summit

6.2—Pipestone Pass

3.6—Summit
3—Head Blacktail Creek

1.2—Beacon

0—I-15

M I L E S

6400
7126
7311
7975
6950
7560
7237
6418
7407
6960
7209
6300

8,000'   7,000'   6,000'   5,000'

E L E V A T I O N

Deer Lodge Pass to
Lower Seymour Lake — 36.6 Miles

Introduction: Travel on roads continues as the trail climbs from the grasslands at Deer Lodge Pass southwest of Butte into heavy forests on Fleecer Ridge enroute to the crest of the divide.

Where open, the divide offers remarkable views that extend westward across the Anaconda Range, eastward to the Highland Mountains, and to the Pioneer Mountains to the southwest.

The trail follows a combination of auto roads, jeep roads and pack trail as it completes its half-circle around the mining city of Butte.

The impacts of the timber and mining industries, vital to the region's economy, are evident from the top, and the trail passes through the Hungry Hill Mine.

Creeks are crossed regularly and Larkspur Spring, a good campsite, is only a short distance off trail.

Difficulty level: Easy, on a combination of auto and jeep roads and pack trail.
Scenery: Fair during the initial stretch through grassland and heavy forest with some clear-cuts, but excellent from higher elevations, with views of the Anaconda Range and Highland and Pioneer mountains.
Water availability: Good, in Larkspur Spring and numerous creeks.
Maps: USFS—Deerlodge National Forest visitor/travel map. USGS (7.5 minute series)—Burnt Mountain, Dickie Peak, Lincoln Gulch and Lower Seymour Lake; (15 minute series)—Butte South.
Supply Points: There are no supply points convenient to the trail. Lower Seymour Lake, at hike's end, is 7.4 miles on Forest Service Road 934 from its junction with Hwy. 274.

Finding the trailhead: Deer Lodge Pass, on I-15, is seven miles north of the town of Divide, and 16 miles southwest of Butte. The trailhead lies about a half-mile south from the Continental Divide at the junction of Forest Service Road 96 and the Frontage Road.

Trail description: Head west on Forest Service Road 96 across the broad grasslands, with Mount Fleecer, 9,436 feet, dominating Fleecer Ridge to the southwest. Cross over the railroad tracks and continue west along the main road, with the North Fork of Divide Creek to the left.

The road forks at .6 mile just before the main branch crosses the creek. Bear right and, in a short distance, bear left onto a jeep trail, Forest Service Trail 125, that climbs gradually into forest.

The trail climbs steadily, soon entering heavy forest that obscures views. Stay on the main track, reaching the forested crest of the divide at 1.8 miles.

Burnt Mountain, 8,383 feet, can be glimpsed to the west from an open spot on the divide. Descend gradually into the broad basin of the North Fork of Divide Creek, striking a good gravel road, Forest Service Road 8505, at 3.6 miles. Turn right (north) and climb gradually through the bottom of the basin.

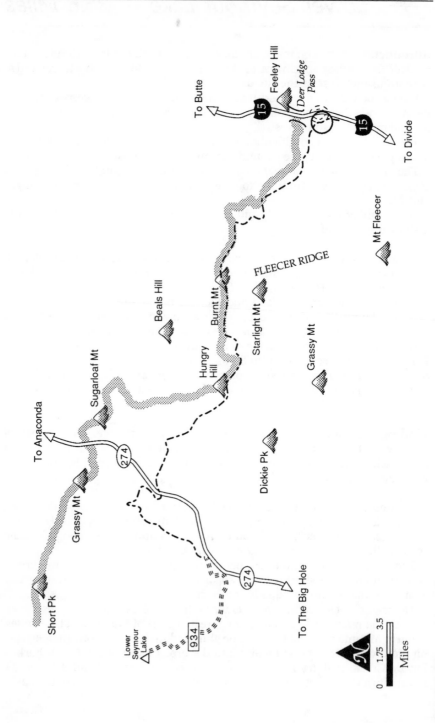

Bear left at the next road junction onto Forest Service Road 1594 and begin a gradual climb to the divide, reached at five miles.

Turn west and follow along the forested crest of the divide, climbing steeply in places and across talus before reaching an open spot atop a 7,489-foot knoll at 6.4 miles, with good views of the Highland Mountains.

Reenter forest and climb gradually along the crest of the divide, with the forested and clear-cut upper basin of the North Fork of Divide Creek spreading below to the southwest. Burnt Mountain, on the north end of Fleecer Ridge, can be seen to the west from an open spot at 7.4 miles atop a 7,841-foot knob.

Drop once more into forest and cross to the base of Burnt Mountain. The climb to the top, at 8.2 miles, is steady, but the views are rewarding, with a sea of peaks to the northeast and southeast. To the southwest, close at hand, spreads the forested and clear-cut basin of Flume and Jerry creeks.

Join Forest Service Trail 94, a jeep track, at the summit, and follow it west along the crest before leaving the divide at 10.6 miles to drop into the head of Jerry Creek, staying on the main track. Good views are seen here of Fleecer Mountain. Larskspur Spring, a reliable water source and a possible campsite, is to the left of the trail at 12.6 miles.

Regain the divide at 13.6 miles and remain close to the crest, avoiding a jeep road that joins at the head of Minnesota Gulch. There are excellent views here to the west of the jagged Anaconda Range. The Pioneer Mountains lie to the southwest beyond the Big Hole Valley, with 9,116-foot Dickie Peak and 9,157-foot Granulated Mountain closer at hand.

Stay on the main road as the trail rounds the head of Long Tom Creek and climbs to the Hungry Hill Mine, reached at 14.8 miles, a good campsite but without water. There are good views here, with the Highland Range to the east.

Descend along the jeep track, dropping gradually into the head of American Creek. Mount Haggin, 10,610 feet, looms ahead to the northeast along the descent, with Short Peak, 10,227 feet, just to the south. The Anaconda Range spreads westward.

The road improves as elevation is lost, and water is available in the creek's lower reaches. There are good campsites here in the streamside flats.

Stick with the road where it bends away from American Creek at 18.2 miles and climbs a low ridge before dropping alongside Little American Creek. Continue west, with good views of the Anaconda Range ahead. Hwy. 274 comes into view as the jeep road nears the valley floor, and is reached at 21.2 miles.

Cross the highway and follow the good gravel road the bends to the northeast toward the ranch complex ahead. Here are excellent views of the eastern peaks of the Anaconda Range, with Mount Evans, 10,641 feet, and Mount Howe, 10,472 feet, prominent.

Pass the ranch complex and bear left (northwest) at the next intersection onto Forest Service Road 2483 at 22.2 miles. Take the next left and follow as the road swings to the southwest, paralleling Hwy. 274 across the valley.

Walking is easy in this open country, with unobstructed views of the high peaks. Water is plentiful in the creek criss-crossing the valley floor.

Swing toward Hwy. 274; reach an intersection with Forest Service Road 934 at 29.2 miles and turn right. The road begins as graded gravel but turns to asphalt. Along its lower reaches are pleasant views of open, rolling foothills leading to the high bare peaks.

Deer Lodge Pass to Lower Seymour Lake
Elevation Chart

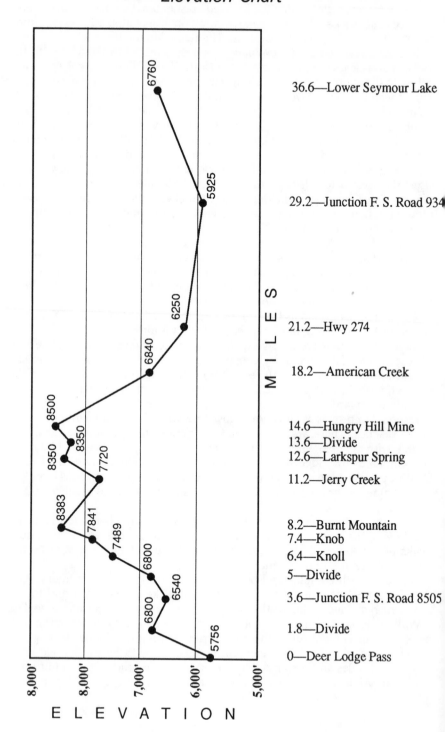

36.6—Lower Seymour Lake

29.2—Junction F. S. Road 934

21.2—Hwy 274

18.2—American Creek

14.6—Hungry Hill Mine
13.6—Divide
12.6—Larkspur Spring

11.2—Jerry Creek

8.2—Burnt Mountain
7.4—Knob
6.4—Knoll
5—Divide

3.6—Junction F. S. Road 8505

1.8—Divide

0—Deer Lodge Pass

Elk are common along much of the Continental Divide Trail, with the bull's high-pitched bugle call heralding the annual rutting season. Photo Chris Cauble.

The views become obscured as you travel further west and enter the first of thick stands of lodgepole pine along the range's flanks. Lower Seymour Lake, reached at 36.6 miles, has developed campsites and is popular with recreational vehicle users.

A mile beyond Lower Seymour Lake is the trailhead for Seymour Lake Trail 131, well-blazed and trodden by pack trains and marked with a Continental Divide Trail marker.

GLACIER
NATIONAL
PARK

■—·—■—·—■—·—■
Continental Divide
Scenic Trail

Kalispell ○

○ Great Falls

○ Missoula

M O N T A N

○ Helena

*ANACONDA-PINTLER
WILDERNESS*

Butte ○

○ Bozeman

○ Wisdom

YELLOWSTONE
NATIONAL
PARK

I D A H O

W Y O M I N G

ANACONDA-PINTLER WILDERNESS

Lower Seymour Lake to Chief Joseph Pass — 69.6 miles

Introduction: The route follows a winding pack trail that leads up and along the divide's craggy crest through the rugged Anaconda Range, west of Butte, past high mountain lakes to the rolling, tree-covered Pintler Range, west of Wisdom.

The trail is well marked and easily followed in the Anaconda-Pintler Wilderness, which features spectacular, sheer peaks that rise with vertical abruptness above forested valleys.

But the divide becomes flatter and tree-covered along the southwestern portion of the hike, and logging roads in the Schultz Saddle area challenge orienteering skills.

Water is plentiful until near the end of the section, and campsites abound. The area is rich in wildlife. Bands of elk and deer are in virtually every drainage, and mountain goats can be seen climbing the cliffs in cirques above high lakes. Rainbow trout are found in several beautiful lakes reached along the route, with especially good fishing in Warren and Johnson lakes.

The trail crosses the divide at four passes, including 9,036-foot Cutaway Pass, the highest named pass on the divide in Montana, and Pintler Pass, 8,378 feet, named after Charles Pintler, an early day settler and miner.

Much of the hike is on the divide's open crest, with expansive views extending northward to the Garnet Range and southward to the divide as it winds through the Bitterroot and Beaverhead mountains that border the historic Big Hole Valley.

Rugged peaks occasionally force the trail downward to easier traveling along drainages.

Granite is encountered along much of the hike. The white boulders and outcrops bespeak the cataclysmic forces that created this range, part of the immense Sapphire Block.

Geologists believe the Sapphire Block was formed between 70 and 75 million years ago when a huge mass of molten rock slid some 50 miles eastward from present day Idaho, leaving behind the gap of the Bitterroot Valley. The range's eastern end is mostly sedimentary rock that folded tightly over and over ahead of the moving mass.

The Garnet Range to the north and the Flint Creek Range to the east mark the limits of the Sapphire Block.

The Pintler Range extends westward from the Anaconda Range high above the Big Hole Valley. Geologists believe the valley was formed when another molten mass, the Pioneer Block, slid eastward to form the Pioneer Range.

The Big Hole Valley is rich in history, and is the site of an 1877 rout of General John Gibbon and troops by Chief Joseph and his Nez Perce band who

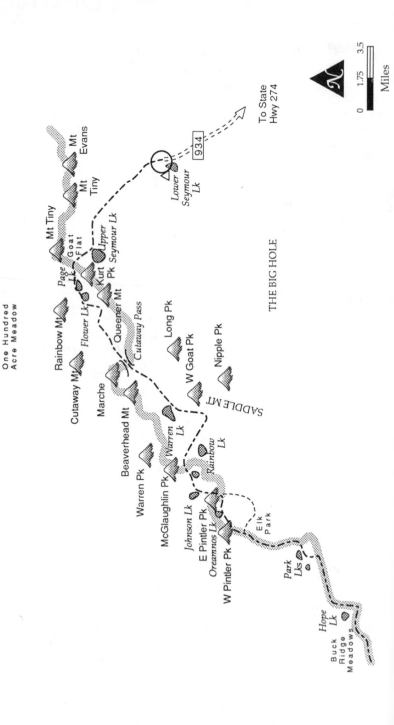

One Hundred Acre Meadow

Mt Evans

Mt Tiny

Mt Tiny

Rainbow Mt

Page Lk

Goat Flat

Kurt Pk

Upper Seymour Lk

Flower Lk

Cutaway Mt

Queener Mt

Cutaway Pass

Marche

Long Pk

Beaverhead Mt

W Goat Pk

Nipple Pk

SADDLE MT

Warren Pk

Warren Lk

McGlaughlin Pk

Rainbow Lk

Johnson Lk

E Pintler Pk

Oreamnos Lk

W Pintler Pk

Elk Park

Park Lks

Hope Lk

Buck Ridge Meadows

Lower Seymour Lk

934

To State Hwy 274

THE BIG HOLE

N

0   1.75   3.5

Miles

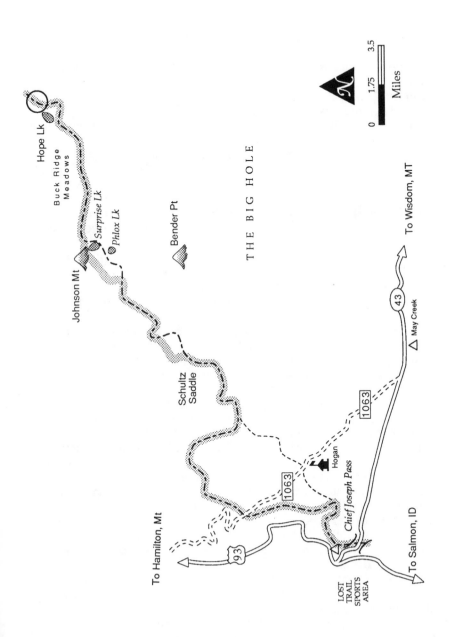

rallied after their sleeping camp was murderously ambushed at dawn.

In his pursuit of the Nez Perce, Gibbon followed the route William Clark blazed in 1806 through the Trail Creek Valley. Gibbons Pass is named after the general and Chief Joseph Pass in honor of the Indian chief.

Heavy clear-cutting, the heaviest since leaving the Helena National Forest, is encountered in the Pintler Range beginning at Bender Point and extending beyond Schultz Saddle.

The town of Wisdom, a possible resupply point, was named by Meriwether Lewis after one of President Thomas Jefferson's traits.

Difficulty level: Easy, on well-marked trail with some short, moderately steep climbs.

Scenery: Excellent in Anaconda Range, rugged high peaks and alpine lakes, but views more obscured in Pintler Range closer to Chief Joseph Pass.

Water availability: Good, in numerous creeks and lakes, becoming more scarce between Trail Creek and Chief Joseph Pass.

Maps: USFS—Deerlodge National Forest (west half). USGS (7.5 min. series)—Lower Seymour Lake, Mount Evans, Storm Lake, Carpp Ridge, Warren Peak, Kelly Lake, Mussigbrod Lake, Bender Point, Schultz Saddle, Elk Creek, Lost Trail Pass.

Supply Points: There are no supply points convenient to the trail. Chief Joseph Pass is 26 miles west of Wisdom, Montana, a full-service community, on busy Highway 43.

Finding the trailhead: The trailhead is a mile beyond Lower Seymour Lake in a parking area 8.4 miles on Forest Service Road 934, which intersects Highway 274 about 21 miles southwest of Anaconda, Montana.

Trail description: From the parking area the trail enters thick lodgepole in the flat bottomland along Seymour Creek but quickly emerges into more open woods sprinkled with small parks that offer views of the rugged divide ahead.

Soon reach a boundary sign marking the edge of the Anaconda-Pintler Wilderness, and a hiker registration box.

Spruce mixes with the lodgepole as the trail climbs gradually along the stream, passing a good level campsite at three miles. Streamside campsites are plentiful until four miles, where the creek forks.

There are good views from the trail to the northeast of Mount Howe, 10,472 feet, with a long jumble of granite boulders extending to the foot of the trail.

Cross the east fork of Seymour Creek on a footbridge and continue climbing a bit more steeply along the stream's west fork. The climb is steeper still after the trail swings away from the creek but soon levels out briefly on a bench that offers good views of the sheer headwall of the divide ahead.

Soon cross another fork of Seymour Creek and continue the steep ascent for a short distance before leveling off near the shores of bright blue Upper Seymour Lake, at 5.5 miles.

The lake lies at the base of a cirque formed by 9,961-foot Kurt Peak and 10,149-foot Queener Mountain, both peaks sheer-faced and stern, rising abruptly above the tree-covered basin.

The lake is popular with trout fishermen. Campsites abound, but sites on the northern and eastern shores get the most afternoon sun. Livestock is

Lower Seymour Lake to Chief Joseph Pass
Elevation Chart

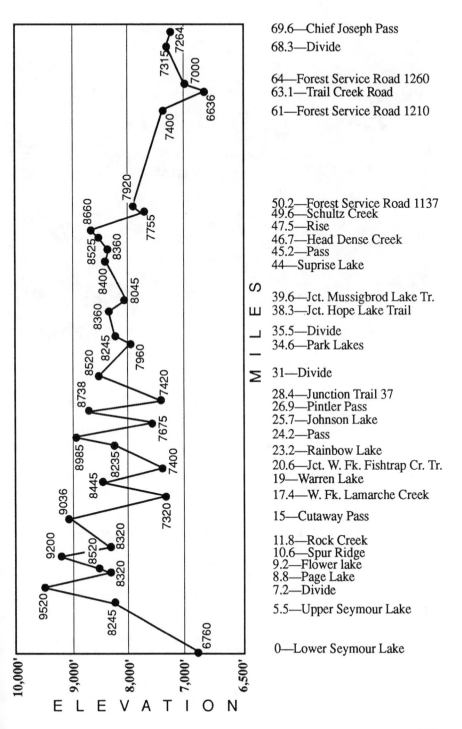

69.6—Chief Joseph Pass
68.3—Divide

64—Forest Service Road 1260
63.1—Trail Creek Road
61—Forest Service Road 1210

50.2—Forest Service Road 1137
49.6—Schultz Creek
47.5—Rise
46.7—Head Dense Creek
45.2—Pass
44—Suprise Lake

39.6—Jct. Mussigbrod Lake Tr.
38.3—Jct. Hope Lake Trail

35.5—Divide
34.6—Park Lakes

31—Divide

28.4—Junction Trail 37
26.9—Pintler Pass
25.7—Johnson Lake
24.2—Pass
23.2—Rainbow Lake
20.6—Jct. W. Fk. Fishtrap Cr. Tr.
19—Warren Lake

17.4—W. Fk. Lamarche Creek

15—Cutaway Pass

11.8—Rock Creek
10.6—Spur Ridge
9.2—Flower lake
8.8—Page Lake
7.2—Divide

5.5—Upper Seymour Lake

0—Lower Seymour Lake

M I L E S

E L E V A T I O N

10,000'   9,000'   8,000'   7,000'   6,500'

Tiny Flower Lake lies at the base of Kurt Peak in the Anaconda-Pintler Wilderness. Alpine lakes are common in the Pintlers, and offer excellent camping.

prohibited here; those on horseback must camp at nearby Queener Pond, to the southwest.

The trail skirts the lake's eastern shore and begins ascending through forest toward the divide, with good views of a hump-shaped 9,989-foot ridge to the northeast.

Climb through forest to the base of a series of sweeping switchbacks which carry you upward on a narrow rocky trail to impressive vistas above Upper Seymour Lake.

The views here are excellent, especially as you cross an open talus slope, with Upper Seymour Lake shining blue and clear and a smaller pond nestled at the base of Kurt Peak.

Mount Tiny, 9,848 feet, comes into view as the trail tops the divide at 7.2 miles and crosses a fragile, grassy plateau near Goat Flat. Stones have been placed in the shape of a cross atop the divide just to the northwest of the trail. Perhaps it is a medicine wheel placed by prehistoric Indians that points to the sun as it rises over the divide.

There are good views all around from this high flatland with the Big Hole, ringed by peaks, to the southeast and the Bitterroot and Beaverhead mountains extending beyond.

The trail soon peters out in the grassy flat but a white stake can be seen to the north in the distance toward Mount Tiny. The stake marks a junction with Trail 9, which heads to the left (west), and Blodgett Trail 40 and Storm Lake Trail 111.

Take Trail 9, also referred to on trail signs as the Page Creek Trail, and begin a contouring descent through a lovely stand of bright green alpine larches, the same deciduous pines last seen along the divide in the Bob Marshall Wilderness.

There are good views to the west along the descent of the "100-Acre Meadow," a vast open park surrounded by forest.

The tributary of Page Creek crossed along the descent at 7.5 miles is likely to be dry in late September. Grasses grow thicker and taller here in the lee of the larches, whose lacy needle-like leaves contrast sharply with the dark green of the surrounding forest.

Later the trail switchbacks to the south and drops into the head of Page Creek Basin, high above timberline with excellent views of Kurt Peak and an unnamed 9,454-foot pyramid-shaped summit with a talus skirt at its base.

The larches give way along the descent to more traditional evergreens, and the trail passes through an old burned area, marked by dead tree trunks bleached white by the sun.

The descent becomes steeper on short switchbacks, and views are obscured where the rocky trail drops into whitebark pine, spruce and fir. Cross a branch of Page Creek at 8.7 miles, a reliable water source. There is good camping a short distance ahead on the shores of Page Lake, shallow and surrounded by low cliffs.

Ahead, at 9.2 miles, lies smaller Flower Lake, reached after a short moderate climb along switchbacks. Nestled in a cirque at the base of Kurt Peak, Flower Lake is more scenic than Page Lake, with good campsites and running water in the meadow at its head.

Cross the lake's outlet stream and reach a signed junction with a trail leading north to East Fork Reservoir, and another heading northeast, downstream. Continue straight (southwest) and descend gradually before beginning a steady climb to a spur ridge leading from the divide, crossing tributaries of Page Creek with water at 9.5 miles and 9.75 miles.

There is good camping at 10 miles near a small pond at the base of the final ascent to the spur ridge. Stay on the main route that forks to the northeast near the pond: the side trail dead-ends ahead in a grassy meadow used by horse packers at the base of cliffs near Rainbow Mountain.

The trail ascends through larches along switchbacks that offer good views to the southeast over Flower Lake, cradled in stringers of talus extending from Kurt Peak and the unnamed pyramidal summit. The views to the southeast expand to include Page Lake and the course of the divide as the trail rises above timberline. Rainbow Mountain, 9,643 feet, a long bare ridge with forest covering its northern tip, can be seen to the northwest.

Reach the crest of the spur ridge at 10.6 miles, with rewarding views of Queener Basin below and to the southwest. Cutaway Pass lies across the basin, just to the left of 9,225-foot Cutaway Mountain. Marche Mountain, 9,823 feet, and an unnamed 9,808-foot peak loom to the northwest beyond the pass: Beaverhead Mountain, 9,656 feet, lies to the south, and Carpp Ridge, its striated rock spreading like a fan, stretches to the southwest. (See view map.)

The trail begins a long, winding descent into Queener Basin, dropping along long switchbacks into another old burn area regrowing with whitebark pine.

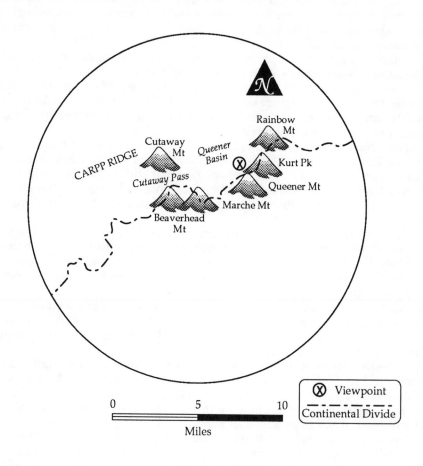

Viewpoint
—·——·——·—
Continental Divide

0   5   10

Miles

Anaconda-Pintler Wilderness View Map

Reaching the crest finds rewarding views of Queener Basin below and to the southwest. Cutaway Pass is across the basin, just to the left of 9,225-foot Cutaway Mountain. Marche Mountain, 9,823 feet, and an unnamed 9,808-foot peak loom to the northwest beyond the pass; Beaverhead Mountain, 9,656 feet, lies to the south and Carpp Ridge, its striated rock spreading like a fan, stretches to the southwest.

The trail again reaches larch trees as it contours around the base of Queener Mountain.

Cross a mucky area on a wooden boardwalk, then boulder-hop a fork of Rock Creek at 11.8 miles, a reliable water source. A small clearing about 40 yards ahead and to the left of the trail is a possible campsite.

Reach the junction with the East Fork Portal Trail just before crossing a second branch of Rock Creek at 12.8 miles. Head south on the Cutaway Pass Trail, cross the creek, and continue contouring to the northwest through forest before beginning a steady climb to Cutaway Pass.

Water is plentiful along the climb to the base of the larch-covered divide. The final ascent to 9,036-foot Cutaway Pass is along a series of short switchbacks that climb past a granite boulder field.

Trees cover the pass, reached at 15 miles, but through them can be glimpsed the course of the divide extending past Marche Mountain and its unnamed rival to Beaverhead Mountain. Trail 111 continues along the crest of the divide and heads northwest toward Maloney Basin and Carpp Creek. Stay on Trail 9, which heads southwest and descends to the West Fork of LaMarche Creek, with good views to the north of Queener Basin.

Beaverhead Mountain, a three-topped hulking giant, dominates this section of the trail, which contours high above the creek then drops steeply along switchbacks to a trail junction at 17.25 miles.

Bear right (southwest), and continue descending, crossing the West Fork of LaMarche Creek at 17.4 miles on a footbridge. Climb along the creek's left bank for a short distance in heavy forest. The trail soon swings away from the creek and climbs steeply along switchbacks to Warren Lake, at 19 miles.

Ringed with a band of larches and reflecting the divide's rugged face, Warren Lake is perhaps the prettiest of all the lakes reached on this hike. Unnamed peaks of red and black rocks form a crescent above the water, and alpine meadows stretch to its shore.

Loons come here, the insane laughter of their calls echoing around the cirque at dusk, and rainbow trout feed just off shore in lazy rises.

The trail climbs from the lake to a saddle at 19.1 miles, with good views to the southeast of the Big Hole. Closer at hand rise huge West Goat Peak, 10,793 feet, the highest mountain in the Anaconda Range and the eighth highest peak in Montana, and Saddle Mountain. Both overshadow the trail as it drops into the forested basin of the east fork of the West Fork of Fishtrap Creek.

The initial descent is steep and along switchbacks, but the drop moderates as the trail swings through forest strewn with chunks of granite. The trail passes through an old burn area at 20 miles, offering views of the basin cut by the west fork of Fishtrap Creek and of 10,463-foot Warren Peak, the dominant summit on the divide.

Descend to a signed trail junction at 20.6 miles and turn right (west) to climb steadily through forest along the west fork of Fishtrap Creek.

The trail is away from the creek and passes a talus slide on the right at 21.2 miles with good views ahead of Warren Peak rising sharply above treeline.

Cross the creek at 21.3 miles and continue ascending steadily along the left bank. The trail forks during the approach to the canyon headwall beneath McGlaughlin Peak, 9,487 feet. Bear left to reach Rainbow Lake: the right fork dead-ends in a meadow used by horse packers.

The trail continues level from the fork, then drops to cross the shores of a small pond. Rainbow Lake, at 23.2 miles, is half-ringed with 9,000-foot peaks and surrounded with a band of larches. This pretty spot gets heavy use, and the most secluded campsites lie along the lake's western shore.

The trail skirts the western shore and begins a climb along switchbacks that gain some 750 feet in .7 mile up an unnamed, crescent-shaped peak on the divide. There are dramatic overviews along the ascent of Rainbow Lake, which gleams in a crowd of summits dwarfed by the backdrop of West Goat Peak.

Views are unobstructed from the open pass and, to the northwest, include McGlaughlin and Warren peaks. To the west extends a breathtaking vista that encompasses Martin and Johnson lakes in the basin below, Pintler Pass and East Pintler Peak beyond, and, on the horizon, the dominant mass of Trapper Peak in the Bitterroot Range. (See view map)

The trail leaves the pass and heads straight toward McGlaughlin Peak before bending downward for a winding descent into the tree-filled basin below, crossing the outlet creek for Martin Lake at 25.3 miles. Beautiful Johnson Lake, reached at 25.7 miles, is heavily used, and camping is restricted to the eastern shore. Camping regulations are posted on trees along the lake's fragile shoreline.

West Goat Peak, 10,793 feet, the highest mountain in the Anaconda-Pintler Wilderness, rises high above Rainbow Lake. The lake is a popular destination for weekend hikers.

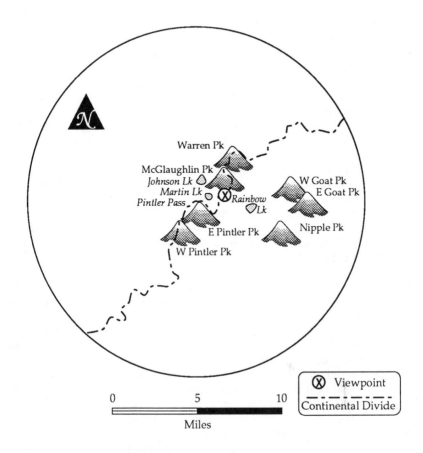

Warren Pk

McGlaughlin Pk
Johnson Lk
Martin Lk
Pintler Pass

Ⓧ Rainbow
Lk

W Goat Pk
E Goat Pk

E Pintler Pk

Nipple Pk

W Pintler Pk

| 0 | 5 | 10 |

Miles

Ⓧ Viewpoint
Continental Divide

Anaconda-Pintler Wilderness View Map

*Dramatic overviews of Rainbow Lake gleaming in a crowd of summits
that are dwarfed by the backdrop of West Goat Peak, 10,793 feet. To the
northwest rise McGlaughlin Peak, 9,487, and Warren Peak, 10,456; the
west offers a breathtaking vista that encompasses Martin and Johnson lakes
in the basin below, Pintler Pass and East Pintler Peak beyond and, on the
horizon, the dominant mass of Trapper Peak in the Bitterroot Range (not
shown).*

Reach a trail junction in a meadow near the head of the lake, with good views of 9,486-foot East Pintler Peak rising directly ahead. Head left (southeast) on the Pintler Pass Trail and climb steeply to 8,738-foot Pintler Pass, gaining 1,058 feet in just over a mile.

Boulder-hop the Falls Fork of Rock Creek twice before leveling out in a beautiful alpine meadow—an excellent campsite —at the base of short switchbacks leading to Pintler Pass.

The character of the divide changes abruptly at the pass, 26.9 miles. On the northwest 9,496-foot West Pintler Peak, its base scarred with a mining road, is the last of the Anaconda Range's sheer, rugged peaks. The divide ahead, to the southwest and west, is the Pintler Range—lower and more tree-covered though still rugged.

Views to the south and southeast reveal the high peaks of the Beaverhead Mountains making their circuit around the Big Hole Valley.

Ignore the faint foot trail that climbs east along the divide. Drop over the pass, heading west to descend into the Pintler Creek basin.

There are good views along the descent of West Pintler Peak and the wide basin below containing Oreamnos and Sawed Cabin lakes. Oreamnos is the scientific name of the American mountain goat, Oreamnos americanus.

The descent is gradual through open forest but becomes steeper along switchbacks as the trail drops below treeline and nears the basin floor. At 27.4 miles the trail forks in a meadow in an open clearing. The trail to the right, leading to Oreamnos Lake, will become the official trail once a route is constructed up the rugged shoulder of West Pintler Peak and along the crest of the divide.

But for now the sheer divide forces the trail along an alternate route that regains the divide past Elk Park.

Bear left from the junction and head downhill through forest, crossing the main stem of Pintler Creek on some logs at 28.2 miles. There is good camping in streamside meadows to the right of the trail.

Soon reach a signed junction with Trail 37 in a heavily used campsite that straddles the trail near the confluence of the outlet stream for Sawed Cabin Lake and Pintler Creek. Head right (west) and ascend through forest: The trail to the south leads in four miles to Pintler Meadows.

Cross the outlet stream on a footbridge and climb gradually to reach two small parks at 29.4 miles. Continue straight through the unsigned intersection with a well-used game trail. There is good camping in the parks, with water a short distance up the trail in a tributary of Sawed Cabin Lake's outlet stream.

The trail shown on the Kelly Lake quadrangle topographic map that forks to the left in the vicinity is no longer in use and not apparent on the ground. The main trail is well-trodden and easily followed.

The trail levels out briefly at the parks before ascending anew. Stay straight through the next unsigned intersection and cross a small creek. From here the trail climbs along a wooded ridge top upward to the divide, reached at 31 miles.

The trail follows the divide for a short distance before intersecting Trail 9 which, to the east, leads to Mystic Lake. Bear right (west) along Trail 9 and climb gradually through open forest with good views all around.

Rock cairns guide the way and are the only trail sign as the route climbs on lichen-covered rock above treeline, reaches a talus slide and crests the divide at 31.2 miles. There is good camping in a meadow at the head of Bear Creek, a short scramble down from the path, and near shallow Bear Lake, visible from the trail.

The trail swings to the west side of the divide beyond the Bear Creek basin and soon intersects East Fork Trail 443 at 31.8 miles. There are good views to the southwest here of the high jagged peaks of the Bitterroot Mountains. Continue south on Trail 9, descending gradually through heavier forest. Near the bottom on the descent, at 34 miles, pass a big park to the left of the trail and a small lake to the right, the first of the Park Lakes. A big park to the right of the trail, with pools of standing water, is reached at 34.6 miles. Stay on the trail and cross a trickling stream on a footbridge at the head of the park. The best camping is in a park a few hundred yards ahead to the left of the trail; it is bisected by a small, reliable creek.

Cross a larger creek, an unnamed tributary of Park Creek, and fill water bottles: The next convenient water is a spring-fed creek 8.5 miles ahead.

Ascend gradually through forest, reaching a signed intersection on top of the divide at 35.5 miles. Trail 9 bears right (west), and Trail 31 continues south, leading to Trail 7 and Mystic Lake.

Stay on Trail 9 and ascend, steeply in spots, passing through openings that offer good views to the southeast of the Big Hole. The trail levels off once on the crest of the divide then swings to its westward side and descends past an unsigned trail junction. Stay straight here, following the Continental Divide Trail markers.

Intersect the Hope Lake Trail at the base of a saddle, reached at 38.3 miles. Hope Lake, .8 mile to the north, is a quiet spot with good camping and reliable water.

Continue from the junction on Trail 9, heading west and climbing, with good views of the Big Hole. Continue southwest along Trail 9 from its junction with the Mussigbrod Lake Trail, reached at 39.6 miles.

Reach another trail junction a short distance ahead, near a burned-over meadow. The Buck Ridge Meadows Trail heads north. Stay on Trail 9, and head west across the meadow, into the mature forest beyond.

Once in the trees the trail begins a gradual descent to an intermittent creek, at 40.6 miles. The creek was dry in late September. Climb along switchbacks from the creek bed and regain the divide at 42.2 miles, where there are good views to the southeast of Mussigbrod Lake, with the Big Hole Valley beyond.

A good, spring-fed creek running through a meadow is reached at 43.5 miles, just after the trail swings away from the divide and begins dropping toward Surprise Lake, at the base of the white colored cliff ahead.

Surprise Lake, at 44 miles, is starkly beautiful and shallow, with delicate grasses growing around its edges. Evidence of an old burn is everywhere, with bleached white trees scattered about and covering the granite white cliffs. This is a good campsite.

The trail descends from the lake and crosses a small creek in a meadow. Keep a sharp eye out for cairns, as the trail peters out in the tall grasses.

Reach a signed junction with Trail 435 and continue south, leaving the Anaconda-Pintler Wilderness and entering the Beaverhead National Forest.

Soon cross the outlet creek for tiny Violet Lake, lying upslope in about 100 yards. The trail in this area appears to get little use, but is well blazed.

East Pintler Peak cradles Martin Lake (left) and Johnson Lake in a high mountain basin in the Anaconda-Pintler Wilderness. The trail is easily followed along the divide's bare spine.

Descend gradually toward Hell Roaring Creek, in the canyon below. Intersect Trail 17 near the bottom of the descent, at 44.9 miles. Head west from the junction into the meadow ahead, keeping an eye out for blazes on trees directly west. Ignore the prominent blaze on the tree to the south. Heading south leads to Trail 17.

There is no discernible footpath through the meadow, but head west, first crossing a marshy area and then a small stream before entering light forest in about 100 yards.

Keep a sharp eye out for blazes and old saw logs from past trail maintenance efforts. The trail becomes easier to follow as the forest thickens. Continue climbing toward the saddle on the divide on the northwest side of the basin, reached at 45.2 miles.

There are good views to the east straight down Hellroaring Canyon of Mussigbrod Lake and the Big Hole beyond.

The trail climbs steeply from the saddle up the hill directly to the west and remains along the divide. Once atop the hill the trail levels out, and the hiking is pleasant through open whitebark pine forest. There are good views to the west of the rugged Bitterroot Range, and to the east of the expansive Big Hole.

Pass a high spot on the trail, marked by a cairn splashed with orange paint, and begin descending gradually to the southeast. There is no discernible footpath in many sections of this open forest, so keep a sharp eye on the tree blazes.

The descent becomes steeper as the trail enters thicker forest above a big meadow. Large clear-cuts can be seen to the southeast, with the Beaverhead Mountains beyond. Skirt above the meadow and follow the trail as it swings to the southwest, still descending.

The trail at this point is marked almost exclusively by cairns as it stays near the rocky crest of the divide above the head of Johnson Creek, then swings west to a saddle at the head of Dense Creek, reached at 46.7 miles. The view into the Dense Creek canyon is impressive, with sheer vertical walls plunging steeply. Keep an eye on the skies above the canyon for golden eagles that soar on the updrafts created by the steep walls.

The trail climbs west from the saddle, steeply in places, before leveling in open forest. The trail soon forks at an unsigned intersection in a small clearing on the divide; the right fork is Trail 462, which leads northwest along the top of Dense Creek canyon. Take the left fork, marked only by blazes, to head south along the flat ridge top of the divide.

Clear-cuts are quite extensive on the low, tree-covered hills to the south and below the trail. Dip, then rise to the top of the knoll ahead, where larch trees mingle with the remains of others that burned long ago. There are good views to the west of the Bitterroot Range as the trail circles above the Balsam Creek basin.

Topping the next rise, at 47.5 miles, reveals a spectacular panorama, encompassing the high peaks of the Anaconda Range, the Beaverhead Mountains beyond the expansive Big Hole, and the Bitterroot Range. Wisdom is the town visible in the grassy valley below.

Keep a sharp eye out for cairns and blazes as the trail dips, then climbs gradually to the next summit. There is no discernible footpath here as the trail descends slightly and swings west through open forest along the crest of the divide.

Blazes mark where the trail leaves the ridge and swings southwest into heavy forest, where the footpath once again is followed easily. Continue straight through an unsigned intersection at the bottom of the descent and begin climbing to the southwest.

Top the tree-covered hill ahead, then descend, steeply in places, before leveling out in a meadow at 49.6 miles. Schultz Creek is at the base of a tree on the far side of the meadow. There is sheltered camping in the forest beyond.

Just inside the forest is an unsigned trail junction near the stone foundation of an old building. An obscure trail leads left (east) toward a meadow. The official trail heads straight (southwest) through forest.

Cross a small creek and an old jeep road that has been blocked off with logs. Continue heading southwest, intersecting another jeep road that has been blocked by logs to the left, but is open to the right.

Stay straight (southwest) here and soon intersect a pack trail joining from the west. A sign here says the trail leads to Tie Creek in 3.5 miles.

Continue southwest to strike a good logging road, Forest Service Road 1137, just south of 7,920-foot Schultz Saddle, a tree-covered pass.

Cross the logging road and continue along the blazed pack trail, staying on the main path. The trail soon joins Forest Service Road 725 and follows it to a fork.

Logging activity in this area has created new roads that aren't shown on Forest Service maps. Bear right at the fork and hike to the southwest along good gravel road, soon passing a clear-cut to the left of the trail. Stay on the main road, passing a meadow bordered by a pole fence at 52.3 miles that marks the head of Tie Creek. Continue straight on the road past its junction with Trail 375 at 59.3 miles.

Dense lodgepole pines limit views in this area, and the divide is flat-topped and rolling. Reach a "Y" in the road at 59.8 miles, with the main branch forking left to eventually dead-end and a jeep road forking right. You've gone too far if you pass an extensive clear-cut on the left.

Trail 62, the Trail Ridge Trail, lies just inside the woods at this "Y," angling in a gradual ascent to the southwest between the main road and the jeep road. There is a trail sign just inside the woods, but it is not visible from the road junction.

Trail 62 marks the beginning of an alternate route of the official Continental Divide Trail. The official trail, when constructed, will remain along the divide and cross Gibbons Pass.

The alternate route travels mostly through forest, veering away from the divide to drop to Trail Creek before rejoining the crest near Chief Joseph Pass.

Climb gradually through lodgepole and level off before reaching a signed junction. Trail 62 veers left (southeast): continue straight (west), and begin descending gradually. Reach another logging road, Forest Service Road 1210, at 61 miles.

Directly across the road, at a culvert containing Elk Creek, is a trailhead. Elk Creek Trail descends to the left (east), and Hogan Creek Trail 106 heads right (west).

The official route follows the Hogan Creek Trail, but it's easier to head west on Forest Service Road 1210. Hogan Creek Trail climbs slightly through forest and passes along the edge of a large clear-cut that is bisected by another logging road. The trail, the logging road and Forest Service Road 1210 all intersect a short distance ahead.

Rejoin the footpath at the intersection and descend through lodgepole pine. Forest Service Road 1210 soon veers away from the trail, and a large clear-cut becomes visible to the southwest across the valley.

Soon reach Hogan Creek and reliable water. The trail breaks into an open meadow heavily grazed by cattle at the bottom of the descent and crosses Trail Creek Road at 63.1 miles. The trail follows gravel roads and jeep roads from here to Chief Joseph Pass.

Head west on the side road that leads to the group of buildings on the far side of the meadow, the Forest Service's Hogan Guard Station. Cross Trail Creek on a bridge just before the guard station, and stock up with water: the next convenient source is 22.3 miles ahead, beyond Big Hole Pass.

Bear left onto the Hogan jeep road at the guard station and head west past the log barn, keeping to the main track through a burned area and passing two spur roads. The road soon forks, with a jeep road bending hard to the left (southwest). Continue straight, ascending gradually to a barbed wire gate on the edge of a large burned over and clear-cut area. Cross the gate and continue climbing, following the jeep road as it swings south to intersect Forest Service Road 1260, at 64 miles.

Bear left and head east, passing through a desolate burned area with dead, standing trees. To the south are views of the tree-covered divide, with the meadow containing Hogan Guard Station in the valley below.

The road soon enters living lodgepole, which obscures views except in clear-cut areas. Stay on the main track, ignoring side routes, and reach the divide at 68.3 miles. Continue on the main route, ignoring the jeep road that enters from the left and another road that enters from the right a hundred yards beyond.

Leave the main road at 68.6 miles and bear left along the jeep road that ascends along the edge of a clearing to reach Chief Joseph Pass. (If desperate for water, continue straight here to reach in about one mile Lost Trail Pass and the junction of U.S. 93 and Highway 43. There are water fountains at Lost Trail Pass at a roadside table.)

The jeep road climbs gradually through forest and crosses the divide before heading straight to tree-covered Chief Joseph Pass on Highway 43, at 69.6 miles, where there is no water.

A sign just before the 7,241-foot pass marks the spot where Forest Service officials gathered on June 21, 1989 to dedicate the Montana-Idaho segment of the Continental Divide Trail.

Highway 43 is well-traveled and hitching a ride to and from Wisdom, a full service community 26 miles to the east, is easy.

Ringed with larches and multi-hued cliffs, Warren Lake is a pool of solace with rainbow trout cruising the shallows.

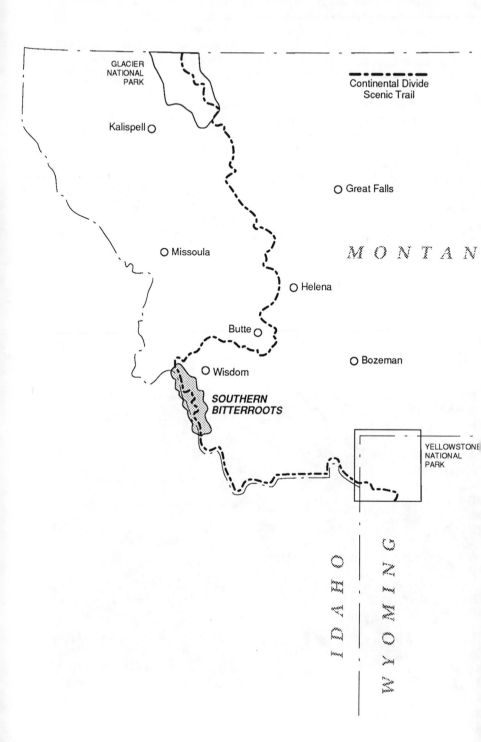

THE SOUTHERN BITTERROOTS

Chief Joseph Pass to Big Hole Pass — 13.5 Miles

Introduction: The trail follows along the mostly forested crest of the divide from Chief Joseph Pass, west of Wisdom, Montana, to Big Hole Pass, east of Gibbonsville, Idaho.

Water is scarce here on top, and the hiker either must conserve his supply or drop into drainages. Flat campsites similarly are limited, with the best spot slightly off trail at Nez Perce Camp.

The route initially follows a good jeep road, then becomes pack trail that occasionally peters out in meadows along the divide's open crest. Jeep tracks again are followed near the end of the segment.

Forest obscures views for much of the hike but gives way in places to reveal the expansive Big Hole Valley, the Pioneer Mountains, and, ahead on the divide, the Beaverhead Mountains. The familiar Anaconda Range also can be seen along this hike.

The trail appears to get little use, except during hunting season. Elk and mule deer are likely to be encountered, as well as blue grouse and spruce grouse.

Difficulty level: Easy, with some short, steep climbs and drops on trail that generally is well-marked and follows the crest of the divide.

Scenery: Good, of rugged peaks with some expansive vistas extending to the Beaverhead Range and Anaconda Range.

Water availability: Poor, none convenient to the trail until beyond Big Hole Pass.

Maps: USFS—Beaverhead National Forest (west half). USGS (7.5 minute series)—Lost Trail Pass, Gibbonsville, Big Hole Pass.

Supply Points: There are no supply points convenient to the trail. Big Hole Pass, at hike's end, is 20.5 miles from Wisdom, Montana, on Forest Service Road 79, and 8.3 miles from Gibbonsville, Idaho, on Forest Service Road 79. The road is traveled infrequently, except during hunting season.

Finding the trailhead: The trail begins at Chief Joseph Pass along Highway 43, 26 miles west of Wisdom, Montana.

Trail description: The well-marked trail crosses tree-covered Chief Joseph Pass, 7,241 feet, and heads south through lodgepole pine, descending gradually to the Anderson Mountain Jeep Road at .2 mile. The gravel road is passable by car and is marked with blue diamond blazes.

Turn left (southeast) and climb gradually along the divide through forest, remaining on the main track. Pass some small clear-cuts and places frequented by firewood gatherers.

Chief Joseph Pass to Big Hole Pass

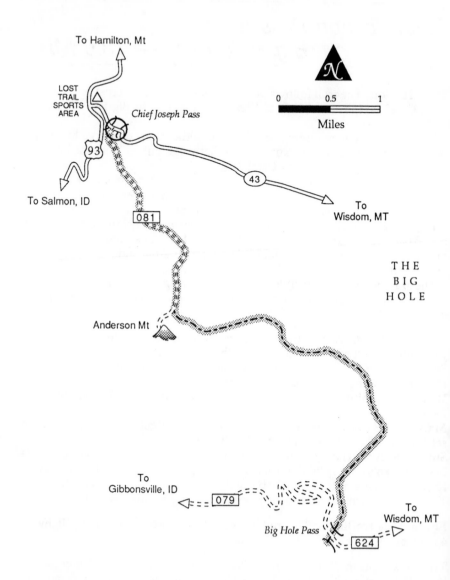

To Hamilton, Mt

LOST
TRAIL
SPORTS
AREA

Chief Joseph Pass

93

To Salmon, ID

081

43

To
Wisdom, MT

THE
BIG
HOLE

Anderson Mt

To
Gibbonsville, ID

079

Big Hole Pass

To
Wisdom, MT

624

0   0.5   1
Miles

The road climbs, then levels off, with a good jeep road angling to the right and descending at .8 mile. Grasses cover the floor of the lodgepole forest, which is fairly thick and obscures the views.

At 1.5 miles intersect the Richardson Creek Trail, a cross-country ski trail that in two miles leads to Hwy. 43. Continue on the main track, ascending gradually. Good views to the southwest reveal a line of tall peaks beyond the North Fork of the Salmon River, which winds through the forested valley below.

Break out of forest and descend to a small meadow at 2.7 miles. Old mining prospects dot the trailside and good views to the southwest overlook a forested basin. Reenter forest and begin climbing. At three miles intersect the Cabinet Creek Trail, a cross-country ski trail that in three miles leads to Hwy. 43.

An old log cabin lies below the trail to the right at 3.2 miles. The road bends to the south at four miles and enters a small meadow at 4.7 miles, with good views to the west.

Climb more steeply from the meadow, reaching the divide at a signed intersection of jeep roads at 5.5 miles. Turn left (south), following the sign for Divide Way, and continue through forest.

Leave the jeep road and turn right (east) at 5.75 miles onto a blazed pack trail then descend gradually through forest. Soon reach two small meadows with good southward views of 9,858-foot Sheep Mountain and Pyramid Peak, 9,616 feet, both snow-sprinkled and looming beyond Big Hole Pass.

Reenter forest and climb slightly along the crest of the divide before dropping through a third meadow, steeply in places. Pass a state line boundary marker and reenter forest, descending to a tree-covered saddle at 6.3 miles. The Threemile Creek Trail veers right (southeast) here, descending.

Climb from the saddle, steeply in places, and break out onto the divide's open crest, with good views ahead to Sheep Mountain and Pyramid Peak. The walking is pleasant here, through parks interspersed with stands of trees.

Climb, passing to the right of the 7,852-foot summit ahead, then drop to another tree-covered saddle at 7.5 miles. Switchback up an 8,230-foot hill, reaching at 8.4 miles a signed intersection with the Nez Perce Trail, Threemile Ridge Trail and Nez Perce Camp, all leading southeast. Another sign points to a spring about a quarter-mile to the southeast, at the head of a tributary of Nez Perce Creek.

Continue on level trail along the divide's crest through open timber that bears the scars of an old forest fire. Soon reach another intersection with Nez Perce Ridge Trail, Nez Perce Camp and Threemile Ridge Trail, leading to the southwest. The spring at the head of Nez Perce Creek is a half-mile from this junction.

Continue east through an open park just below the crest of the divide. Ponderosa pines grow here, and there are good views ahead to the south of the high peaks of the Beaverhead Mountains. The Big Hole Valley lies to the east, with the Pioneer Mountains beyond.

The trail drops steeply from the meadow to a saddle covered with open forest at 9.4 miles. Climb from the saddle, steeply in places, up the tree-covered hill ahead, emerging into a small meadow near its summit at 10 miles.

From the crest, the rugged Anaconda Range is visible to the northeast and the Big Hole Valley spreads to the east. Finish the climb through forest and continue along the crest of the divide on level trail. In a small meadow, look westward into Idaho to see line upon line of tree-covered ridges.

Chief Joseph Pass to Big Hole Pass
Elevation Chart

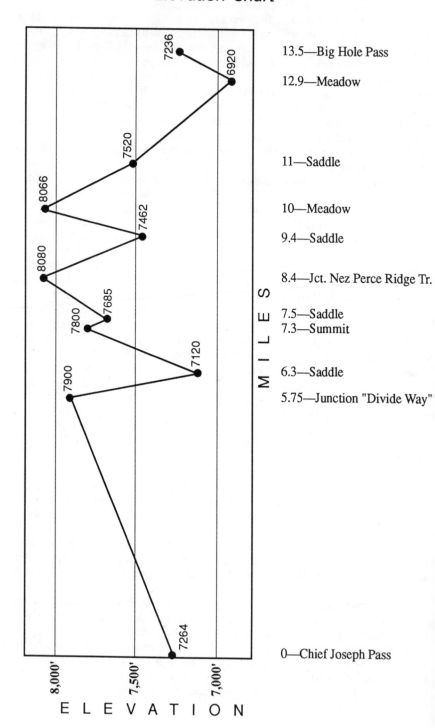

13.5—Big Hole Pass

12.9—Meadow

11—Saddle

10—Meadow

9.4—Saddle

8.4—Jct. Nez Perce Ridge Tr.

7.5—Saddle
7.3—Summit

6.3—Saddle

5.75—Junction "Divide Way"

0—Chief Joseph Pass

M I L E S

8,000'   7,500'   7,000'

E L E V A T I O N

7236
6920
7520
8066
7462
8080
7685
7800
7900
7120
7264

Drop steeply through forest, with good views of rugged Sheep Mountain dead ahead to the southeast. Reach a low saddle at 11 miles, then climb steeply up the next tree-covered hill, circling to the right of its summit.

Descend steeply at first, then gradually level off on a ridge top covered with lodgepole pines, heading south past several state line boundary markers. Grasses carpet the forest floor and large Douglas firs mingle with the pines.

Top a hill and join a jeep track in a small meadow at 12.9 miles. Follow the track as it descends gradually, climbs, then drops to a gravel road traversing Big Hole Pass, 7,236 feet, at 13.5 miles.

Wisdom, Montana, lies to the left (east) and Gibbonsville, Idaho, to the right (west). The trail continues to the south along Forest Service Road 78, toward Morgan Mountain.

Big Hole Pass to Goldstone Pass — 62.75 Miles

Introduction: This segment between Big Hole Pass and Goldstone Pass in southwestern Montana contains some of the best scenery and most rugged hiking encountered along the divide as the trail circles high above the historic Big Hole Valley.

Water is plentiful and wildlife abounds, with trout in all but the highest lakes and elk herds in virtually every drainage. Mountain goats live on the open summits surrounding Homer Youngs Peak, and black bears haunt high valleys that are visited only infrequently by hikers.

Rugged terrain forces the trail off the divide along two alternate routes that descend and climb along drainages. Much of the trail follows jeep roads, jeep tracks and pack trails, but a few rugged segments make cross-country hiking a must.

The most difficult hiking occurs along the climb from Montana's South Fork Sheep Creek basin and the descent into Idaho's Fourth-of-July Creek. Another challenging stretch is near the end of the segment between Cowbone Lake and Goldstone Pass.

Cowbone Lake is named for the bones of about 90 cattle that drowned in the 1920s; they still lie on the lake's bottom. The cattle, being driven across the divide in a snowstorm, crashed through a thin coat of ice that had formed on the lake's surface.

Evidence of mining appears throughout the hike. Included are trailside test pits and the abandoned Jahnke mine, complete with rusting steam engine and rotting stacks of cordwood.

Clear-cuts also occur, particularly in the vicinity of Twin Lakes. But the scenery in portions of this segment is unlike any other on the divide. The peaks are rugged and sheer, the lakes clean and clear, and the long miles of forested valley travel are well worth the breathtaking sights from the top.

Difficulty level: Moderate, with some cross-country hiking and steep climbs and drops.

Scenery: Excellent, of rugged and wild high peaks; some of the best along the divide.

Big Hole Pass to Goldstone Pass

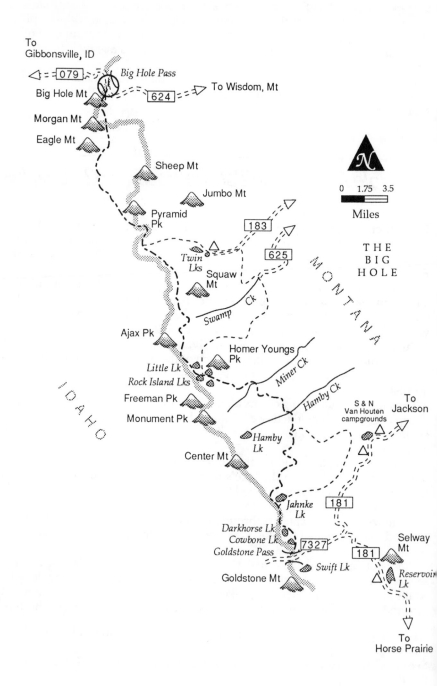

Water availability: Good throughout, in alpine lakes and numerous streams.
Maps: USFS—Beaverhead National Forest (west half). USGS (7.5 minute series)—Big Hole Pass, Shewag Lake, Jumbo Mountain, Ajax Ranch, Homer Youngs Peak, Miner Lake. (15 minute series)—Goldstone Mountain.
Supply Points: No supply points are convenient to the trail. Goldstone Pass, at hike's end, is reachable by four-wheel-drive vehicle along Forest Service Road 7327. The pass is about four miles west of Forest Service Road 181, which gets much summer travel by recreational vehicle users visiting campgrounds at Reservoir and Van Houten lakes.

Finding the trailhead: The trailhead is at Big Hole Pass, reachable by car, 20.5 miles southwest of Wisdom, Montana, on Forest Service Road 79.

Trail description: Head south from 7,236-foot Big Hole Pass on Forest Service Road 78, a gravel road that winds atop the forested crest of the divide toward cone-shaped Morgan Mountain.

Walking is easy as the road alternately rises and dips, and glimpses appear through the trees of the sheer, high masses of Sheep Mountain, 9,858 feet, and Pyramid Peak, 9,676. Break into a small meadow, where the road splits. The road rejoins just before the crest of the next 7,243-foot hill, at .75 mile, which the Forest Service map also shows as Big Hole Pass.

Crest the hill and drop through forest before ascending anew. Keep an eye out for large blazes marked on trees on either side of the trail. This point marks the start of a short bushwhack to Pioneer Creek; the Forest Service hadn't yet constructed the connecting link when we hiked.

Leave the road and head east-southeast, dropping through open forest to reach a jeep road paralleling Pioneer Creek, at 1.5 miles. Be careful not to head too far to the south along the descent, or you will wind up in steep tributary drainages choked with brush.

Turn right (southeast) and climb gradually along the jeep track to a gate marking the border between Montana and Idaho. Stay with the main track and descend into Bradley Gulch, with good views ahead of the divide stretching from Sheep Mountain to Pyramid Peak.

The rocky jeep track drops along switchbacks, steeply in places, before joining a small creek at 2.1 miles. The descent becomes more gradual as the basin broadens, and the trail passes through forest containing some very large fir trees.

Cross the North Fork of Sheep Creek on some logs just below the jeep ford, at 3.6 miles. Stay on the jeep track, which veers away from the creek after the crossing but soon swings back to parallel its left bank. There is a good campsite here just to the left of the trail.

Pass a miner's log cabin to the left of the trail. There is good camping along this stretch in grassy parks above the creek.

The jeep track forks just beyond the cabin. Take the left fork and descend gradually through forest. Bear left onto a well-worn pack trail just before the jeep track dead-ends in a gully.

Soon come to an unsigned "T" intersection with the South Fork Sheep Creek Trail, at 3.9 miles. There is good camping here, but a better spot lies a short distance to the west on the opposite side of the North Fork of Sheep Creek.

Head left (east) from the junction and begin climbing steadily and steeply along switchbacks up the ridge separating the north and south forks of Sheep Creek. Mule deer are plentiful in this gullied, broken country.

From the high point of the trail, at 4.7 miles, are good views of the South Fork of Sheep Creek rushing through a narrow canyon below. Its basin is heavily timbered, with patches of talus poking through the trees.

Drop into the canyon, steeply at first, then more gradually. Large Ponderosa pines and Douglas firs grow at trailside. Cross the creek at 5.5 miles and begin climbing gradually along its right bank.

Skirt the edge of a bit of talus just before boulder-hopping the creek again at six miles. A camp could be made in a rocky flat just beyond the second crossing.

Continue climbing gradually along the stream's left bank, passing through the bottom of two avalanche chutes with lodgepole trunks tossed about like pick-up sticks.

Boulder-hop the creek again where it forks and continue along the right bank for a short distance. The trail soon veers away from the creek and climbs, steeply in places, to gain the forested ridgetop ahead.

The trail forks at 7.2 miles just before cresting the ridge. Bear left (northeast) onto the newly constructed path, built and blazed in 1989. The trail climbs along the ridgetop, steeply in places, high above the unseen creek roaring in the canyon below.

Pyramid Peak can be seen ahead rising high above the treeline. A sharp-sided spur ridge curls to the southwest to separate the South Fork of Sheep Creek drainage from Fourth of July Creek.

Trail construction was not completed when we hiked, and the path ended abruptly in the forest. Maintaining a course along the ridgetop leads to the base of talus slopes slanting down from the spur ridge that extends to the southwest from Pyramid Peak. Walking is easy along the edge of the forest, with unobstructed views of the course ahead.

A spring bubbles from the base of the talus at eight miles, with good camp-sites nearby. Choose a route across the talus that leads to the prominent notch on the spur ridge just to the right (south) of Pyramid Peak. Watch for pikas along the ascent.

Views to the southeast from the notch are impressive, with the tree-covered Fourth of July Creek basin spreading below and the steep peaks of the divide curling around its head. The Bitterroot Range can be seen parading to the northwest beyond the South Fork Sheep Creek basin.

Hike cross-country and drop steeply toward Fourth of July Creek, angling to the southeast as much as is safely possible. Reach the creek at 9.1 miles and head upstream. There is no visible trail here, and deadfall is thick in stands of insect-damaged lodgepole pine.

Stay with the main branch of the creek, bearing along the left fork at every confluence. Break out of the forest near the head of the creek and climb the steep slope ahead. Reach a flat bench at 10 miles, where there is good camping at streamside.

Leave the creek, climbing through open forest toward the obvious gap to the south between two unnamed peaks on the divide, at 10.6 miles.

Views from the top are magnificent, with the dome-shaped hulk of 10,404-foot Squaw Mountain rising to the southeast beyond the upper valley of Big Lake Creek, its head circled by the sheer cliffs of the divide. The Big

Big Hole Pass to Goldstone Pass
Elevation Chart

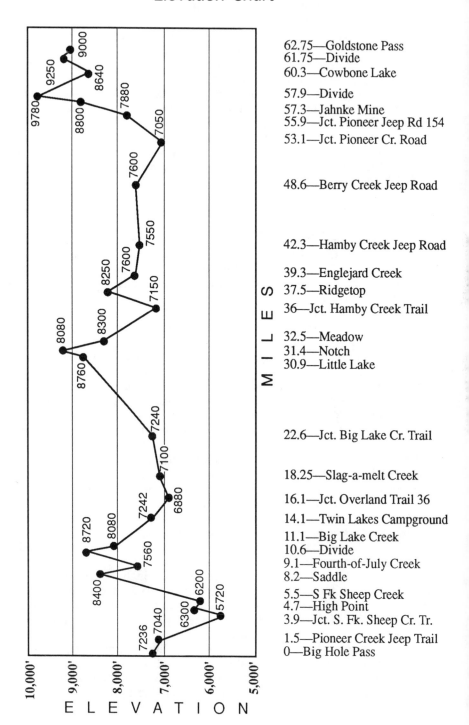

62.75—Goldstone Pass
61.75—Divide
60.3—Cowbone Lake

57.9—Divide
57.3—Jahnke Mine
55.9—Jct. Pioneer Jeep Rd 154
53.1—Jct. Pioneer Cr. Road

48.6—Berry Creek Jeep Road

42.3—Hamby Creek Jeep Road

39.3—Englejard Creek
37.5—Ridgetop
36—Jct. Hamby Creek Trail

32.5—Meadow
31.4—Notch
30.9—Little Lake

22.6—Jct. Big Lake Cr. Trail

18.25—Slag-a-melt Creek

16.1—Jct. Overland Trail 36
14.1—Twin Lakes Campground
11.1—Big Lake Creek
10.6—Divide
9.1—Fourth-of-July Creek
8.2—Saddle

5.5—S Fk Sheep Creek
4.7—High Point
3.9—Jct. S. Fk. Sheep Cr. Tr.

1.5—Pioneer Creek Jeep Trail
0—Big Hole Pass

Hole Valley can be seen to the east, with the Pioneer Mountains rising beyond.

The trail will one day continue southward from here just below the crest of the divide, but for now is forced downward by the rugged terrain into an alternate route that follows Big Lake Creek.

Keep a sharp eye at the pass for a blaze marking the alternate route, which descends southeast into the basin. The path becomes easier to follow as it enters thicker forest. Cross the head of Big Lake Creek at 11.1 miles and begin descending gradually along its right bank.

Boulder-hop to the left bank of the creek and continue the descent, passing through a meadow at the base of an unnamed, 9,646-foot mountain to the north. Watch for elk feeding on the open slopes.

The trail becomes less rocky and more level as it nears Twin Lakes, passing some large, grassy parks. Beavers have been at work in the stream here, and the trout fishing is especially good in pools formed by their dams.

Reach the head of Twin Lakes at 13.4 miles, where numerous sheltered campsites wait along its north shore. Pass a cabin complex to the right of the trail near the foot of the lake and soon reach Forest Service Road 183, at 14.1 miles.

Twin Lakes has a developed campground at its foot, and is popular with recreational vehicle users who come for the excellent fishing and views of Squaw Mountain and the peaks of the divide. A Forest Service ranger station, fresh water wells, and pit toilets all are here. From the campground it is about 24 miles to Wisdom, Montana.

Head east on Forest Service Road 183, descending gradually through lodgepole forest. Reach a signed intersection with Overland Trail 36 at 16.1 miles and turn right (east) into the forest, striking a "T" intersection with a jeep track almost immediately. Turn right (south) and follow the jeep track as it backtracks a short distance before swinging east to boulder-hop Big Lake Creek. There are good campsites in the willow-lined flat beside the crossing.

Follow the jeep road as it reenters forest and climbs gradually past the remains of an old log cabin. The track soon levels off on a grassy bench and reaches a signed intersection. Bear right (east) onto the lesser used jeep track and stay on the Overland Trail. Climb gradually, keep straight past an unsigned intersection just before the crest. Continue straight (southwest) at the next unsigned intersection, with views of Squaw Mountain ahead.

Reach an unsigned three-way intersection and bear left (southeast), watching for trail markers. Follow as the jeep track swings east and becomes a pack trail that heads into heavier forest and begins climbing.

Good views open to the west with gains in elevation. Jumbo Mountain, 9,723 feet, can be seen rising across the valley of Big Lake Creek above a wooded ridge containing some large clear-cuts.

Top the crest of the ridge at 17 miles. Drop through a narrow notch and descend through forest, reaching Sawmill Creek, dry in mid-October, at 17.6 miles. Follow the Overland Trail as it curves to the right (south) and heads up the left side of the dry creek bed. Squaw Mountain comes into view to the southwest.

The trail reenters forest, then swings east to climb a series of short switchbacks before dipping and rising along a wooded ridge top. There are good views from the ridge top to the east cross the Slag-a-melt Creek basin of the Big Hole Valley, with the Pioneer Mountains rising beyond.

Drop into the basin through lodgepole and spruce forest, boulder-hopping the creek at 18.25 miles. Enter a regrowing clear-cut on the opposite side, where there are good views to the southwest of Squaw Mountain and the peaks of the divide. The top of Ajax Peak, 10,028 feet, pokes above the divide to the south.

Head southeast on a faint foot trail that leads across the clear-cut and soon reach a gravel road. Turn left (north) and head away from the divide. The Big Hole Valley and Pioneer Mountains are to the north.

Descend gradually, swinging east past another clear-cut area containing a directional trail sign for Overland Trail 36. Head east across the clear-cut, and soon reach Forest Service Road 625, the Big Swamp Creek Road. Cross the road and head east into forest, remaining on the Overland Trail, now a pack trail. Cross Big Swamp Creek at 20 miles on a logjam. There are good campsites in the streamside flats.

Head east from the creek, cross a jeep track and reenter forest on its opposite side. Strike a "T" intersection with another jeep track on the edge of a regrowing clear-cut.

Cairns guide the way as the trail crosses the jeep track and heads diagonally to the left (east), ascending. Keep a sharp eye for blazes that sometimes are hard to see on the young trees. The trail climbs, then swings to the south before leveling near the end of the clear-cut.

The path is better defined as it enters the stand of mature lodgepole ahead and climbs, before swinging back to the east. Drop to cross a low spot containing a dry creek bed, then climb steadily through lodgepole to crest the ridge ahead. The tree-covered basin containing Little Lake Creek can be glimpsed ahead through the trees.

Impressive 10,621-foot Homer Youngs Peak, its steep sides rising well above treeline, first is seen along the initial descent to Little Lake Creek. Pass through mixed spruce and lodgepole forest enroute to the broad valley floor, with sagebrush growing in open areas along the slope.

Reach a signed junction with Little Lake Trail 87 at 22.6 miles. Bear right (southwest) and begin a gradual ascent, passing the remains of some mining prospects and two log cabins before reaching the creek at a jeep ford. Good campsites are all around, but the best is on the opposite side of the jeep ford.

Follow the rocky jeep track upstream along the creek's right bank and enter forest. Soon reach a pretty meadow that offers excellent views of Homer Youngs Peak, gigantic and hump-shaped, flanked by the cliffs of the divide. Continue on the jeep track, climbing alternately through stands of trees and small meadows as the trail swings away from, then toward, the creek.

The trail skirts marshy meadows as it nears the head of the creek and passes beneath the looming half-dome of Homer Youngs Peak. The jeep trail peters out and becomes a pack trail that continues along the creek's right bank and swings halfway around the base of Homer Youngs Peak.

The trail forks where the main branches of the creek join. Head left and boulder-hop the nearest branch of the creek. Continue ascending along the right bank of the other branch.

Soon cross over to the left bank of the creek as you continue climbing toward the basin's headwall and the sheer cliffs of the divide ahead.

Cross a beautiful and fragile alpine meadow. The terrain becomes rockier here, with large granite boulders sprinkled throughout the forest. Watch for blazes and cairns to guide you through open areas.

Cross the creek twice and begin climbing steeply along a series of switchbacks. The worn footpath peters out in spots, but orange paint blazes on rocks guide the way.

Reach an unsigned intersection in an open area at 30.5 miles. Head south, watching for cairns on the climb up the low ridge ahead. Whitebark pines predominate in this high grassy basin below the cliffs of the divide. Top the ridge for good views of Homer Youngs Peak, connected to the divide by a spur ridge.

Descend along rocky trail, reaching beautiful Little Lake at 30.9 miles. Water is in the inlet stream and good campsites are on the lake's northern shore. Little Lake marks the end of the alternate route of the Continental Divide National Scenic Trail.

Drop to the lake's northwest shore and cross the rock-strewn inlet stream. Aim for the middle of three notches on the spur ridge, avoiding the notch just to the right of Homer Youngs Peak and the notch at the head of the inlet stream.

Climb along switchbacks on the cairn-marked path, passing beneath the face of a rocky outcrop midway along the ascent. Yellow splashes of paint mark the trail, which is easier to follow as elevation is gained. Watch for pikas scurrying among the rocks, and stately mountain goats on the higher ledges.

The view from the top, at 31.4 miles, is impressive. Homer Youngs Peak dominates the scene to the northwest, with the divide's stony spine trailing along. Southeast lies the upper valley containing the Rock Island Lakes; Freeman Peak, 10,273 feet, lies to the south, with 10,323-foot Monument Peak rising over its shoulder. (See view map.)

Descend into the Rock Island basin along a rocky trail that soon parallels a rowdy creek. The first of the Rock Island Lakes can be seen below and to the right from an overlook just off trail. Descend to pass the first of the lakes, which offers good camping and cutthroat trout.

The trail drops more steeply between the first and second lakes, crossing the outlet stream of a small pond in a meadow between the two lakes, at 32.5 miles.

Well-worn side trails lead to the second lake, which has good sheltered camping near its foot. Elk often visit the lake at dusk and dawn, feeding in the lush grassy meadows that slope to the southwestern shore.

Descend gradually through forest and away from the third lake. Strike a jeep track at 32.9 miles. Turn right to reach the foot of the third lake, left (northeast) to continue the hike.

Descend along the rocky jeep track through forest, which limits views of the high basin, and cross some side creeks before swinging to touch the upper reaches of Miner Creek. The trail soon veers away from the creek and passes through parks, the largest of which has some mucky spots.

Reach an intersection with the Ridge Lake Trail at 34.7 miles and continue descending, soon passing through a jumble of tree trunks in the bottom of an avalanche chute.

The trail swings back toward Miner Creek and continues north through a signed intersection for the Miner Lakes Trail. Pass the remains of a log cabin before reaching a well-signed intersection with Hamby Creek Trail 203, at 36 miles.

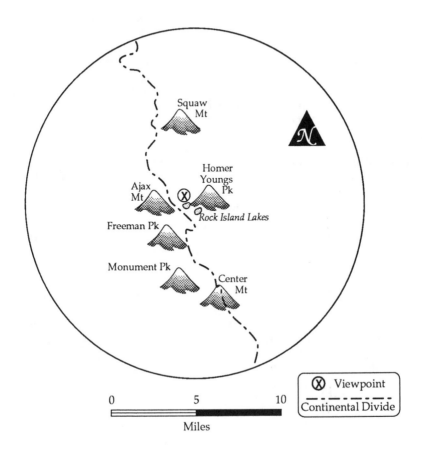

Saddle above Rock Island Lakes View Map

The view from the saddle is impressive. Homer Youngs Peak dominates the scene to the northwest, with the divide's stony spine trailing along. Southeast lies the upper valley containing the Rock Island Lakes; Freeman Peak, 10,273, lies to the south, with 10,323-foot Monument Peak rising over its shoulder.

Leave the jeep track and bear right (southeast) on a pack trail that drops to cross Miner Creek, then climbs the wooded ridge ahead on switchbacks that are very steep in some places. Good views can be had near the top, 37.5 miles, with Homer Youngs Peak looming across the valley and the Big Hole Valley and Pioneer Mountains to the north and northeast.

Descend gradually through forest, crossing tiny Englejard Creek at 39.3 miles. Climb for a short distance from the creek, then continue descending through lodgepole forest, which opens up a bit and becomes interspersed with meadows during the final approach to Hamby Creek.

Reach a good jeep road and a signed intersection at 42.3 miles. There is good camping here in the meadows on either side of Hamby Creek.

Head southeast from the sign post and cross Hamby Creek on a beaver dam. Head for the large tree with the prominent blaze in the middle of the meadow. More blazes mark the trail's entrance into the forest.

The trail climbs gradually to a wooded ridge top, then dips and climbs again, offering good views from the high point of heavily-forested Berry Creek basin, to the southeast. The trail later swings to the southwest on the descent to Berry Creek, revealing the rugged divide, dominated by 10,362-foot Center Mountain.

The jagged peaks and rough terrain again force the trail downward into easier valley travel along an alternate route. The official trail one day will climb through the broken country ahead to rejoin the crest of the divide above Pioneer Lake.

Reach Berry Creek and the Berry Creek Jeep Road on the valley floor at 48.6 miles. Bear left (northeast) on the jeep road and pass the remains of an old log cabin to the right of the trail. The flat grassy park at streamside is Berry Meadows, a good campsite. Pan-sized brook trout thrive in the upper reaches of this creek.

The hike along the creek is uneventful, passing through a vast lodgepole pine forest that obscures views. Later the trail begins a gradual ascent and breaks out of the forest into open sagebrush meadows. Pass through a meadow containing a fenced spring at 51.1 miles.

The trail at 52.3 miles touches the banks of Berry Creek, a good campsite. Reach a "T" intersection with another jeep track joining from the left (west). Bear right (east) and boulder-hop two creeks within the next 75 yards.

Another jeep track joins from the left in an open sagebrush flat at 52.7 miles. The high peaks of the divide can be seen to the southwest while crossing this flat. Pass some rickety wooden fence that is formed into a square near the end of the meadow. Reach an intersection of jeep roads a short distance beyond, at 53.1 miles.

Continue straight from this junction to reach Forest Service Road 181. Van Houten Lake, a popular campground with recreational vehicle users, is a half-mile beyond.

Turn right (southwest) at the junction and head toward Pioneer Creek along a jeep road that crosses the sagebrush flat. The divide, directly ahead, juts above the forest; snowbanks linger on the higher peaks. The jeep road becomes a jeep track as it enters lodgepole forest, passing a grassy meadow on the left.

Cross a small creek and follow the tracks across sagebrush, stepping across another small creek just before reentering the forest. Soon hear gurgling Pioneer Creek, reached at 53.8 miles.

Homer Youngs Peak, a 10,621-foot cone of snow-spangled rock, rises above Little Lake in the Southern Bitterroot Mountains. Elk and mountain goats will be your only company at this seldom visited spot at the base of the divide.

Boulder-hop the creek and continue along the jeep track, avoiding pack trails that branch to the right. Keep a sharp eye for a trail sign just as you enter the next sagebrush meadow. Leave the jeep track and turn left (southeast) and cross the meadow on Overland Trail 36.

From here putty-colored Center Mountain, rising well above treeline, dominates the view of the divide.

The trail is easier to follow after it enters woods on the far side of the meadow and begins ascending slightly. The walking is pleasant on the floor of the lodgepole pine forest, which is carpeted with bright green grass.

Climb more steeply, contouring south along the ridge ahead before switching back to the northeast, then back again to the south for the final ascent.

Descend gradually through parks interspersed with open forest into the Jahnke Creek basin. Reach a signed intersection and Pioneer Jeep Trail 154 at 55.9 miles. Head left (southeast) along the jeep track, remaining on the Overland Trail.

Soon intersect well-traveled Jahnke Lake Trail 113, a good jeep road, and bear right (southwest), ascending gradually. The trail contours high above Jahnke Creek, passing through open parks mixed with forest. The good views of the divide ahead later are obscured by heavier forest.

Reach a barricade closing the road to jeep traffic. The trail forks just beyond the barricade. Take the wider left fork and continue ascending. The canyon narrows, with old avalanche chutes streaking the steep walls on its south side.

Cross a good creek near the canyon headwall and soon ascend a series of switchbacks, reaching the abandoned and junk-strewn Jahnke Mine at 57.3 miles. The jeep track peters out here on the edge of the mine compound. A path to the northwest leads in a short distance to bright blue Jahnke Lake, half-surrounded by the high cliffs of the divide. Trees offer good sheltered camping.

The Forest Service hadn't yet built a short section of trail linking the Jahnke Creek Jeep Road to a mining road just below the crest of the divide when we hiked.

The quickest route to the top crosses the mining camp and heads west past the rusting ruins of a steam engine. Cross a stream flowing from the base of a huge tailings pile and climb the tailings along a faint trail past the mine's sealed shaft.

The trail peters out midway up the unnamed 9,780-foot mountain ahead. Continue climbing cross-country through open forest toward the summit, striking a mining road at 57.9 miles, just before the crest. The road has been carved into the side of the mountain and leads south along the crest of the divide.

This mining road marks the end of the alternate route of the Continental Divide Trail.

Excellent views are to be had from the road looking east over the Jahnke Creek basin, with the Big Hole Valley beyond. Stay on the road as it follows the crest, descending to a spur ridge that separates Jahnke Creek from Darkhorse Creek. Bear right just before reaching the spur ridge onto a well-worn pack trail that climbs gradually toward the divide, high above an unnamed pond lying in a cirque below.

Reach the divide and cross briefly into Idaho before swinging back into Montana. There are good views here to the north of the Big Hole Valley. The trail begins a sharp descent, passing some prospects and mining equipment before joining a jeep road at the head of an abandoned mining camp, the Darkhorse Mine, at 59.3 miles.

Jeep roads not shown on either the USFS or USGS maps can be confusing here, and there was no sign of a footpath leading to the shores of Darkhorse Lake, as indicated by the Forest Service's Continental Divide National Scenic Trail guide map.

However, Darkhorse Lake can be reached by following the jeep roads, thereby avoiding some cross-country hiking through dense forest that obscures views.

Pass an open mine shaft to the right of the trail before entering the mining camp. The trail levels out here and swings to the northeast. Bear right (east) at a fork in the jeep road at the camp. The jeep road is part of a snowmobile route, and is marked with yellow snow course markers and fluorescent orange blazes.

The jeep road descends through forest, reaching the foot of cobalt blue Darkhorse Lake at 59.8 miles. The lake is reachable by four-wheel-drive and all-terrain vehicles, and receives heavy camping use. A dilapidated log cabin rots beside the outlet stream.

Stay on the jeep road and cross the outlet, remaining in forest. A conspicuous

Dilapidated cabins at the Jahnke Mine in the Southern Bitterroot Mountains speak of a bygone boom gone bust. Old mines and prospects are sprinkled along the divide as it winds high above Montana's famous Big Hole Valley.

flat, grassy spot passed to the right of the trail is all that remains of Alpine Lake.

The road passes deep blue Cowbone Lake at 60.3 miles. Whitebark pine covers the lake's basin at the base of a cirque below the divide's steep cliffs. Campsites here are good, though heavily used.

The jeep road ends at a campsite on the lake's east shore, but the trail continues along a poorly maintained footpath. Keep a sharp eye for weathered tree blazes.

The trail heads above the lake's shoreline in a southerly direction toward the canyon headwall but soon veers to the southeast away from the lake and begins climbing. The path peters out as it enters a stand of young whitebark pine, but can be picked up on the opposite side.

The trail later swings to the southwest, with views ahead of your destination: a notch between the divide and a spur ridge that forms the southeastern wall of the Darkhorse Creek basin. The trail breaks out of the trees into more open country, but fades in the tall grasses. Head south cross-country toward the headwall and the divide.

A well-worn trail can be seen climbing diagonally to the left across a talus slope at the base of the headwall. Reach the base of the trail above a tiny, unnamed lake, a possible campsite. The trail appears to be little used by hikers but is a favorite path for mountain goats, whose sign is prevalent throughout the upper basin.

Reach the 9,780-foot notch on the divide at 61.75 miles— the highest point on the trail since leaving Canada—with good views to the southeast of the divide stretching beyond Goldstone Pass and into the Beaverhead Range. Goldstone Mountain, 9,909 feet, mostly covered with trees, looms to the southeast, and a line of unnamed peaks marches westward into Idaho across the upper valley of Pratt Creek. The vast opening for Horse Prairie lies to the northeast.

The path here was poorly maintained when we hiked, with the only trail sign being ancient blazes on the bleached white trunks of trees burned long ago. Descend to the southeast from the notch and contour to the shoulder of the spur ridge leading from the divide. From here looking eastward you can see a jeep road snaking upward along Pratt Creek. The road leads to Goldstone Pass.

Contour east-southeast across the slope through open whitebark pine forest and strike a well-blazed jeep track. Turn right and follow the jeep track to the southeast as it descends past some mining prospects.

Strike the Pratt Creek Jeep Road at 62.75 miles and turn left (northeast). Reach 9,090-foot Goldstone Pass a short distance ahead. The pass is marked by cairns, and there is a hiker's registration box a short distance along a jeep track that forks to the left on the summit.

Goldstone Pass to Lemhi Pass — 29.8 Miles

Introduction: The character of the divide changes abruptly along this short segment between Goldstone Pass and historic Lemhi pass on the Montana-Idaho border.

The rugged high peaks that are the hallmark of the Southern Bitterroot Range give way to a series of flat-topped, tree-covered hills.

Forests obscure views along much of the hike, opening only near the end of the segment to reveal spectacular vistas of Idaho's Lemhi Range and Lemhi Valley.

Logging activity here perhaps is the heaviest along the entire divide, and the maze of logging roads and jeep tracks that criss-cross the trail can lead the traveler astray.

Forest Service crews had yet to clearly mark the trail's official route when we hiked. Unless the trail is obvious, we recommend following Forest Service roads beyond Eunice Creek that shadow the divide just below its crest.

Cattle graze along the length of the hike, and water should be filtered for safety.

This segment is rich in history. Lewis and Clark first reached slopes that drain to the Pacific at 7,373-foot Lemhi Pass in 1805. Sacajawea Camp is named after the explorers' female Shoshone Indian guide.

Bloody Dick Creek and 9,812-foot Bloody Dick Peak are named after an Englishman named Richards who settled in the area; his favorite adjective was ''bloody.''

Difficulty level: Easy, along pack trail that follows the crest of the divide and along graded gravel roads.

Scenery: Excellent from above Goldstone Pass, but obscured by forest until Lemhi Pass.

Water availability: Good, in spring-fed creeks.

Maps: USFS—Beaverhead National Forest (west half). USGS (15 minute series)—Goldstone Mountain; (7.5 minute series)—Kitty Creek and Lemhi Pass.

Supply Points: Reachable by car, Lemhi Pass, at hike's end, is 12 miles east of Tendoy, Idaho, on Forest Service Road 13. Tendoy has a post office (ZIP 83468) that adjoins a small grocery store and gas station.

Finding the trailhead: Goldstone Pass, 9,000 feet, is reachable by four-wheel-drive vehicle, and lies four miles up Forest Service Road 7327. Forest Service Road 7327 is about 20 miles southwest of Jackson, Montana, via Highway 287 and Forest Service Road 181.

Trail description: Head south from Goldstone Pass, following fresh tree blazes toward the 9,731-foot ridge ahead on the divide. Climb steadily above treeline across talus slopes and top the ridge at one mile.

The views here are impressive, with the high sawtooths of the Lemhi Range marching to the south and southwest and other Idaho ranges in the background. The Bitterroot Range and the divide winds to the north all the way to the Anaconda-Pintlers. The Big Hole Valley and Pioneer Mountains are to the northeast, while the eastern view overlooks Bloody Dick and Park Creeks winding around an unnamed 9,149-foot peak. Tiny Swift Lake glimmers below.

Looking south-southwest, the divide changes abruptly at the head of Eunice Creek from a procession of rugged peaks to a series of flat-topped, tree-covered hills. (See view map).

Head south along the divide's open crest, remaining on the backbone of the ridge as it dips and rises. Contour to the right of a dome-shaped, 9,404-foot knob at seven miles. Clear-cuts come into view to the northeast in the Bloody Dick Creek basin.

Drop below treeline, keeping a sharp eye out for tree blazes and signs of deadfall removal. There is no defined footpath except where the trail crosses talus slopes.

Cairns help guide the way across the talus slopes as the trail begins descending into forest well above the head of Eunice Creek. The footpath is well defined here but appears to end suddenly in a pile of deadfall at 11.5 miles.

Keep straight for about 30 yards and pick up the trail again. It soon intersects a jeep trail not shown on either USFS or USGS maps. Bear right and walk a short distance along the jeep track before reaching a three-way intersection.

Bear left here along the heavier-traveled track, descending along a winding trail that heads generally to the southeast. Pass two trees marked with double blazes at 12.5 miles. This is the junction of the Eunice Creek Trail.

Remain on the main track, ignoring all side routes, and reach the Kenney Creek Road at 15.5 miles.

A myriad of logging roads and jeep tracks that criss-cross the forest makes for difficult trail finding in this area. The Forest Service had yet to adequately

Goldstone Pass to Lemhi Pass

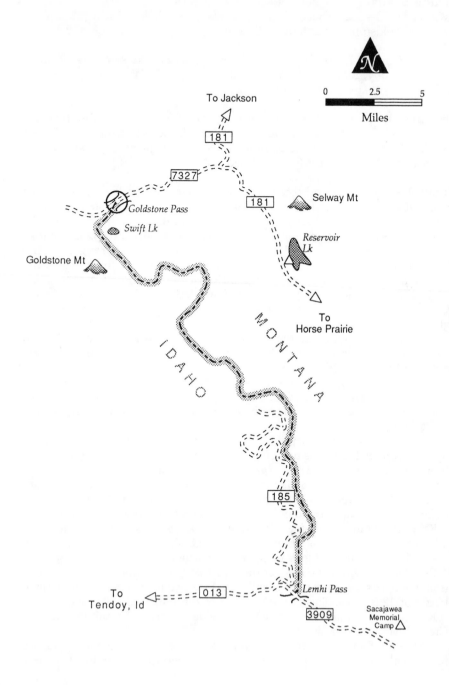

To Jackson

181

7327

Goldstone Pass

Swift Lk

Selway Mt

181

Reservoir Lk

Goldstone Mt

To Horse Prairie

MONTANA

IDAHO

185

To Tendoy, Id

013

Lemhi Pass

3909

Sacajawea Memorial Camp

0   2.5   5
Miles

Goldstone Pass to Lemhi Pass
Elevation Chart

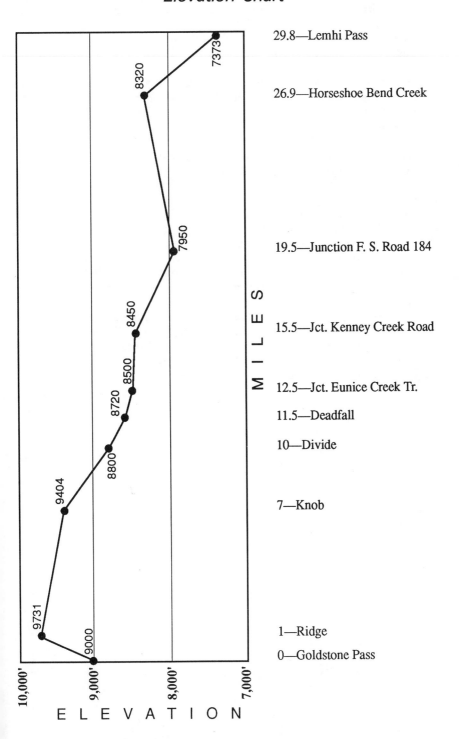

29.8—Lemhi Pass

26.9—Horseshoe Bend Creek

19.5—Junction F. S. Road 184

15.5—Jct. Kenney Creek Road

12.5—Jct. Eunice Creek Tr.

11.5—Deadfall

10—Divide

7—Knob

1—Ridge

0—Goldstone Pass

M I L E S

E L E V A T I O N

sign and blaze this segment of trail when we hiked. Much of the route is through forest, which obscures views and makes it difficult to locate landmarks. Unless the trail is obvious it may be better to stay on roads, as we did, to Lemhi Pass.

Stay on the Kenney Creek Road, passable by car, and round the head of the East Fork of Kenney Creek, passing through an intersection with the Eunice Creek Snowmobile Trail.

The road swings from the Kenney Creek Basin into the Pattee Creek basin, passing through a rare open area at 17.3 miles. There are good views here of the Lemhi Range and Lemhi Valley. Forest Service Road 185 can be seen snaking upward along Pattee Creek.

Intersect Forest Service Road 185 at 19.5 miles. Just ahead across the meadow is Pattee Creek, a dependable water source. Good camping is here and in flat meadows just ahead and to the right of the road.

Follow Forest Service Road 185 to contour below the heavily forested crest of the divide, passing a lumbered area on the left.

Circle around the head of Horseshoe Bend Creek, where there are good views of the Lemhi Range and the broad Lemhi Valley. Spring water flows through a culvert under the road at 26.9 miles.

The forest becomes more open near the end of the hike and gives way to sagebrush-covered slopes during the final descent to Lemhi Pass. Flume and Agency creeks flow in the valley to the west; see Forest Service Road 13 winding upward toward the divide from Tendoy, Idaho.

Pass under power lines and reach Lemhi Pass at 29.8 miles. The views here are impressive, with the Lemhi Range dominating to the southwest. The eastward view overlooks Horse Prairie and Trail Creek.

Water and good campsites lie a short distance ahead on the Montana side of the divide at Sacajawea Memorial Camp.

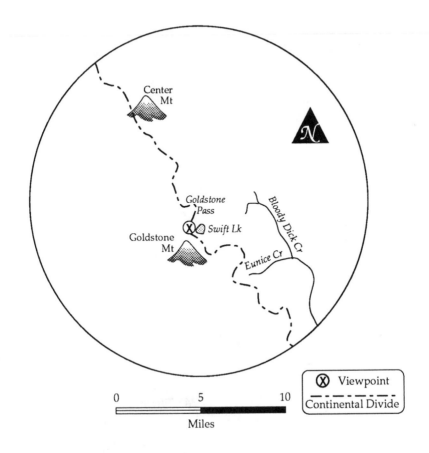

Divide Above Goldstone Pass View Map

Goldstone Mountain, 9,909 feet, dominates on the south, although views are impressive all around from this high, open vantage. In the distance, the high sawtooths of the Lemhi Range (not pictured) march to the south and southwest, and other Idaho ranges are even farther in the background. The Bitterroot Range and the divide winds to the north all the way to the Anaconda-Pintlers. The Big Hole Valley and Pioneer Mountains are to the northeast, while the eastern view overlooks Bloody Dick and Park creeks winding around an unnamed 9,149-foot peak. Tiny Swift Lake glimmers below. Looking south-southwest, the divide changes abruptly at the head of Eunice Creek from a procession of rugged peaks to a series of flat-topped, tree-covered hills.

GLACIER
NATIONAL
PARK

━ ━ ▪ ━ ▪ ━ ━
Continental Divide
Scenic Trail

Kalispell O

O Great Falls

O Missoula

M O N T A

O Helena

Butte O

O Bozeman

O Wisdom

*THE BEAVERHEAD
RANGE*

YELLOWS
NATIONAL
PARK

I D A H O

W Y O M I N G

THE BEAVERHEAD RANGE

Lemhi Pass to Bannock Pass — 26.5 miles

Introduction: The trail follows the crest of the divide through high grasslands mixed with stands of forests from historic Lemhi Pass, 12 miles east of Tendoy, Idaho, southeastward to Bannock Pass, 13 miles east of Leadore, Idaho.

A combination of jeep roads and jeep tracks is used, but there is some cross-country orienteering through lodgepole and whitebark pine forests. There are springs near the divide, but water must be conserved for fairly long stretches in this dry country.

Lewis and Clark first crossed the divide and reached Pacific slopes at 7,373-foot Lemhi Pass in 1805. A developed campsite with a good spring on the Montana side of the pass was named in honor of Sacajawea, the explorers' female Shoshone Indian guide.

Lemhi is a corruption of the word "Limhi," a character in the Book of Mormon. The Mormon Church founded a colony nearby in 1855, and later settlers misspelled the word.

Lemhi Pass is along an ancient Indian route between Idaho's salmon rivers and Montana's buffalo country, and became known as the "Blackfoot road."

The trail climbs steadily from the open pass to the 9,100-foot level, with excellent views of the divide northward to the Anaconda-Pintler Wilderness and southward to Italian Peak and the Red Conglomerate Peaks.

Cattle graze extensively in the highlands and the open sagebrush country near Bannock Pass, 7,484 feet. There are numerous mining prospects along the trail, and some clear-cuts near Grizzly Hill.

Bannock Pass also was along an important Indian trail linking Idaho salmon country to Montana buffalo grounds. Nez Perce War combatants crossed the Rockies here in 1877 on their way from the Big Hole battlefield to Yellowstone country.

The Gilmore and Pittsburgh, one of the nation's oldest railroad firms, built a line near the pass in 1810, and remnants of the old grade and a 75-foot-long tunnel near the summit can be seen from the trail.

Difficulty level: Moderate; some steep climbs and cross-country hiking through forests.
Scenery: Excellent, of high peaks from the open divide.
Water availability: Fair, with dry stretches 8.7 and 7.9 miles long.
Maps: USFS: Beaverhead National Forest (west half). USGS (7.5 Min. series): Lemhi Pass; Goat Mountain, Bannock Pass.
Supply Points: There are no convenient supply points along the trail. Bannock Pass, at hike's end, is 13 miles from Leadore, Idaho along Idaho Route 29, which is traveled infrequently. Leadore (ZIP 83464) has a post office, grocery stores and lodging.

Lemhi Pass to Bannock Pass

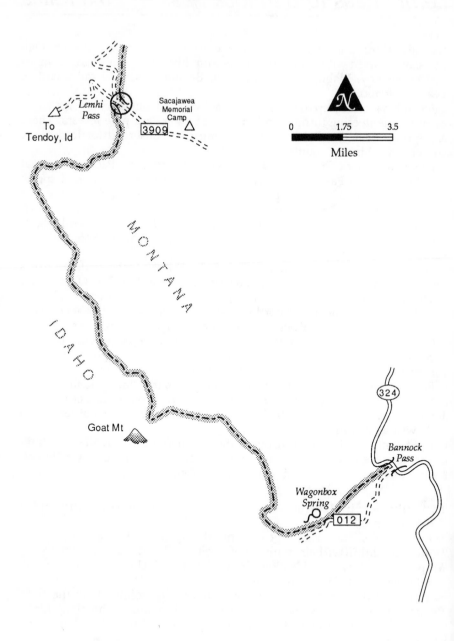

To
Tendoy, Id

Lemhi
Pass

Sacajawea
Memorial
Camp

3909

MONTANA

IDAHO

Goat Mt

Wagonbox
Spring

012

324

Bannock
Pass

N

0   1.75   3.5

Miles

Finding the trailhead: Lemhi Pass, reachable by car, is 12 miles east of Tendoy, Idaho, on Forest Service Road 13, and six miles west of Montana Route 324.

Trail Description: Get plenty of water from the spring at the Sacajawea Memorial Camp on the Montana side of Lemhi Pass before starting: The next water source is 8.7 miles away.

Cross to the Idaho side of the pass and turn left onto the gravel jeep road that climbs gradually to the south over sagebrush slopes mixed with pine.

Stay on the main jeep road as it criss-crosses the divide, generally climbing through high open meadows and stands of lodgepole.

Keep straight (southwest) at two miles, where a jeep track joins from the southeast, and descend past some mining test pits and into forest. Pass through a four-way intersection of jeep roads just beyond the bottom of the descent, at 2.6 miles, and begin a short, steep climb that soon levels off on an open ridgetop.

The divide swings from west to south here, and its tree-covered bulk dominates the skyline to the left of the trail. Continue the climb through forest and open sagebrush, reaching a flat open spot at 4.5 miles, with good views of the rugged Lemhi Range to the west and to the east of the rounded Tendoy Mountains, named after a Bannock Indian chief.

Stay with the main jeep track as it dips, then climbs steeply through forest for a short stretch. Later, from the open divide, are good views to the west of the Lemhi Valley, backed by the Lemhi Range.

The trail is level at seven miles, passing through a clump of aged-white tree trunks draped with bright green, moss-like plants.

Bear left at a triangular intersection at 8.5 miles onto the descending jeep road and drop steadily through a whitebark pine forest. The road soon makes a sharp "S" curve; keep a sharp eye out where the road bends sharply to the right for a cairn at the edge of a open, flat bench, a good campsite.

The cairn marks the head of a short side trail that leads north across the meadow and in about 40 yards drops to strike a small spring near a mining test pit. If you cross a steep mining road in the search for water, you've descended too far.

Climb from the meadow, following the jeep track through whitebark pine trees to the divide, at nine miles. The country is open here, and the walking is pleasant in grasslands at 9,100 feet that abound with lupine and Indian paintbrush. Looking west, the sawtoothed peaks of the Lemhi Range are at eye level.

A sweeping panorama unfolds within a half-mile, exposing the divide southeastward from steep-sided Goat Mountain, looming ahead, to high Italian Peak and the Red Conglomerate Peaks well beyond. To the rear (northwest) the divide extends from Lemhi Pass beyond the Big Hole to the high peaks of the Anaconda-Pintler Wilderness. The Pioneer Mountains are closer at hand to the northeast, and the Lemhi Range lies to the west.

Stay on the jeep road, contouring to the right of a 9,205-foot peak overlooking the Left Fork of Peterson Creek. The jeep road peters out, becoming jeep tracks that climb steeply from a grassy saddle at 13 miles to a notch between the divide and Goat Mountain, jutting to the southwest. A reliable spring lies to the right of the trail in a meadow at the head of the right fork of Peterson Creek, reached by crossing the barbed wire fence and descending west about 150 yards.

Climb along the jeep tracks, staying on the Montana side of the fence to avoid steep talus on the west slope. Contour to the right around the rocky knob near the top and gain the 9,240-foot notch, with Goat Mountain looming to the west.

Here begins a short cross-country stretch that ends at the jeep track traversing the half-forested, half-sagebrush-covered mountain to the east, across the valley.

Descend from the notch, steeply in places, and head east through open whitebark pine forest until a rockslide of red boulders is reached. Follow the edge of the rockslide downhill; a good spring, corralled by a broken down fence, rises at its base, at 13.8 miles. Fill water bottles here; the next reliable source is a spring 7.9 miles ahead.

Climb eastward to top the ridge ahead and descend along the treeline to the jeep track, reached at 14.5 miles.

The jeep track shadows the divide as it climbs steadily, exposing stunning views of Goat Mountain's steep, avalanche-streaked southern face high above the head of Little Eightmile Creek Basin, with the Lemhi Range beyond.

Climb along the jeep track and top the first in a series of small summits, passing a graveyard of bone-white tree trunks all blown over in the same direction. Alpine buttercups, asters and lupines prosper here, along with mountain bluebirds and Clark's nutcrackers.

The hiking is easy in this high rolling country as the trail passes through sagebrush meadows and stands of trees, descending to the north then climbing to reach the high, cone-shaped knoll in the distance, at 16 miles.

There are good eastward views from this vantage of tree-covered Grizzly Hill, in the foreground on the divide, and of 10,194-foot Elk Mountain beyond Bannock Pass.

Descend, steeply in places, on rocky jeep track that soon parallels a rickety fence line. A trail sign at the bottom of the descent, 17 miles, points the way to Little Eightmile Creek. There is a lovely view here to the southwest: Goat Mountain and Grizzly Hill form a sharp notch above Little Eightmile Creek, with the Lemhi Range in the background and a shallow pond in the grassy foreground.

A gravel jeep road joins from Idaho at the pass ahead; cross to the Montana side and continue along the fence line, climbing the open slope.

To remain on the official trail, leave the gravel road where it bends left on the crest, and descend southeast cross-country along the barbed wire fence. The road rejoins the official route near a spring, at 21.7 miles.

Faint jeep tracks join from the left along the descent. Follow them into the flat, grassy park ahead. A sign on a tree to the left near the head of the park points north to a spring—the one shown on the topo map at the head of the North Fork of Divide Creek. Cattle had trampled the spring into a useless bog when we hiked in early August, and the creek was dry.

Follow the barbed wire fence to where it enters thick forest and becomes a dilapidated wooden fence. Continue on the well-used game trail that crisscrosses the fence line and ascends gradually through the forest. Keep a sharp eye on the collapsed fence in areas with heavy deadfall as elevation is gained: saw marks and axe-cut rail ends are your trail markers.

Follow the fence line until it levels off and begins descending from the ridge top. Head right (southwest) and hike cross-country through open forest to reach

Lemhi Pass to Bannock Pass
Elevation Chart

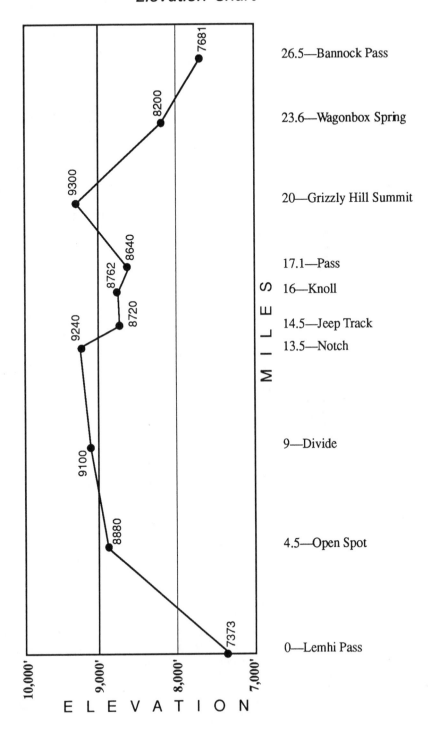

26.5—Bannock Pass

23.6—Wagonbox Spring

20—Grizzly Hill Summit

17.1—Pass

16—Knoll

14.5—Jeep Track

13.5—Notch

9—Divide

4.5—Open Spot

0—Lemhi Pass

7681
8200
9300
8640
8762
8720
9240
9100
8880
7373

M I L E S

10,000' 9,000' 8,000' 7,000'

E L E V A T I O N

the tree-covered summit of Grizzly Hill, at 20 miles.

Here the official route bends to the southeast, following the gentle crest of the divide through forest that obstructs views. The official trail was not yet blazed when we hiked, so we opted to descend westward from Grizzly Hill to reach a jeep road that parallels the divide and soon rejoins the official route.

Turn left (south) and follow the road through a clear-cut, with good views to the southeast of the Lemhi Range. Soon reach a clearing with a microwave relay station and tower that is not shown on the topo map.

Turn left onto a jeep track that by-passes the station and crosses the divide at a gate and fence of offset logs, at 21.5 miles. A good spring and sheltered campsite lie about 200 yards ahead on the jeep track. The gravel road bypassed earlier swings past this spring.

Turn right (northeast) at the gate and follow the fence line of offset logs on the divide through lodgepole pine forest. Cross the gravel road and continue along the fence.

Stay straight along the fence line through intersections with two jeep tracks and a jeep road, which are not shown on the topo map. Pass two state line boundary markers; the eastward view from the second, at 22.5 miles, includes grassy Elk Mountain, on the divide, and Maiden Peak, 10,227 feet.

At 23 miles the fence line emerges into a sagebrush meadow bisected by Forest Service Road 12, a gravel road. To get to Wagonbox Spring, the last reliable water for nearly seven miles, cross the meadow and turn left on the gravel road.

Reach a signed intersection in a half-mile and turn left, crossing a sagebrush meadow. The spring—two sources with a livestock watering trough—and good campsites are just ahead in the forest.

Continue on the jeep tracks from the spring and fork right at the next road junction, descending through sagebrush. The countryside opens ahead toward Bannock Pass, wide rolling grass- and sageland with fingers of trees reaching up the gulches.

Reach the pass and a good gravel road at 26.5. Leadore, Idaho, a possible resupply point, is about 13 miles east on Idaho Route 29.

Bannock Pass to
Medicine Lodge Pass — 53.5 Miles

Introduction: The three tallest peaks on the divide in Idaho and Montana lie along this segment between Bannock Pass and Medicine Lodge Pass in extreme southwestern Montana.

And the trail for the first time tops the 10,000-foot level, reaching its second highest point on the divide at the summit of 10,194-foot Elk Mountain.

Forests predominant in the previous segment give way to high, rolling slopes covered with grass and sagebrush that rise above broad valleys.

Views are excellent and extensive. This part of the Beaverhead Range is true Big Sky country.

The trail climbs steadily from historic Bannock Pass, 7,484 feet, an ancient

Indian traverse between Idaho salmon rivers and Montana buffalo plains.

The Gilmore and Pittsburgh, one of the nation's oldest railroads, built a line and tunnel through the pass in 1910, remnants of which can be seen from the trail.

Water is generally scarce on the divide's crest and must be conserved for stretches of 11.75, 10.15, and 8.3 miles. Cattle graze extensively along the entire route.

Water availability improves when the divide's sheer cliffs force the trail downward into drainages along the bases of Baldy Mountain, 10,773 feet, 11,024-foot Cottonwood Peak, 11,141-foot Eighteenmile Peak—the highest on the Montana-Idaho Divide—and 10,998-foot Italian Peak.

Beautiful Morrison and Deadman lakes are known for good trout fishing, and Nicholia Creek harbors native westslope cutthroat trout within its banks. Game abounds: elk, mule deer, pronghorn antelope, big horn sheep, moose, black bear, coyote and sage hens are likely to be seen.

Much of the trail is well marked and follows jeep tracks, but a combination of jeep tracks and pack trails is used in rugged sections. Hiking is rigorous in places, with some steep climbs and drops.

Medicine Lodge Pass, 7,650 feet, also known as Bannack Pass, was an important crossing point for Indians. It is named for a 60-foot-high medicine lodge that Blackfeet Indians reportedly built in the area for ceremonies that would protect them in battle.

Difficulty level: Moderate, with some rigorous climbs and descents.
Scenery: Excellent, of high rugged peaks and expansive vistas.
Water availability: Fair, improving to the south. Dry stretches of 11.75, 10.15 and 8.3 miles.
Maps: USFS—Beaverhead National Forest (west half). USGS (7.5 min. series)—Bannock Pass, Deadman Pass, Tepee Mountain, Morrison Lake, Cottonwood Creek, Eighteenmile Peak, Deadman Lake.
Supply Points: There are no supply points convenient to the trail. Medicine Lodge Pass, at hike's end, is on Montana Forest Service Road 951, which is traveled infrequently.

Finding the trailhead: Bannock Pass, reachable by car, is 13 miles north of Leadore, Idaho, on Idaho Route 29, also known as Railroad Canyon Road, and 20.25 miles south of Grant, Montana, on Montana Route 324.

Trail description: Climb northeast in open country from Bannock Pass on the good jeep road that follows a fence line along the grassy crest of the divide. Golden eagles and redtail hawks hunt these rolling grasslands, and use the fence posts for perches.

The rugged Lemhi Range comes into view to the west as elevation is gained, and there are good views all around from the divide, especially to the southwest from above Deadman Pass overlooking Whiskey Spring Creek.

Remnants of a railroad grade and tunnel also can be seen near Bannock Pass from this vantage.

Drop steeply to Deadman Pass, at 3.75 miles; a cattle trail angles down to willow-lined Whiskey Spring Creek, a reliable water supply with possible campsites if cattle aren't about.

Bannock Pass to Medicine Lodge Pass

Crest the 8,186-foot summit beyond the pass and continue along the jeep track, climbing steeply in places, toward the 9,393-foot peak ahead with a rocky outcrop on its summit.

There are good views to the northeast beyond Bannock Pass, with Goat Mountain dominating the divide close at hand.

Pass through a lovely stand of whitebark pine near the summit and continue along the open, rocky crest where the jeep tracks peter out.

Grass-covered Elk Mountain soon looms into view ahead, tawny and massive across Rough Canyon. Contour to the right of the dome-shaped 10,153-foot summit ahead to avoid steep scree slopes, then descend along the long, grassy ridge line leading to Elk Mountain's north summit.

Look down the saddle's sheer east side for bright blue Dad Creek Lake and a small pond lying in a cirque some 850 feet below. The steep walls of Rough Canyon Creek open to the west.

Climb a footpath that traverses Elk Mountain's north summit, then angle back and hike cross-country to gain the divide, at 9.45 miles. Elk Mountain's southern summit, the second of two bumps ahead, is 10,194 feet, the second highest point reached on the trail in Montana and Idaho.

The view here is impressive, extending westward over the Lemhi Range to the Lost River Range and 12,666-foot Borah Peak, Idaho's tallest mountain. Medicine Lodge Pass lies to the southeast, with Garfield Mountain and the Red Conglomerate Peaks beyond. Views to the northwest extend beyond Goat Mountain and Lemhi Pass to the peaks of the southern Bitterroot Range.

Drop cross-country from the second summit and follow along the crest of the divide as it curves to the left (southeast) around the head of Pass Creek. Tepee Mountain, 9,227 feet, lies across the Pass Creek basin at the end of a spur ridge.

Strike a faint set of jeep tracks in open whitebark pine forest near the bottom of the descent. Follow the tracks into open country and crest the hill ahead, with a state line boundary marker on top.

Find compass bearing 120 degrees and descend to the southeast through open whitebark pine. Your goal is the minor summit on the divide ahead that is topped with rocks and lies opposite of Tepee Mountain.

Strike a blazed jeep track near the summit, reached at 10.75 miles, and follow as it switchbacks steeply down talus into forest before leveling out on a grassy ridge top, reached at 11.65 miles.

There is reliable water but no flat campsites at Reservoir Creek, about 400 yards from the ridge top. Reach the creek by following the well-worn footpath that descends to the right just inside the treeline along the edge of the meadow. The next reliable water is nearly nine miles ahead.

Follow the jeep tracks across the meadow and into forest. Take the footpath that forks to the left at the edge of the forest and contour around a hilltop to rejoin the jeep track on the divide.

The track climbs to the northeast, but then curves south along the top of the long, bare ridge ahead. Baldy Mountain, 10,773 feet, looms beyond the ridge, snow-dotted and grand.

The view from the ridge crest rivals any on the entire divide, with Elk Mountain to the rear, the Lemhi Range and valley to the southwest, and the bare dome of Baldy Mountain looming ahead.

The hiking for the next 4.75 miles is pleasant, though with a few short, steep climbs, and the jeep track is easily followed as it rolls through open country fringed with whitebark pines.

The jeep track forks at 20.1 miles at the head of a big sloping meadow. To get to a good spring and sheltered campsite less than a mile ahead, take the right fork, descend across the meadow, and bear left at the head of Big Bear Creek, where the tracks criss-cross.

Morrison Lake lies 1.75 miles ahead on the more heavily traveled left track, which leaves the divide and drops steeply through a gully. Bear right at the next fork, climb the ridge ahead then drop through sagebrush, reaching the bright blue lake at 21.9 miles.

Its spring-fed waters are popular with rainbow trout fishermen and shoreline campsites abound. There is a pit toilet just beyond the lake's southern shore.

The trail is well marked here, a jeep track that skirts the lake and climbs to the southeast across tawny colored sagebrush and grass meadows. The cliffs of the divide, stratified and multi-colored, loom to the right of the trail above a skirt of scree.

The trail soon levels out as it skirts a whitebark pine forest at the base of the divide, and high peaks pop one by one over the horizon until the full expanse of the divide is exposed clear down to the Red Conglomerate Peaks.

Cross a barbed wire gate above the tree-lined basin of Simpson Creek, a reliable water source, and begin descending. The trail curves sharply to the (left) northeast midway along the descent, while a less used track continues straight. Cross Simpson Creek at 23.8 just below a series of willow-lined, shallow lakes.

Continue on the jeep track as it climbs the hill ahead, avoiding a lesser used track that veers to the south. Pronghorn antelope and sage hens are likely to be seen in this high rolling country, and mule deer and elk like the wooded draws.

The trail climbs, then drops into the Tex Creek basin, crossing a jeep track that joins from the left just before the stream is reached. The view upstream through the canyon is quite pretty, with the creek's headwaters circled by the divide's rocky cliffs.

Boulder-hop the creek at 25 miles and continue upstream along its left bank to enter the canyon's mouth. There is sheltered camping in a stand of trees at the entrance.

Skirt the base of a red and gray talus slope streaming down the canyon's south wall and cross the creek again. Continue ascending along its right bank, with good views ahead of the canyon headwall and two unnamed peaks rising above the 10,600-foot level.

Veer left (southeast) onto a signed pack trail that joins the jeep track about two-thirds of the way up the canyon. Drop to boulder-hop Tex Creek again, at 26 miles and cross a small meadow with good views and excellent camping.

The pack trail bends sharply to the east in the meadow and climbs into forest, switchbacking in moderate bursts up out of the Tex Creek basin before contouring south through open forest just below the crest of the divide.

The pack trail becomes jeep track once more in a meadow, and cairns guide the way as it skirts clumps of trees before breaking out into open sagebrush country.

Here again are excellent eastward views of the broad basin below, with the high peaks of the divide forming a backdrop. A jeep track joins from the left,

Bannock Pass to Medicine Lodge Pass
Elevation Chart

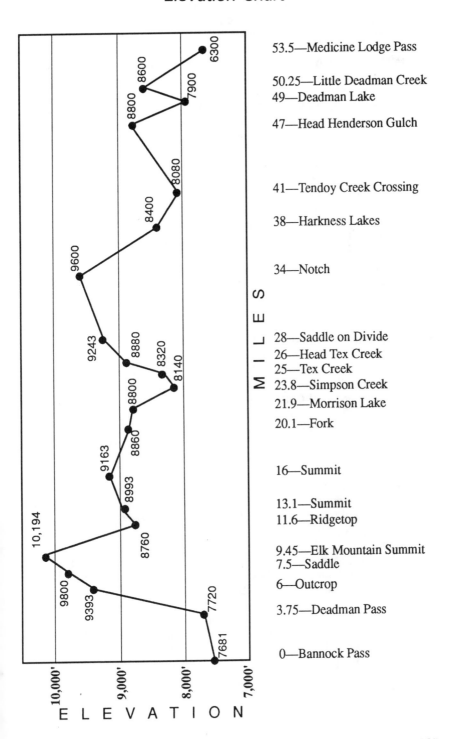

53.5—Medicine Lodge Pass

50.25—Little Deadman Creek
49—Deadman Lake

47—Head Henderson Gulch

41—Tendoy Creek Crossing

38—Harkness Lakes

34—Notch

28—Saddle on Divide
26—Head Tex Creek
25—Tex Creek
23.8—Simpson Creek
21.9—Morrison Lake
20.1—Fork

16—Summit

13.1—Summit
11.6—Ridgetop

9.45—Elk Mountain Summit
7.5—Saddle

6—Outcrop

3.75—Deadman Pass

0—Bannock Pass

M I L E S

E L E V A T I O N

10,000'   9,000'   8,000'   7,000'

and the trail makes a sharp 90-degree turn to the west, heading straight for the divide.

Top a low ridge at the head of Coyote Creek, 27.25, with westward views of gigantic, striated cliffs rising from an expansive talus slope. The basin is tree-covered, cradled by high grassy summits.

The jeep track becomes pack trail again as it drops into the basin and crosses Coyote Creek, which was dry in late September. Ascend gradually along the creek bed, reaching the divide at a 9,243-foot saddle at a signed intersection.

The trail bends east, ascending in the open, then swings south, climbing steeply in places and passing a small seep near the summit. The trail peters out in the high grassland, but the divide can be seen plainly rolling along from south to southeast in a line of grassy peaks.

Top the knoll ahead, then drop to a low spot where a spring above Chamberlin Creek has been trampled by cattle. Contour to the right of the 9,743-foot peak ahead to rejoin the crest of the divide as is curves to the southwest above the Meadow Creek basin.

Massive 11,024-foot Cottonwood Peak, the second highest mountain on the Montana-Idaho Divide, comes into view across the basin, with the divide's snow-capped peaks trailing in a line to the east. The Lemhi Range is the solid procession of summits to the west.

Descend and contour to a saddle at the head of Meadow Creek. Climb the steep, grassy hill ahead (southeast), swinging to the south at mid-ascent to cross a fence line and reach the crest of the divide, at 9,840 feet.

The view from the top is phenomenal, with the Lemhi Range to the west, Cottonwood Peak in the center and 11,141-foot Eighteenmile Peak, the divide's highest mountain in Montana and Idaho, peeking over Cottonwood's shoulder. The high summits of the divide can be seen curving from southeast to east as far as Garfield Mountain and the Red Conglomerate Peaks.

Descend along the crest, circling the rocky outcrop to reach a notch and trail sign at the base of Cottonwood Peak, at 34 miles. Here the route bends east on pack trail, forced by Cottonwood Peak's mass to descend quickly into the tree-lined basin, reaching a spring and good campsite in a half-mile.

The trail climbs slightly from the spring, then drops through a stand of whitebark pine to cross another branch of Meadow Creek, 35 miles, where there also is good camping.

Boulder-hop the creek and ascend to the southeast, first through whitebark pine, then through open sagebrush. Top the ridge ahead and cross the fence along the crest above the tree-lined basin of Rock Creek, with Eighteenmile Peak looming beyond.

Cross the creek at 36 miles, where there is a sheltered campsite, and continue descending along its right bank past a stand of beautiful aspens. Later, walk through a stand of spruce and begin veering to the east, away from the creek.

Here the pack trail becomes a jeep track that descends through forest before emerging in open country at 36.9 miles beside a shallow pond. There is good camping here in a tree-sheltered nook at the base of Eighteenmile Peak.

That jeep track peters out in the meadow. Continue southeast along the shore of the pond, ascending the ridge ahead for a short distance along the edge of the forest. Keep a sharp eye out for blazes marking the trail as it enters the forest.

The trail soon becomes jeep track once more and emerges into rolling grasslands. Here there are good views of Cottonwood and Eighteenmile peaks and the divide's grassy crests. Further south, above Tendoy and Nicholia creeks, the mountains of the divide becomes more rugged and tree-covered.

The trail descends into the Cottonwood Creek basin, where a willow-lined stream and a smattering of small ponds, the Harkness Lakes, offer reliable water. There is good camping along Cottonwood Creek and a lovely view of an old log cabin in a meadow at the base of the divide's putty-colored cliffs. Campsites at the Harkness Lakes, 38 miles, are exposed to wind and livestock.

Top the ridge ahead and begin a long, winding descent toward the valley floor, reaching a triangular road junction near Bear Creek. Bear right (southwest) and boulder-hop the creek. Bear left (southeast) onto the less used track at the fork on the creek's opposite bank and climb the sagebrush-covered hillside ahead.

Cottonwood Spring, developed for livestock, is on the crest. Descend to a road junction at 40 miles, where a jeep track joins from the west. Strike out cross-country here, following a series of cairns southeast to Tendoy Creek, emerging from a narrow canyon dominated by high, rocky mountains into an aspen-lined basin.

Boulder-hop the creek and descend in open sagebrush along its right bank, soon striking a jeep track that veers away from the creek and climbs into open country. Continue heading downstream, joining a good jeep road passable by car at 41.8 miles near the confluence of Tendoy and Nicholia creeks.

Turn right here, following the jeep road upstream across a sagebrush flat into the canyon ahead. The road ends at a barrier gate, but a jeep track continues the gradual ascent, soon reaching a junction with Nicholia-Deadman Pass Trail 91 in a grassy flat spot at streamside, a good campsite.

Continue upstream on Trail 91, a pack trail along the right bank that skirts the edge of the willows; ignore the jeep track, which climbs steeply to the right.

Beavers have been at work in Nicholia Creek, and their dams create deep pools and riffles that contain pan-sized westslope cutthroat. Moose favor the dense willows in the bogs.

Continue the gradual ascent along the right bank, crossing two good side creeks, the second with an excellent campsite. The canyon narrows ahead, pinched to a bottleneck on the left by a bare ridge with a rocky outcrop and on the right by a tree-covered summit slashed by an avalanche chute.

Climb through forest, soon reaching a junction with a jeep track that joins from the left (south). Follow the jeep track, dropping to boulder-hop Nicholia Creek, then climbing to contour downstream along the base of a steep ridge.

Head northwest along a well-worn pack trail, marked by a cairn, that forks to the right where the jeep track fords a tributary to Nicholia Creek.

Top the sagebrush-covered ridge ahead, with a cairn on its crest. There are good views here to the southeast of 10,998-foot Italian Peak, the third highest mountain on the divide in Montana and Idaho, at the head of the steep canyon.

Drop into a gully and continue heading northwest. Bear right and head north, ascending, at the next cairn; ignore the level trail that continues to the northwest. Climb in the open, then drop to the base of a 9,361-foot summit that is partially covered with whitebark pine.

The trail again forks here; bear right (northeast) and climb steadily from the Nicholia Creek basin to crest the low spot on the ridge ahead. Cross the

Unusual cliffs protrude above the sagebrush in this view toward the divide from Coyote Creek in the Beaverhead Mountains. Post and trail markers guide the way through this big country.

grassy plateau on the ridgetop and drop through the notch dead ahead into Henderson Gulch. Pass a spring that has been trampled by cattle midway along the descent and strike a good jeep road, shown as a four-wheel-drive road on the topo map, at the bottom, at 48 miles.

Turn right and ascend along the jeep road to cross a cattle guard. Bear right at the next fork, ascending steadily to the southwest along the heavier-traveled road. The road becomes jeep track along the summit and swings to the east before dropping steeply to cross Deadman Creek at the foot of Deadman Lake.

Westslope cutthroat trout also live in these waters, and there is good camping at the head of the lake.

The jeep track forks at the foot of the lake; bear left (northeast), and climb, steeply in places, out of the basin, passing a spring that has been developed for livestock use.

There are good views from the ridgetop of the divide extending to the northwest all the way to Elk Mountain, and the Red Conglomerate Peaks looming ahead, to the northeast, beyond the Little Deadman Creek basin.

Stay on the jeep track and drop to Little Deadman Creek, at 50.25 miles, its channel to the valley floor guarded on both sides by jagged rock outcrops. Looking down the channel to the north is a view of Island Butte, the black cone rising from the valley floor. Fill water bottles here; the next convenient source is beyond Medicine Lodge Pass at Buffalo Spring, 8.3 miles ahead.

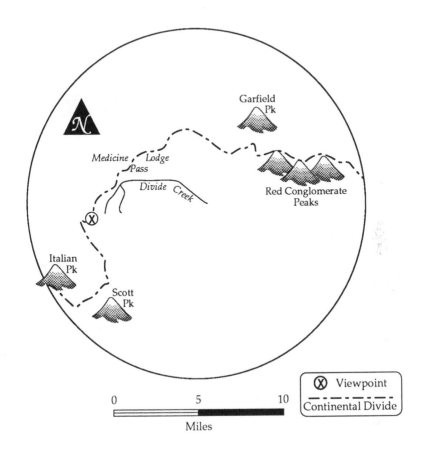

Bannock Pass to Medicine Lodge Pass View Map

The view is a near panorama from 8,890 feet, with the divide stretching south-to-north from Italian Peak to 10,194-foot Elk Mountain (not shown), and ahead, to the east, beyond Medicine Lodge Pass, 7,060 feet, to 10,961-foot Garfield Mountain and the Red Conglomerate Peaks.

Regain the divide at a low saddle, with eastward views over the Divide Creek basin to the Red Conglomerate Peaks. The trail swings to the north along the divide, climbing the steep, 8,890-foot summit.

The view from the top is splendid, a near panorama with the divide stretching from Italian Peak to the northwest beyond Elk Mountain, and ahead, to the east, beyond Medicine Lodge Pass to Garfield Mountain and the Red Conglomerate Peaks. (See view map.)

Descend along the rocky jeep track, steeply in places, to the grassy saddle below, then top the ridge ahead. To the northeast, across the open expanse of Medicine Lodge Pass, are white rocky outcrops that are being mined.

The jeep track forks at the bottom of the descent; bear left along the heavier-traveled track and drop through a stand of trees, the last trees encountered for several miles.

Descend gradually through open country, reaching Medicine Lodge Pass and a good gravel road, Forest Service Road 951, at 53.5 miles.

Medicine Lodge Pass to Monida Pass — 37.2 Miles

Introduction: Massive red mountains highlight this hike through high grasslands along Montana's extreme southwestern border with Idaho.

The well-marked trail is mostly jeep track that follows along the open crest of the divide before being forced downward by a string of 9,700 to 10,100-foot peaks.

Seldom-visited Garfield Mountain, 10,961 feet, and the sheer-faced Red Conglomerate Peaks, 10,250 feet, are the main features of the hike. The peaks shelter Little Sheep Creek, its basin an oasis of forest in this open rangeland that abounds with wildlife.

Elk, mule deer, pronghorn antelope, moose, coyote, grouse and sage hens can be seen in a single day's hike.

This area of Montana was home to horsepackers long before gold was struck to the north and boom towns sprang to life. Cattle still graze extensively, and are encountered all along the trail, as are camps used by cowboys.

Water is generally available at springs, most of which are developed with livestock watering troughs, or in tributaries. Near the end of the hike is an 11.6-mile dry stretch between Shineberger and Horse creeks, but two reliable springs only slightly off-trail offer relief.

The trail passes a calcium carbonate mine in some pretty white cliffs just beyond 7,650-foot Medicine Lodge Pass. Distances between stands of trees in this big open country can be measured in miles.

The pass, broad and sagebrush-covered, lies along a historic Indian trail, and was named for a 60-foot-tall medicine lodge Blackfeet warriors reportedly built in the area for pre-battle ceremonies.

The pass is sometimes called Bannack Pass, not to be confused with Bannock Pass, to the north.

Big horn sheep roam the high rolling mountains in the Beaverhead Range. Photo Chris Cauble.

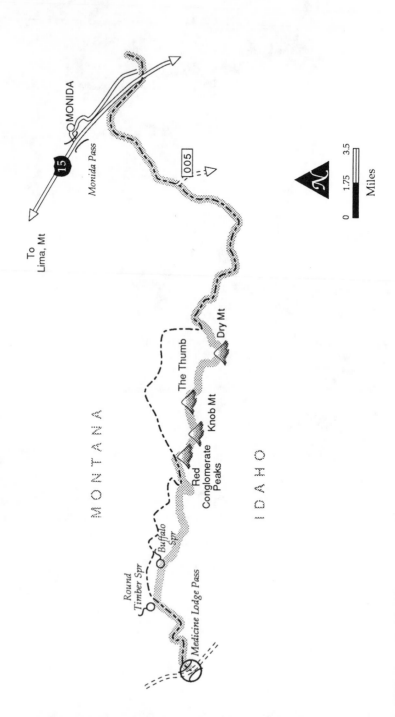

The trail generally climbs from the open country at the pass to the forested shoulder of the Red Conglomerate Peaks, with summits like a cresting wave frozen in stone.

Knob Mountain, 9,762 feet, and a curious peak called "The Thumb" force the trail downward to traverse tree-lined drainages in broken country at the base of the divide.

The trail later regains the treeless divide and begins much up-and-down travel in spectacular open country before dropping to the broad, gentle swath cut by 6,823-foot Monida Pass.

Monida began as a stagecoach stop between the gold camps and Salt Lake City that later evolved into a railroad border station. A train dispatcher is credited with naming this now nearly deserted town, combining the names of Montana and Idaho to get Monida.

Difficulty level: Easy, in mostly open country along well-marked pack trail and jeep track.

Scenery: Excellent, with expansive views from the open divide, highlighted by a string of rugged peaks.

Water availability: Good, except for an 11.6-mile dry stretch between Shineberger and Horse creeks.

Maps: USFS—Beaverhead National Forest (west half). USGS (7.5 min. series)—Deadman Lake, Fritz Peak, Gallagher Gulch, Edie Creek, Lima Peaks, Snowline, Tepee Draw, Paul Reservoir, Monida.

Supply points: There are no supply points convenient to the trail. Monida, at hike's end, on Interstate 15, has a public pay telephone, but no other services. Lima, a full-service community, is about 16 miles north of Monida on the busy Interstate.

Finding the trailhead: Medicine Lodge Pass, reachable by car, is 23 miles from Dell, Montana, via gravel Forest Service roads 257 and 951.

Trail description: Head northeast in open country from Medicine Lodge Pass on the jeep track that climbs gradually along the Montana side of the fence. A huge, solitary chunk of calcium carbonate—the same kind of rock mined from the prominent white cliffs ahead along the divide—lies in a cattle pasture to the right of the trail.

Bear left and head to the northwest where the trail forks just below the crest of the divide. Climb gradually to gain the crest, then swing east and northeast on the open ridge top to circle the head of Pine Creek.

Flocks of mountain bluebirds, the females drab and the males a brilliant blue, are likely to be seen perched along fence lines, winging ahead for short distances as you approach.

Reach the base of the white cliffs, at 2.3 miles, and leave the jeep track to continue east on a well-traveled mining road. Traverse the cliff face, ignoring side routes to the north and east, then switchback to the west and follow the mining road to the cliff top.

Bear left onto a lesser-traveled jeep track and continue west along the cliff top; the trail soon curves east and intersects the more heavily traveled route bypassed earlier. Bear left (southeast) at the next fork and top the low ridge ahead.

Medicine Lodge Pass to Monida Pass
Elevation Chart

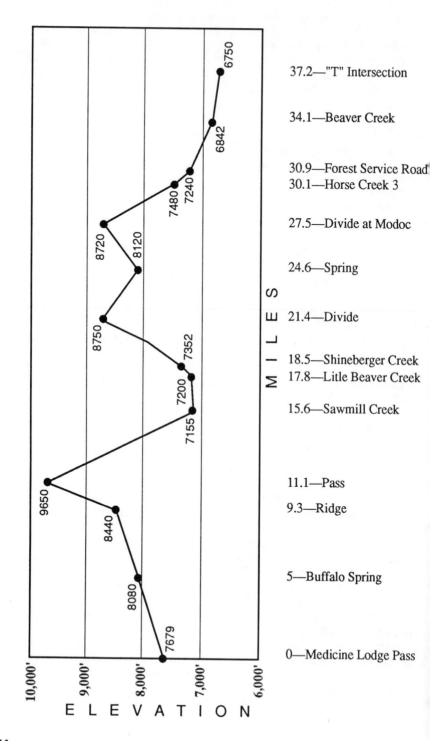

37.2—"T" Intersection

34.1—Beaver Creek

30.9—Forest Service Road
30.1—Horse Creek 3

27.5—Divide at Modoc

24.6—Spring

21.4—Divide

18.5—Shineberger Creek
17.8—Litle Beaver Creek

15.6—Sawmill Creek

11.1—Pass

9.3—Ridge

5—Buffalo Spring

0—Medicine Lodge Pass

Here there are good views ahead of Garfield Mountain and the Red Conglomerate Peaks, with the course of the divide plainly seen as it winds to the northeast and east.

Stay on the jeep tracks, generally ascending through grasslands, and follow the prominent guideposts. The jeep track soon peters out in the open country, but the guideposts make for easy cross-country travel.

The trail drops steeply and heads due north, joining a set of jeep tracks that crosses a low, open saddle at 4.9 miles. There are good views to the east of Garfield Mountain and the Red Conglomerate Peaks, both streaked with red, rising above the tree-lined basin of Little Sheep Creek.

Drop eastward from the saddle along a jeep track and cross the fence. Leave the jeep track here and and follow a pack trail that bends sharply to the south along the fence line.

The trail soon passes trickling Buffalo Spring, at five miles, which is unprotected from cattle. Slopes are too steep for camping here, but campsites and water are plentiful in the forest a short distance ahead.

The pack trail is well blazed and easily followed as it descends steadily from the spring and enters the forested basin below. Later, the trail emerges from pine forest and swings east across a sagebrush-covered meadow to descend through a beautiful stand of aspens.

Cross a tributary of Little Sheep Creek at the bottom of the descent, at 5.75 miles. A good campsite lies 100 yards ahead in the stand of trees on the hilltop to the right of the trail.

Cross another tributary at the bottom of the next gradual descent and soon cross a fence. The trail, now on jeep tracks, forks here; head right (northeast) along the faint jeep tracks and descend, joining a blazed pack trail on the edge of the forest.

Leave the pack trail in a small clearing and swing to the southeast, keeping a sharp eye out for trail blazes. Pass through a stand of mature fir trees, ascending slightly, and cross two more tributaries, both with good campsites at trailside.

The trail swings to the southeast from the second stream crossing, at 6.75 miles, generally descending alternately through stands of dense pine and open meadows fringed with aspens.

Cross another tributary at 7.5 miles and climb the grassy ridge ahead, soon reaching a fence along its top. Cross the fence and climb along its left side for a short distance before leaving the fence line as the trail swings left (east).

The trail alternately climbs and drops to cross small tributaries as it continues eastward opposite Garfield Mountain high above the main branch of Little Sheep Creek. Keep a sharp eye out for tree blazes when crossing open meadows, especially as you near the Red Conglomerate Peaks.

The trail breaks out of the forest atop an open grassy ridge at 9.3 miles, offering excellent views of the Red Conglomerate Peaks. The line of jagged summits resembles a wave that was frozen in stone while breaking from right to left. The base of the mountain is covered with a thick mat of dark green trees interspersed with tawny patches of grasslands.

Both Garfield Mountain and the Red Conglomerates are in plain view as the trail makes a wide sweep to the east around the head of Little Sheep Creek, reaching an open saddle and fence line at 9.9 miles.

Climb northward along the fence line and contour to the left of the rocky, cone-shaped peak ahead before dropping slightly to cross a wooded swale.

Continue climbing, alternately through open country and stands of trees, reaching a spring-fed creek and good campsite at 10.8 miles, just below a pass near the divide.

The final ascent to the pass is steep in places, but the views are rewarding, with a procession of summits marching westward from Italian Peak beyond Medicine Lodge Pass to Baldy Mountain. Low rolling hills and a broad bare valley spread to the northeast, with the Snowcrest Range rising in the distant haze. (See view map.)

Cross the fence at the pass and descend eastward into a gully marking the head of Sawmill Creek. The pack trail soon turns to jeep trail and continues contouring eastward through forests and open country below the base of the divide.

Knob Mountain, 9,762 feet, soon becomes visible to the southeast as the trail breaks out into open country. "The Thumb," a 9,782-foot summit with a bulbous pinnacle of red rock on its top, is visible further to the east.

Follow the jeep track as it begins a long, gradual descent along a ridge line between two branches of Sawmill Creek. A spring and livestock watering trough lie to the right (southeast) as the trail swings abreast of Knob Mountain.

Leave the jeep track as the trail nears the valley floor and follow a well-

The divide winds around the edge of a high alpine basin in the Beaverhead Mountains. The Red Conglomerate Peaks (center) can be seen rising above the high, dry country from as far as 90 miles.

blazed pack trail through forest. The trail soon emerges crosses a branch of Sawmill Creek at 15.6 miles, where there is a heavily used campsite.

Cross the good gravel road at the trailhead for the Sawmill Creek Trail and follow the jeep track to the northeast, again boulder-hopping Sawmill Creek.

Here the trail begins alternately climbing, contouring and descending as it continues eastward, crossing drainages at the base of the divide enroute to regaining the crest at the head of Shineberger Creek, at 18.5 miles.

The trail is well-marked and easily followed in open sagebrush country mixed with stands of aspen and lodgepole pine, ideal habitat for sage hens and ruffed grouse.

There is especially good camping at Little Beaver Creek in a clearing where the trail first reaches water, at 17.8 miles. Be careful to avoid getting sidetracked here on heavily used livestock trails. The official route, after reaching the stream, bends downstream and follows the left bank for a short distance before crossing and climbing out of the basin.

Fill up water bottles along the lower stretches of Shineberger Creek, the last good water supply and campsite until Horse Creek, at 30.1 miles. Shineberger's upper reaches are likely to be dry.

The climb to regain the open divide, 21.4 miles, is strenuous in places, and,

Garfield Mountain (left) rises high above the Little Sheep Creek basin, one of the most prolific wildlife areas along the trail. The red rocks on the mountain's flanks contrast sharply with the deep green forest and tawny brown grasslands.

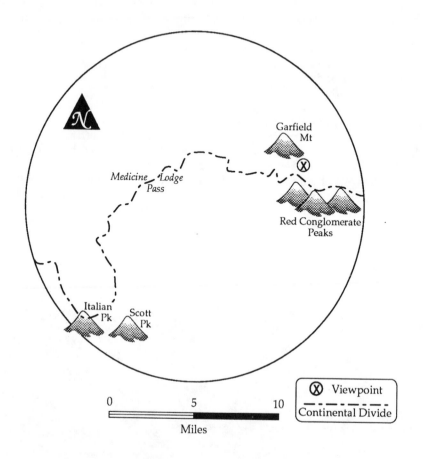

View from pass above Sawmill Creek

Views are rewarding, with a procession of summits marching westward from Italian Peak to Baldy Mountain (not shown). Garfield Mountain, 10,961 feet, thrusts up on the north; to its west points of interest include Medicine Lodge Pass, 7,060 feet, Italian Peak and Scott peak, off the divide. Low rolling hills and a broad bare valley spread to the northeast, with the Snowcrest Range rising in the distant haze.

once on top, the trail follows a jeep track along a fence line over a procession of steep summits that roll from east to northeast high above the valley floor.

The views are extensive, and the high grassy hillsides are favorite haunts for elk and mule deer. From the crest looking west you can see the Lima Peaks rising above rings of forests circling their bases.

Water and good campsites are scarce on top. A trickling spring and small campsite at the head of the East Fork of Middle Creek, at 24.6 miles, lie about a quarter-mile from the divide. There is another spring and livestock watering trough visible from the trail at the head of the West Fork of Poison Creek, at 25.2 miles.

Stay on the jeep track and follow the fence line along the divide, with drainages fanning out on either side into Montana and Idaho. Keep a sharp eye out for where the fence makes a 90-degree turn to the north above Modoc Creek, at 27.5 miles.

Continue along the fence line and follow it northward above the steep basin of Horse Creek. Drop sharply into the basin along a dirt road that bisects the fence line. Horse Creek, at 30.1 miles, has good water and flat campsites.

Reach Forest Service Road 005, also known as the Modoc Road, at 30.9 miles and bear left, heading northwest into open sagebrush flats grazed heavily by cattle. Stay on the main track, crossing Beaver Creek, a reliable water source, at 34.1 miles.

The divide is the procession of rolling hills to the northeast that taper into the broad, flat swath cut by 6,907-foot Monida Pass.

Interstate 15 lies ahead. Leave the gravel road where it bends sharply to the southeast at 35.2 miles and cross the interstate for a shortcut to Monida, which lies about 1.5 miles to the northwest.

The trail follows the gravel road and heads southeast parallel to the interstate before reaching an underpass at 37.2 miles.

Reach a "T" intersection just beyond the underpass. Bear left to reach Monida, right to begin the Centennial Mountains segment of the hike.

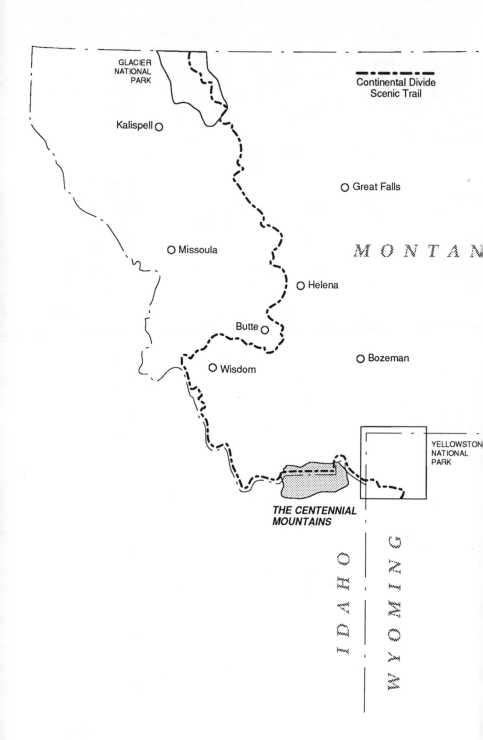

CENTENNIAL MOUNTAINS

Monida Pass to Red Rock Pass — 58.4 miles

Introduction: The Centennial Range offers a variety of terrain as it trends eastward from rolling sagebrush country at Monida, Montana, through a band of thick forest to reach towering peaks and outstanding views over Henrys Lake, Idaho.

Its north face is precipitous, rising some 3,000 vertical feet from the broad floor of Montana's Centennial Valley.

The face is cut by the steep canyon of Hell Roaring Creek, said to be the most distant source of the Missouri River from its mouth.

The valley was favored by the Bannock Indians as a travel route between the Big Hole and Yellowstone rivers. It was settled by whites—mostly livestock growers and loggers in 1876.

The trail straddles the divide much of the way. Water is convenient except for a 12-mile stretch along Taylor Mountain. Jeep tracks, gravel roads and pack trails compose the route, but there is some cross-country travel.

The rugged high faces of Baldy and Slide mountains force the trail from the preferred route along the divide into forested Idaho valleys.

Cattle and sheep graze extensively on the first leg of the hike. This high, rolling sagebrush country near Monida is home to pronghorn antelope and is the favored hunting grounds of golden eagles and a variety of hawks.

Sandhill cranes also forage in the big open fields, their raucous calls echoing at dawn.

Monida began as a stagecoach stop between Salt Lake City and Montana's booming gold camps. The Utah and Northern Railroad laid tracks over the nearby pass in 1880, and a train dispatcher named the station Monida, combining the names of Montana and Idaho.

Forests of lodgepole, fir and spruce cover mountains along the hike's midsection. These harbor elk and mule deer, and, in wet areas, moose that migrate to summertime retreats from the Red Rock Lakes National Wildlife Refuge in the valley below.

The 40,300-acre refuge was established to protect the rare trumpeter swan and is an important nesting and wintering range for a variety of waterfowl.

The mountains, made of complex sedimentary folds, are coated in places with younger volcanic rocks. Forests on high are interspersed with sagebrush meadows and grassland plateaus that sport a variety of wildflowers.

The trees give way to alpine grasslands as the trail reaches its high point along 9,855-foot Taylor Mountain, with outstanding views for a 50-mile radius.

The majestic Teton Mountains and the rugged Madison, Gallatin, Lemhi, Snowcrest, Gravelly and southern Bitterroots are some of the distant ranges seen from this vantage.

Rugged mountains again force the trail from the divide to circle pristine Blair Lake, known for its cutthroat trout fishing, before descending through Hell Roaring Canyon to the valley floor.

The range's eastern end, at Red Rock Pass, features some of the oldest rock

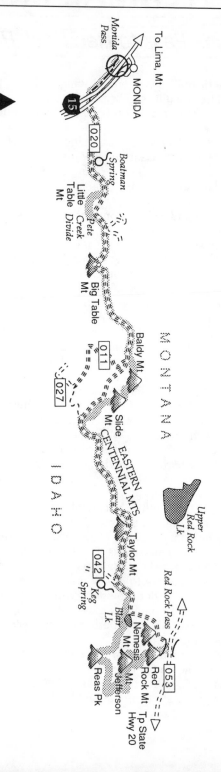

on the divide—metamorphic rock colored white with marble, streaked with gneiss and glimmering with crystals. It is not known how old these so-called "basement" rocks of the continental crust are, but geologists believe they were recrystallized some 2.7 billion years ago.

Difficulty level: Easy, with some steep climbs and cross-country hiking.
Scenery: Excellent, including views of Tetons and six other ranges.
Water availability: Good; one 12-mile dry stretch.
Maps: USFS—Beaverhead National Forest (east half); Targhee National Forest, Gallatin National Forest. USGS (7.5 min. series)—Monida, Corral Creek, Big Table Mt., Antelope Valley; (15 min. series)—Lower Red Rock Lake.
Supply Points: No resupply points are convenient to the trail. Monida is nearly deserted and offers no services other than a pay telephone. Lima, Montana, a full-service community, lies some 16 miles to the north along busy Interstate 15. There are no services at hike's end, at Red Rock Pass on the Red Rock Pass Road, some 23 miles northwest of Macks Inn, Idaho.

Finding the trailhead: Take the Monida exit from Interstate 15, cross the railroad tracks and bear right (southeast) from town onto the gravel frontage road. Cross the indistinguishable divide in one-half mile at grass and sage-covered Monida Pass, 6,283 feet. At three miles strike the official route, where another gravel road joins from the right, emerging from an underpass of Interstate 15.

Trail description: Bear right (southeast) from the Interstate 15 underpass onto the gravel frontage road and, at .1 mile, turn left onto the Long Creek Road, also graded gravel.

Cross the railroad tracks and pass a sign for the Humphrey Ranch and the U.S. Sheep Experiment Station. Both sheep and cattle graze in the fields ahead, segregated by barbed wire fences.

Cross Beaver Creek and follow the road as it climbs across open hillsides covered with sagebrush. The divide lies atop the inconspicuous, rolling hills to the north.

A good campsite is reached at three miles at the shaded head of Long Creek, a reliable water source. Water from a cold spring bubbles across the road at 4.1 miles.

A half-mile beyond, the road strikes a junction with a jeep track leading northeast to Boatman Springs, another reliable water source and a potential campsite.

Stay on the Long Creek Road as it passes a junction with the West Camas Creek Trail at 5.5 miles and swings northward through stands of trees toward the divide.

The road becomes a jeep track as it nears the Montana-Idaho border, and strikes the divide at 6.8 miles on a sage-covered ridge top. Good views to the north overlook the head of the broad Centennial Valley.

Little Table Mountain, its summit a sagebrush-covered plateau surrounded by forest, rises to the northeast beyond a low wall of red cliffs. Follow the jeep tracks to the northeast, first dropping then climbing steeply to gain the cliff tops.

Monida Pass to Red Rock Pass
Elevation Chart

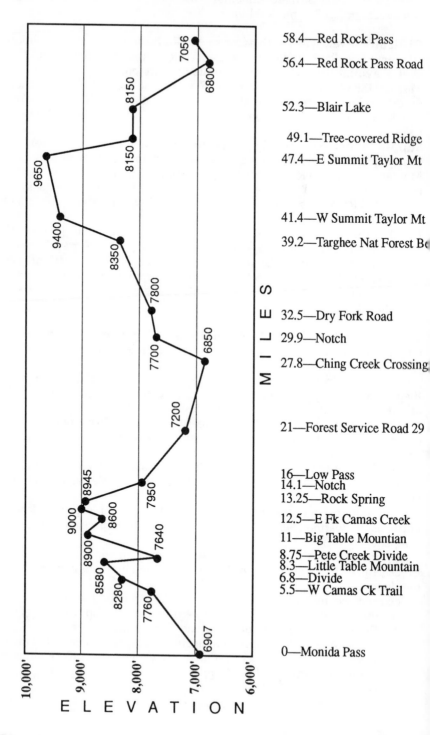

58.4—Red Rock Pass

56.4—Red Rock Pass Road

52.3—Blair Lake

49.1—Tree-covered Ridge

47.4—E Summit Taylor Mt

41.4—W Summit Taylor Mt

39.2—Targhee Nat Forest B

32.5—Dry Fork Road

29.9—Notch

27.8—Ching Creek Crossing

21—Forest Service Road 29

16—Low Pass
14.1—Notch
13.25—Rock Spring

12.5—E Fk Camas Creek

11—Big Table Mountian

8.75—Pete Creek Divide
8.3—Little Table Mountain
6.8—Divide
5.5—W Camas Ck Trail

0—Monida Pass

M I L E S

E L E V A T I O N

10,000' 9,000' 8,000' 7,000' 6,000'

The track forks at 7.7 miles; we stayed left along the more-traveled route toward Little Table Mountain.

The track peters out in a small grassy meadow at eight miles. Head northeast in a cross-country ascent of the low ridge ahead, drop and cross the tree-covered dip, and then climb steeply to gain the summit of Little Table Mountain, reached at 8.3 miles.

Bits of obsidian litter the trail here, and elk and mule deer sign is prolific in forested draws and hillsides.

Cross the summit plateau and contour to the southeast along the ridge top overlooking the tree-covered valley below. The Price-Pete Road can be seen snaking up from the Centennial Valley, reaching its apex at Pete Creek Divide, which separates Little Table Mountain and Big Table Mountain.

Descend to a saddle above Pete Creek Divide and set your sights on the curved section of road peeking through the trees to the north. Drop steeply in a cross-country descent, passing sagebrush meadows and narrow bands of trees before reaching the road at 8.6 miles.

Continue heading northeast, bearing right at 8.75 miles onto a jeep track that in 30 yards reaches 7,640-foot Pete Creek Divide at the head of a meadow. There is good camping here, with water a short distance down the draw to the south in willow-lined Pete Creek.

The trail ascends to the east from the divide along the Table Mountain Trail, an old pack trail that follows the fence line and is marked with new and old blazes.

The climb is gradual at first through a mixture of sagebrush meadows and forest, but becomes steep as the trail by-passes a landslide and, at 11.3, switchbacks through a boulder field.

The trail soon levels off in forest, and begins descending along a tree-covered ridge before striking a meadow spotted with sagebrush. Big Table Mountain, its tree-covered shoulder sashed with tawny grasslands, lies to the northeast.

A blaze across the meadow marks the trail, which winds atop the divide. Climb gently through open forest atop Big Table Mountain, then drop gradually to a "T" intersection with a well-traveled pack trail, at 11.75 miles.

Turn left (northwest) and follow blazes and metal guideposts to contour through parks and stands of trees enroute to the East Fork of Camas Creek.

A good piped spring flows into the creek just below the crossing, and a sheltered camp can be made nearby on the low tree-covered hilltop.

The rocky trail climbs gradually from the creek then bends to the northeast, crossing high stretches of open grasslands and sagebrush enroute to Rock Spring, 13.25 miles. Here find good shaded campsites and fresh water at a livestock watering trough.

Continue climbing alternately through meadows and trees. Keep a sharp eye for blazes, especially where the divide broadens into an open-forested plateau.

Contour around the 9,218-foot summit ahead, circling high above Burnt Canyon to the southeast. Drop to a notch at 14.1 miles for excellent views to the southeast of a vast expanse of plains.

The Centennial Valley, bisected by the Red Rock River, lies to the north; beyond, the rugged sawtoothed tops of the Madison Range are dominated by 11,316-foot Hilgard Peak.

Thermals rise along the faces of the steep ridges here, and golden eagles and a variety of hawks patrol the skies above the divide.

Climb gradually from the notch and contour below the next summit. The divide narrows here to a knife-edged ridge that ends abruptly at the base of a steep rock escarpment ahead.

Here to the northeast find the first unobstructed views of 9,889-foot Baldy Mountain and 9,805-foot Slide Mountain, their summits rising above treeline in a crescendo of rock.

The trail will one day climb along these peaks, but for now it is forced downward along an alternate route through the broken country at their bases.

Descend steeply to the west from the overlook along rocky switchbacks, quickly dropping into thick forest. Soon reach a meadow and a four-way intersection. Head northeast on the Idaho side of the divide along the trail with newer axe blazes.

Here the trail begins following the stout posts of an old fence line, which marks the divide for several miles ahead. Blazes, too, denote the trail, and often are the only clue to its whereabouts when the path crosses grassy meadows.

The pack trail later peters out on a grass-covered knoll, but the route continues along the fence line, joining a jeep track that angles to the northeast through a low pass at 16 miles.

Blazes reappear in forested sections, but the track in open areas has been covered by red Indian paintbrush, purple asters and larkspur, brilliant yellow black-eyed Susans and white umbrella plants.

The divide makes a 90-degree turn to the right at 17.8, and descends, then climbs, along the fence line past meadows fringed with aspens.

Continue the ascent, following the fence posts and occasional blazes after the jeep tracks peter out. But these trail markers, too, soon disappear, ending at a very old blaze at the foot of a steep tree-covered ridge that forms the western wall of the Salamander Creek basin.

Climb the ridge and ascend the game trail along its crest. Salamander Creek lies in the cut below, and Salamander Lake can be seen beyond in a small meadow.

The game trail peters out, but the forest is open and soon gives way to a clearing at the head of the creek. Cross to the opposite bank here and climb the dirt slope ahead.

Continue contouring eastward, angling slightly downhill to reach a bench of open meadows traversed by a blazed pack trail, Trail Creek Trail 11.

Head right (west) a half-mile to reach algae-filled Salamander Pond, a shallow pool with a good inlet stream and meadow campsites.

The trail continues climbing to the east, passing two stagnant pools before dropping into the head of the Trail Creek basin.

Descend through spruce and fir forest, soon reaching the creek to drop along its right bank. Slide Mountain can be glimpsed to the east through the trees.

Reach Forest Service Road 29 and the trailhead for Trail Creek Trail at 21 miles, a possible campsite. Follow the road to the southeast through several clear cuts, and pass the confluence of Trail and Cottonwood creeks.

Crews were clear-cutting in this area when we hiked, and, due to a lack of blazes and confusing logging roads, we were unable to find any sign of the trail, which leaves the road and heads eastward below the divide for 3.7 miles across the Kay and Little Creek basins.

Unless the trail is clearly signed and blazed, we recommend a 4.9-mile-long

Taylor Mountain rises high above the Centennial Valley and Upper Red Rock Lake, part of a national refuge for trumpeter swans. Views extend into Idaho and Wyoming, encompassing the Henrys Lake Mountains and the Tetons.

alternate route that follows well-signed Forest Service roads 29 and 27, the Little Creek Road.

This alternate is along stream beds, and regains the official trail where it strikes a hairpin turn on road 27 near Little Creek.

From this junction the trail climbs gradually through forest along the Little Creek Road for about a mile, then begins a descent to Ching Creek, 27.8 miles, with intermittent views to the southeast of the Antelope Valley.

Stay on the main road as it swings north, passing a clear-cut on the left that extends to the banks of Ching Creek, where there is good streamside camping in a stand of large spruce trees.

Keep a sharp eye for a blaze and a conspicuous pile of rocks to the right of the road at 28.4 miles; these mark the head of an old pack trail that leads to Scalp Creek.

Leave the road and follow the trail east across a dry creek bed. Continue heading east after the trail peters out in a meadow. Climb the low, tree-covered ridge ahead and cross an old logging road near Scalp Creek.

Boulder-hop the creek and ascend along the logging road above its right bank. Dead ahead on the divide is your next objective: a notch immediately to the left (northwest) of the dome-shaped, tree-covered, 8,203-foot summit.

Continue upstream. Bear left onto the next logging road and recross the creek on a log. Bear right at the next intersection, and continue ascending along the creek's left bank.

Follow the road as it bends to the right past a stand of aspens at the base of a tree-covered slope that leads to the notch.

Strike out cross-country and climb to the northeast through open forest, steeply in places, with Scalp Creek below and to the right. Pick up a well-used game trail as the forest thickens and follow it upward along the top of the gully, reaching the notch at 29.9 miles.

An old blazed pack trail leads to the right from the notch and descends through forest. It may well be a better route than the one we took.

We opted to continue ascending cross-country to the northeast through thick forest, soon gaining the divide. Here we turned east and contoured to the north slope of the 8,203-foot summit.

From this vantage the triple summits of Sheep Mountain and the giant grassy mass of Taylor Mountain can be seen to the northeast and east, towering over the sage-covered meadows and tree-covered hills.

But steep slopes and heavy deadfall made for slow going, and we headed north downslope to easier terrain, then struck northeast to contour across small high meadows and narrow bands of lodgepole pine.

This cross-country route leads to the head of a large open slope above the West Fork of Dry Creek, with 9,855-foot Taylor Mountain looming beyond and the divide rolling across the open country in between.

Drop to the creek, 31.4 miles, and fill all water bottles; there is no other reliable water convenient to the trail until Blair Lake, 12 miles ahead.

The character of the divide changes here, as the thick forests gradually give way to high open grasslands.

Climb in the open from the creek and top the ridge ahead. The Dry Fork Road can be seen below, crossing the divide at a low, open pass. Strike a jeep road midway along the descent, and follow as it bends to the southeast to cross the Dry Fork Road, at 32.5 miles.

Guideposts mark the route here. Stay on the jeep tracks as the trail climbs northward toward Taylor Mountain through wildflower-filled meadows mixed with open stands of fir and pine.

Views improve with altitude. Lower Red Rock Lake and the Centennial Valley soon are exposed to the northwest, while Island Park Reservoir sprawls in the valley to the northeast, with the snow-capped peaks of the Teton Mountains towering beyond.

The guideposts peter out at 35 miles, but the grassy crest of the divide can be seen clearly, and axe blazes mark the ridge top trail where it climbs through open forest.

Later, cairns and iron state line boundary posts mark the trail, which reaches a high point at an iron stake at 38.7 miles. Top the next rise on the divide, a half-mile beyond, its summit marked by a cairn, and continue northeast to a second cairn.

Here the trail drops from the crest to join the jeep track descending through the forested gully below. To the north, on the opposite side of the valley, note another jeep track switchbacking across the face of Taylor Mountain.

The trail emerges from the forest at 39.2 miles on a pass at the base of the switchbacks. A sign here marks the state line and the Targhee National Forest boundary.

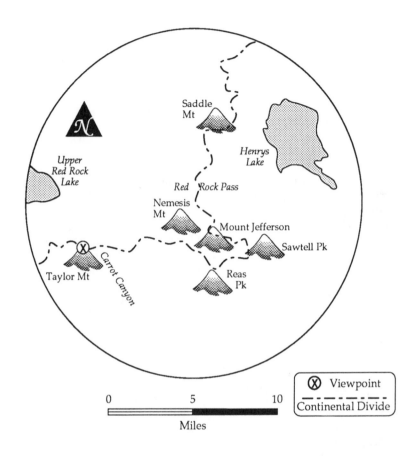

Monida Pass to Red Rock Pass View Map

Mountaintops stretch for miles and miles: The Italian Peaks and the Lemhi Range (not shown) rise in the distance to the west and southwest; across Upper Red Rock Lake, to the north, spread the Centennial Valley with the Snowcrest and Gravelly ranges beyond. The Madison Range extends as far north as Sphinx Mountain; just to the northeast, the Henrys Lake Mountains, on the divide, loom over the blue waters of Henrys Lake. On the divide, which forms a backward "L" running south and bending west, are Mount Jefferson, at 10,196 feet the tallest in the Centennial range; Sawtell Peak, and Reas Peak, 9,376 feet. Jutting off the divide is Nemesis Mountain, 9,439 feet.

Climb gradually along the switchbacks, making three left-hand turns and two right-hand turns before reaching a fork at 40.4 miles. Bear right and continue climbing steadily toward the west summit of Taylor Mountain.

Sheep Mountain lies to the northwest, its gray, stepped cliffs looming some 3,000 feet above the Centennial Valley and Upper Red Rock Lake, which now comes into view. Miners have left a scarred landscape here as the trail climbs eastward below the summit and bends toward the knob ahead.

Climb the knob and head east on level jeep track just below the crest of the divide.

The views here are outstanding. The majestic Tetons rise to the southeast beyond Island Park Reservoir, and Slide Mountain lies to the southwest, flanked by lesser peaks. The westward view encompasses Upper Red Rock Lake and a wide slice of the Centennial Valley with the Gravelly Range beyond.

But the best viewpoint lies ahead, reached by bearing left onto a rocky spur road at 47.4 miles that climbs steeply to the divide near the east summit of Taylor Mountain. (See view map.)

Drop from the divide to regain the jeep track and continue contouring to the east, soon reaching a dead end. Here the route follows a faint pack trail that drops steeply across the talus slopes to the right, then contours east toward the sharp notch ahead on the divide at the head of Carrot Canyon.

Pass a section of low, wind-blasted trees and cross two rock slides before reaching the notch. Climb along the ridge toward the next summit and circle tightly to the left below the peak; too wide a circle will take you to the edge of a steep drop-off, on the northern slope above Tom Creek.

Swing to the Idaho side of the divide through a high, boulder-strewn meadow with good views all around. Here the divide drops steeply, crossing the valley below on a narrow, tree-covered ridge. The jeep road seen traversing the high meadows beyond is the Keg Spring Road.

Use caution along the steep descent: There is no worn footpath, but two iron boundary stakes mark the divide. Get a compass bearing to help guide you across the tree-covered ridge, at 49.1 miles, and stay as close to the crest as possible when crossing to avoid the steep drops on either side.

The trail emerges from forest at the base of a sagebrush-covered meadow. Climb steeply to gain the ridge top ahead and follow along its rocky crest as it swings to the north through open forest above sloping meadows and the Keg Spring Road.

Keg Spring, a reliable water source, lies to the south about one mile off trail. The trail drops to cross the meadow, then follows the Keg Spring Road as it swings to the northeast, climbing gradually through open country before leveling off on a grassy plateau. Nemesis Mountain, rocky and streaked with red, rises above the forest ahead.

Stay on the road as it enters the forest and bear right at the fork. Descend on rocky footing, steeply in places, and soon reach a feeder stream that leads to Blair Lake, lying in a pretty cirque below.

The lake at 52.3 miles, is an oasis in this dry country, and a draw for wildlife. Indian paintbrush, asters and umbrella plants flourish in the meadows along its shore, and cutthroat trout grace its waters. There is excellent camping at the head of the lake, with good views to the northeast of 9,349-foot Nemesis Mountain.

The trail crosses the lake's outlet, and climbs to the southeast through forest before swinging west across an open flat above Hell Roaring Canyon.

From this overlook are good views to the northwest of a multi-spired, 7,722-foot column of red rock rising at the foot of the canyon.

The trail switchbacks down into the canyon and soon intersects a well-traveled pack trail. Turn left (northwest) and descend gradually, soon entering thick lodgepole forest.

Water is plentiful and the trail is mucky in spots where it crosses side creeks. Later, the route climbs then drops into the Corral Creek basin, striking a road on private land in a logged area near the valley floor.

The Forest Service is planning to relocate the trail onto public land in Hell Roaring Canyon.

Turn right (northwest) on the road and descend gradually to the sagebrush-covered valley floor, reaching the Red Rock Pass Road at 56.4 miles. Here are excellent views to the south of the sheer-faced front of the Centennial Mountains.

The Henrys Lake Mountains rise to the northeast, sagebrush- and tree-covered hills except for a few rock outcrops.

Head east on the gravel road, filling water bottles at either Hell Roaring or Cole creeks; water is not convenient to the trail for the rest of the section.

Pass the entrance to the Hell Roaring Ranch and cross onto Beaverhead National Forest land at the foot of Red Rock Pass. Flat campsites are in the grove of trees to the left of the road.

The trail climbs gradually along the road, passing sagebrush meadows frequented by sandhill cranes before reaching 7,056-foot Red Rock Pass at 58.4 miles.

The westward views are outstanding, with the wall of the Centennials trailing above the Red Rock Lakes. Mount Jefferson, Red Rock Mountain and Sawtell Peak rise closer at hand, a sharp contrast with the open, rolling mountains of the divide ahead to the north.

GLACIER
NATIONAL
PARK

Continental Divide
Scenic Trail

Kalispell O

O Great Falls

O Missoula

M O N T A

O Helena

Butte O

O Bozeman

O Wisdom

**HENRYS LAKE
MOUNTAINS**

YELLOWST
NATIONAL
PARK

I D A H O

W Y O M I N G

HENRYS LAKE MOUNTAINS

Red Rock Pass to
Raynolds Pass — 8.75 miles

Introduction: The divide jogs northward over this short, rolling segment of the Henrys Lake Mountains between Red Rock Pass at the eastern end of the Centennial Valley and Raynolds Pass, 22 miles west of West Yellowstone, Montana.

The hike is entirely on well-defined jeep tracks that traverse high sagebrush meadows and cross the divide four times.

Cattle graze this country extensively, and water is available at developed livestock watering troughs.

Red Rock Pass, 7,056 feet, is the named pass closest to Hell Roaring Creek, said to be the most distant source of the Missouri River.

Nearby Squaw Pass, 7,262 feet, was along the Bannock Indians' travel route between the Big Hole and Yellowstone rivers. A favored campsite was near the junction of Squaw and Papoose creeks.

Hawks patrol this high open country, and sandhill cranes and blue grouse forage in the flats. Flocks of mountain bluebirds are sure to be seen perched on barbed wire fences.

The metamorphic rocks exposed in crumbly outcrops along this segment are some of the oldest encountered along the divide. These are "basement" rocks that extend to unknown depths in the continental crust and normally lie beneath all other kinds of rocks.

Raynolds Pass, 6,836 feet, was first crossed by whites in 1810, but was not named until 1860, after Capt. William F. Raynolds crossed it with Jim Bridger.

Difficulty level: Easy hiking through rolling hills.
Scenery: Good, of rugged peaks and broad valleys, improving toward hike's end.
Water availability: Good, at livestock troughs.
Maps: USFS—Gallatin National Forest (west half). USGS 15 min. series—Upper Red Rock Lake; USGS 7.5 min. series—Targhee Peak.
Supply Points: There are no supply points convenient to the trail. Red Rock Pass lies some 23 miles northwest of Macks Inn, Idaho. Raynolds Pass, at hike's end on Route 287, is 22 miles west of West Yellowstone, Montana.

Finding the trailhead: Red Rock Pass lies 46 miles east of Monida, Montana, and 23 miles northwest of Macks Inn, Idaho, on the Red Rock Pass Road.

Trail description: Follow the jeep road angling north from 7,056-foot Red Rock Pass as it climbs gradually across a sagebrush-covered meadow.

The Henrys Lake Mountains roll northward, their open slopes a sharp contrast to the rugged Centennial Mountains, which loom behind and trail to the west high above the Centennial Valley.

Red Rock Pass to Raynolds Pass

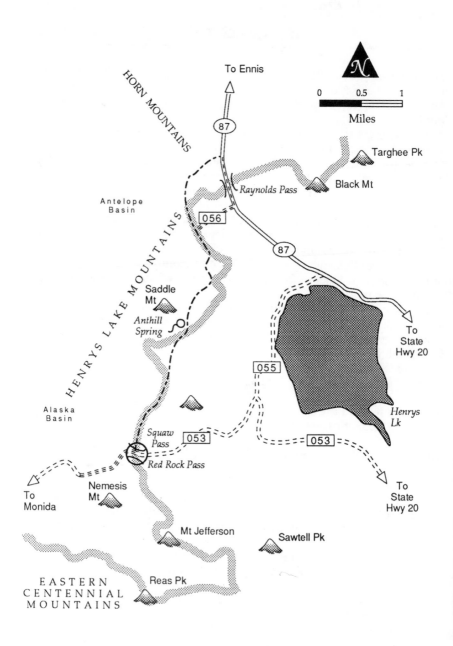

HORN MOUNTAINS

To Ennis

87

N

0   0.5   1

Miles

Targhee Pk

Raynolds Pass

Black Mt

Antelope
Basin

056

87

HENRYS LAKE MOUNTAINS

Saddle
Mt

Anthill
Spring

055

To
State
Hwy 20

Alaska
Basin

Henrys
Lk

Squaw
Pass

053

To
Monida

Nemesis
Mt

Red Rock Pass

053

To
State
Hwy 20

Mt Jefferson

Sawtell Pk

EASTERN
CENTENNIAL
MOUNTAINS

Reas Pk

The Henrys Lake Mountains on the Montana-Idaho border offer some of the most challenging and rewarding hiking on the trail. The rugged Madison Range is constantly in view as the trail climbs to 10,300 feet, the highest point along the 961-mile route.

Stay on the main jeep road as it dips to cross the head of Squaw Pass, 7,262 feet, then continues climbing through meadows grazed heavily by cattle.

The Red Rock Lakes, lying at the base of the Centennials, come into view to the west at about two miles. Saddle Mountain, 8,343 feet, is the triple-spired summit ahead.

The jeep track forks at about three miles near the head of the North Fork of Duck Creek. Bear left on the heavier traveled route and head toward Saddle Mountain.

A spring, livestock watering trough and shallow pond are in a low spot to the right of the road just beyond the intersection.

Cross a cattle guard. Bear right (northeast) at the next intersection and ascend the hill ahead, reaching the divide at four miles. From the top are good views of the Madison Range to the north, and of the Gravelly and Snowcrest ranges to the northwest.

Drop from the crest and descend through open country to Anthill Spring, in the low spot ahead at 4.5 miles.

Good camping is at springside amid a profusion of wildflowers. A jeep track joins from the east here. Head north, still on jeep track, and climb the hill ahead.

Good views from the top reveal the next segment of the Henrys Lake Range,

Red Rock Pass to Raynolds Pass
Elevation Chart

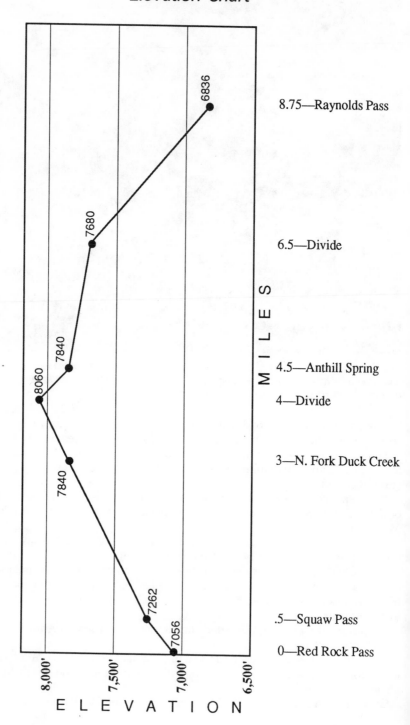

a line of rugged, 10,000-foot peaks rising sharply from Henrys Lake to the northeast. Route 287 winds to the northwest through a broad valley beyond Raynolds Pass, with the Madison Range in the distance.

Stay on the main jeep track as it bends to the northwest and descends gradually into the Poison Creek basin, filled with aspens. Pass another spring and livestock watering trough to the left of the trail along the descent.

The countryside begins losing its wide open character and becomes more tree covered. The track forks at 5.75 miles; bear left and continue circling the head of Poison Creek toward the divide.

Conklin Lake lies below and to the northwest on the fringe of Antelope Basin. The low Horn Mountains are beyond.

The trail descends through a lovely stand of quaking aspens and swings north to begin a gradual climb toward the divide. Near the top of the final ascent, at 6.5 miles, Henrys Lake comes into view to the southeast, with the Henrys Lake Mountains rising steeply from its northern shore.

The trail descends from the high spot into an aspen-filled bowl. Stay on the main jeep track and bear right (northeast) onto the trail's alternate route at the next fork, near the bottom of the descent.

Construction of the preferred route is not complete. It will follow the fainter jeep track that climbs the hill ahead, bypassing Raynolds Pass before reaching the valley floor via Horn Creek.

Ignore the side track that forks to the right just before the alternate trail enters forest and descends. The next track that forks right leads to an unappetizing spring and livestock watering trough, at 7.25 miles.

Stay on the main jeep track as pine forest gives way to more aspens along the final descent to the valley floor. Head north on Route 287, reaching 6,836-foot Raynolds Pass at 8.75 miles.

Raynolds Pass to Lionshead — 19.25 Miles

Introduction: The trail reaches its high point in Montana and Idaho along this stretch of 10,000-foot peaks between Raynolds Pass and Targhee Pass, 9.25 miles west of West Yellowstone, Montana.

Views are spectacular from the 10,280-foot overlook, featuring the Absaroka Range and the plateaus of Yellowstone National Park, Wyoming's Teton and Wind River ranges, and the Centennial, Beaverhead, Lemhi and Madison ranges among the sea of peaks visible.

The divide trends east here, high above Henrys Lake. Water is plentiful and so are sheltered campsites.

Grizzly bears inhabit this wild Lionhead Mountain country, and favor the starkly beautiful Targhee Creek basin at its heart.

The trail is seldom used, and requires some cross-country travel. The climb to the divide from Mile Creek is steep, gaining 3,050 feet in 3.25 miles.

But once on top the hiking is superb, featuring unobstructed views and a basin with a handful of glacial tarns. Later the trail contours along the base of the divide's sheer face before dropping into forest near Targhee Pass, named for Chief Tyghee of the Bannocks.

Chief Joseph and the Nez Perce Indians crossed this pass in 1877 while making their 2,000-mile flight from central Idaho to Canada.

Difficulty level: Very difficult in the first stretch, with some steep, slippery climbs; then moderate as the trail levels.
Scenery: Excellent, with views from the highest point reached on the trail in Montana and Idaho.
Water availability: Good, in spring-fed streams and glacial tarns.
Maps: USFS—Gallatin National Forest (west half). USGS (15 min. series)—Hebgen Dam; (7.5 min. series)—Targhee Peak, Targhee Pass.
Supply points: At hike's end the trail is a half-mile from Montana's Lionshead Ski Resort, on Route 20, with a restaurant, hotel, campground and small grocery store. West Yellowstone, a full-service community, is eight miles beyond.

Finding the trailhead: Raynolds Pass, on Route 287, is 43 miles south of Ennis, Montana, and 22 miles west of West Yellowstone, Montana.

Trail description: Head north on Route 287 from Raynolds Pass across the sagebrush-covered valley floor. Black Mountain, 10,230 feet, rises sharply to the east, the first in a line of 10,000-foot peaks that mark this segment of the Henrys Lake Mountains.

At 3.25 miles bear right (east) on a gravel public access road and head toward the mouth of Little Mile Creek, straight ahead at the base of a peak criss-crossed with mining roads.

Cross Mile Creek in the flat at 4.25 miles, and head southeast along the jeep track above its left bank.

Boulder-hop Little Mile Creek at its junction with Mile Creek and continue upstream, entering the narrow mouth of the Mile Creek canyon at five miles. Sheltered camping is in the trees at streamside.

The jeep track continues climbing above the stream on a bench on the canyon's east side. It soon turns to pack trail that ascends through stands of pine and aspen, overshadowed on both sides by the canyon's steep cliff walls.

A good campsite lies in a small meadow to the right of the stream at 6.75 miles. Another possible campsite is a quarter-mile beyond in a flat area near a rockslide.

The trail peters out where it crosses small meadows at mid-canyon, but is better defined where it passes through stands of trees. At seven miles the path begins a steep climb up the north side of the canyon before leveling out in a meadow at the base of the cliff headwall.

The path peters out here; climb cross-country to the northeast and reach a thick stand of whitebark pines.

Pick up an old pack trail in the trees and continue the climb along switchbacks. The trail later bends to the northwest, crossing two gullies before climbing to a grassy saddle above Little Mile Creek, just east of the 9,536-foot summit shown on the topo map.

The views from the top are impressive; the Madison Range and 11,316-foot Hilgard Peak spread northward beyond Little Mile Creek's steep canyon. Behind, to the south, rocky cliff faces form the headwall of the Mile Creek basin.

Raynolds Pass to Lionshead

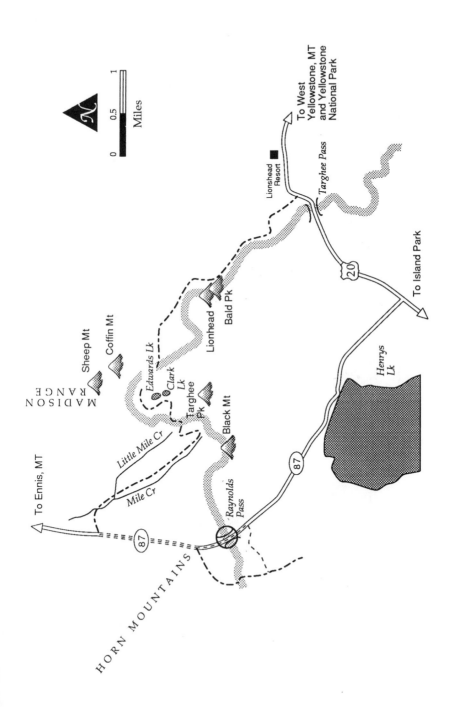

Raynolds Pass to Lionshead
Elevation Chart

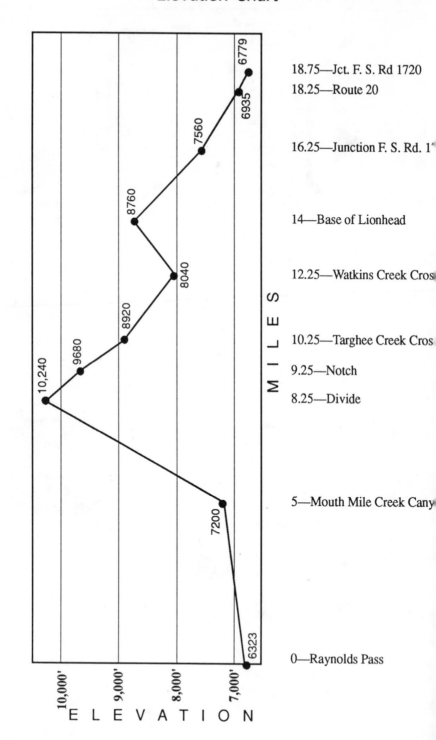

18.75—Jct. F. S. Rd 1720
18.25—Route 20

16.25—Junction F. S. Rd. 1

14—Base of Lionhead

12.25—Watkins Creek Cros

10.25—Targhee Creek Cros
9.25—Notch
8.25—Divide

5—Mouth Mile Creek Cany

0—Raynolds Pass

Alpine lakes and high peaks are main features of the Henrys Lake Mountains on the Montana-Idaho border. The Lionhead, a curious-shaped formation, rises sharply beyond Targhee and Edward lakes on the divide, with Hebgen Lake in the valley below.

Climb east from the saddle and switchback through trees in a cross-country ascent to the open divide, emerging at a notch at 8.25 miles between the 10,388-foot peak to the north and the 10,273-foot summit to the south.

At 10,240 feet reach the highest point attained on the divide in Montana and Idaho; the views are splendid. (See view map).

Head north on the open, rocky crest of the divide along a faint pack trail, circling the headwall of Little Mile Creek. Later the trail swings high above the Targhee Creek basin, to the northeast, with views of tiny Edwards and Tyghee lakes a thousand feet below.

Avoid the spur ridge just to the east and stay on top of the divide, reaching a notch at 9.25, nearly half-way around the basin.

Climb the steep ridge ahead, then follow along the crest as it swings eastward past the head of a steep canyon and drops steadily into the Targhee Creek basin. Sheep Mountain, 10,311 feet, and massive Coffin Mountain, 9,989 feet, are prominent along the descent, with the Madison Range beyond.

The basin is starkly quiet beneath the windy cliffs of the divide and sports a handful of shallow glacial tarns, each a different color.

Head southeast cross-country, passing an unnamed bright green pond and fragile alpine meadows with sweet smelling grasses. An unnamed blue pond at the head of Targhee Creek has running water and better campsites.

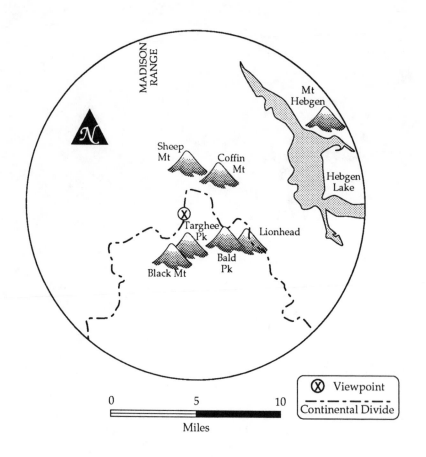

Raynolds Pass to Lionshead View Map

Views from the highest spot on the entire trail extend for 50 miles and more, encompassing ranges as distant as the Beaverhead Mountains, the Tetons and Wyoming's Wind River Range. The rugged Madison Range, dominated by 11,316-foot Hilgard Peak, lies to the north beyond Coffin and Sheep mountains. Hebgen Lake, with Skyline Ridge its backdrop, lies to the northeast. The snow-capped peaks of the Wind River Range jut up on the southeastern horizon over the forested plateau of Yellowstone National Park. Targhee Peak looms close at hand to the south, while Sawtell Peak and all of the Centennial Range and valley trail from southwest to west to Monida and beyond. The Tetons poke through the haze to the distant southwest.

Next reach Edwards Lake, bright blue in its rocky cradle. Here the trail bears east, shooting for the gap across the basin and on the divide just to the left of 10,180-foot Bald Peak.

Cross Targhee Creek at 10.25 miles and climb the hill ahead. Stay to the right of a band of low cliffs as you cross the divide and enter the notch, at the head of Watkins Creek.

Drop and pick up a pack trail in the grassy flat below and follow as it climbs eastward under the gray-streaked cliff faces of Baldy Mountain.

The pack trail peters out in the high meadow, but cross-country travel is easy. Contour eastward below Baldy Mountain's summit, then descend toward the creek in the meadow below, passing a group of springs at its head.

The views here are lovely, with the wildflower-strewn meadow against a backdrop of Hebgen Lake and the Madison Range. There is excellent camping in a stand of whitebark pine at the meadow's edge.

The pack trail becomes well-worn again farther down the left bank of Watkins Creek. Cross the stream on boulders at 12.25 miles just below the turret-like rock formation and curve to the northeast, passing small small meadows and bands of forest.

Climb a tree-covered spur ridge, with good views from the top of Hebgen Lake. Descend, avoiding a jeep track that heads to the left, and continue contouring along the base of the divide as it swings to the east and southeast. Pick up blazes here and there on the trees.

The Lionhead, a 9,574-foot dome of tawny rock, comes into view at 14 miles as the trail emerges into a large meadow with a small pond.

The trail joins the jeep track traversing the meadow and heads southwest, passing just under the Lionhead's maw before continuing to contour to the southeast.

Hiking is pleasant along this stretch below the sheer face of the divide, and the jeep track is followed easily as it dips and rises through meadows and stands of forest.

The eastward view includes some clear-cuts in the foothills below, with the Madison Arm of Hebgen Lake and the town of West Yellowstone in the valley beyond.

Stay on the main jeep track at 16 miles, where a side track forks to the right. Bear left (northeast) at the next fork, and drop to the graveled jeep road below.

Head left and continue descending, soon reaching a barricade and the roadhead for Forest Service Road 1791 at 16.5 miles. Follow the road as it descends through forest, reaching Route 20 just east of Targhee Pass at 18.25 miles.

Head northeast on Route 20, reaching the intersection with Forest Service Road 1720 at 18.75 miles. The Lionshead resort, with a campground, hotel and restaurant, lies a half-mile beyond. West Yellowstone, a full-service community, is eight miles ahead on the busy road.

Lionshead to Black Canyon Road — 16 Miles

Introduction: This mostly wooded segment connects the high peaks of the Henrys Lake Mountains with the forested plateau of Yellowstone National Park.

The trail follows a combination of Forest Service roads, jeep roads, jeep tracks and abandoned railroad grade. Part of the route is along the Two Top National Recreation Trail, popular with all-terrain vehicles in summertime and with snowmobilers in winter.

Clear-cuts are encountered throughout the segment, and afford some views of surrounding peaks. The best panoramas are found in high meadows atop the divide, and include the Centennial Range and majestic Tetons.

Reas Pass, about four miles west of Yellowstone Park, is crossed along an abandoned railroad grade that once bore Union Pacific trains.

Difficulty level: Easy hiking on jeep roads, gravel roads and an abandoned railroad grade.

Scenery: Poor, mostly tree-covered or clear-cut, except for a stunning view of the Tetons.

Water availability: Good, in small streams.

Maps: USFS—Targhee National Forest (east division), Gallatin National Forest (west half); USGS (7.5 min. series)—Targhee Pass; Madison Arm, Reas Pass.

Supply Points: The Lionshead resort, with a small grocery store, is a half-mile northeast of the trailhead on Route 20. West Yellowstone, a full-service town, is eight miles beyond.

Island Park, Idaho, another resort with a good cafe but no grocery, is 8.9 miles from hike's end.

Finding the trailhead: Forest Service Road 1720 is 8.5 miles west of West Yellowstone, Montana, on Route 20, and 20.5 miles north of Island Park, Idaho.

Trail description: Turn right (south) from Route 20 onto Forest Service Road 1720 and begin ascending gradually. Bear left at the first intersection onto the East Fork Denny Creek Road. Stay on the main track where the road forks in a meadow a short distance ahead.

The road ends at .8 mile at a Forest Service gate in a clear-cut area. The trail continues on the jeep road, which is part of the Two Top National Recreation Trail—a snowmobile route marked with orange diamonds.

The trail forks a short distance beyond the gate; continue straight, avoiding the road to the right that climbs toward a clear-cut. Cross the head of Buttermilk Creek, a reliable water source, and pass through another clear-cut area, with flat campsites on the far end.

Stay on the main track and head south where the road forks again. Bear left at the next fork and traverse two clear-cuts.

The jeep road intersects Forest Service Road 1703 at the end of the second clear-cut, at 2.3 miles. Bear right (southwest) and climb gradually along the edge of the clear cut toward the low, tree-covered divide ahead.

Lionshead to Black Canyon Road

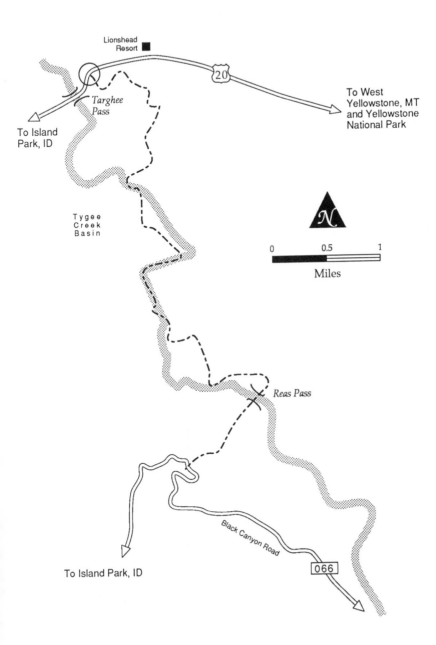

Lionshead Resort

Targhee Pass

To Island Park, ID

20

To West Yellowstone, MT and Yellowstone National Park

Tygee Creek Basin

N

0   0.5   1

Miles

Reas Pass

Black Canyon Road

066

To Island Park, ID

Lionshead to Black Canyon Road
Elevation Chart

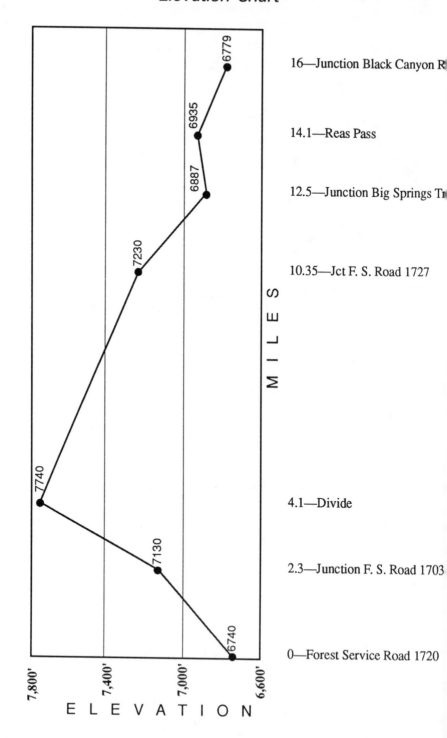

16—Junction Black Canyon R

14.1—Reas Pass

12.5—Junction Big Springs Tr

10.35—Jct F. S. Road 1727

M I L E S

4.1—Divide

2.3—Junction F. S. Road 1703

0—Forest Service Road 1720

7,800'   7,400'   7,000'   6,600'

E L E V A T I O N

There are good views to the west from these clear-cuts of the Lionhead, 9,574 feet, the dome-shaped formation jutting above the cliff face of the divide. To the north lie Hebgen Lake and the Madison Valley.

The jeep road forks at the end of the clear-cut. Follow the diamond-blazed trail to the left, soon passing a culvert with a small creek, a reliable water supply.

Pass through another clear-cut and begin climbing gradually in lodgepole forest. Strike an intersection with Forest Service Road 1703D at the head of the next clear-cut; go straight (south), ignoring the road to the right, and cross another small creek.

The trail levels off on a clear-cut hilltop, offering good views of Hebgen Lake, with Hebgen Ridge and the Madison Range beyond. Cross a small creek at the bottom of the descent into the valley below, and begin a long, gradual climb through several clear-cuts.

The countryside opens up a bit as elevation is gained, and the divide can be seen rolling from the west. West Yellowstone lies in the valley to the east, with the high, tree-covered plateau of Yellowstone National Park beyond.

A jeep road, also marked with orange diamonds, comes in from the left as the trail nears the divide. Bear left and head south through open forest, reaching the open divide at 4.1 miles.

Snowbanks may linger on the divide's northern slopes in this area, which features meadows tinged purple and white with asters and umbrella plants.

A wooden sign astride the divide sports a thermometer and displays a map of the Two Top National Recreation Trail. Head south, following a jeep track marked with orange diamonds.

The views from this high, open country are the best of the segment. Sawtell Peak, 9,866 feet, and the Centennial Range lie across Henrys Flat to the west, while on the southeast jut the impressive snow-streaked peaks of the Tetons.

The trail passes several state line boundary markers on the open ridge above Tyghee Basin before dropping steadily into forest, joining Forest Service Road 1727 in a clear-cut at 10.35 miles.

Forest Service Road 1727 descends gradually through numerous clear-cuts that are in varying stages of regrowth before intersecting the Big Springs Trail at 12.5 miles, near the junction of Forest Service Road 1751.

Bear right (southwest) on the Big Springs Trail and hike through open forest, soon striking an old railroad grade. Turn right and head southwest on level gravel.

Cross tree-covered Reas Pass, 6,935 feet, at 14.1 miles—the last pass on the divide in Montana and Idaho. Stay on the railroad grade to reach the Black Canyon Road at 16 miles.

Turn right (northwest) on Black Canyon Road to reach Island Park, a resort with a good cafe, 8.9 miles away via Forest Service roads 59 and 66.

YELLOWSTONE NATIONAL PARK

Black Canyon Road to Heart Lake Trailhead — 53.5 miles

Introduction: Level, easy walking makes up most of this segment, which begins to the west of Yellowstone National Park and heads east, into the heart of the park's scenic southern half.

Volcanoes erupting over millions of years made Yellowstone National Park what it is today—a wonderland of steam and heat and vivid colors and pungent smells. For beneath much of the earth composing the park's surface is a virtual sea of red-hot magma that fires cool water from the skies to the point where it must boil and sends it bubbling upward to escape through holes and cracks like valves in a pressure cooker.

Geysers, fumaroles, hot springs and paint pots all are nature's way of handling the pressure. No more varied and vibrant example exists than in the Shoshone Geyser Basin, the highlight of the segment. The basin is on the shore of the lovely large lake, once named DeLacy Lake after the gold-seeker who discovered it in 1863. Brown, brook and lake trout all swim in its waters as well as in adjoining Lewis Lake.

The two lakes, connected by the broad Lewis River, are popular with canoeists who must tow their boats upstream to reach Shoshone from Lewis Lake.

Wildlife is abundant, especially on the Moose Creek Plateau above the lakes. Elk, deer and moose all feed in the lush parks beside Moose Creek.

Camping opportunities are many, too, with Shoshone Lake's shores freckled with them and some sites along Moose Creek and on the north side of Lewis Lake.

Much of the trail, especially the first segment, was charred in the 1988 North Fork Fire, one of many that blackened the landscape of Yellowstone in the worst fire season in Montana's history. Some of the fires, lightning-caused, burned without interference as part of the park's emphasis on letting nature take its course. Others, such as the North Fork, were man-caused and firefighters battled them from the start. Nevertheless flames touched an estimated 1.4 million acres in the Greater Yellowstone Area, about 989,000 inside the park's boundaries.

Difficulty level: Easy, with only moderate ups and downs; however, deadfall through badly-burned areas may make the going slow.
Scenery: Poor at first, as the trail follows flat, forested terrain. From the Old Faithful area the geysers and other thermal features for which the park is famous become numerous, and two large, lovely lakes add to the hike's beauty.
Water availability: Poor to Old Faithful, then good as the trail crosses several tiny creeks and larger streams.

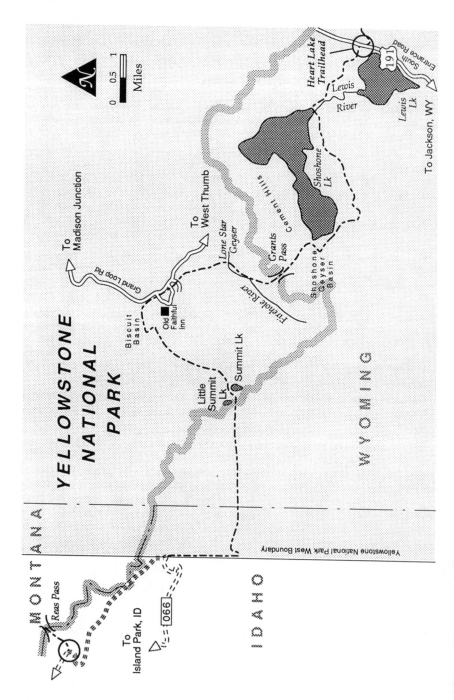

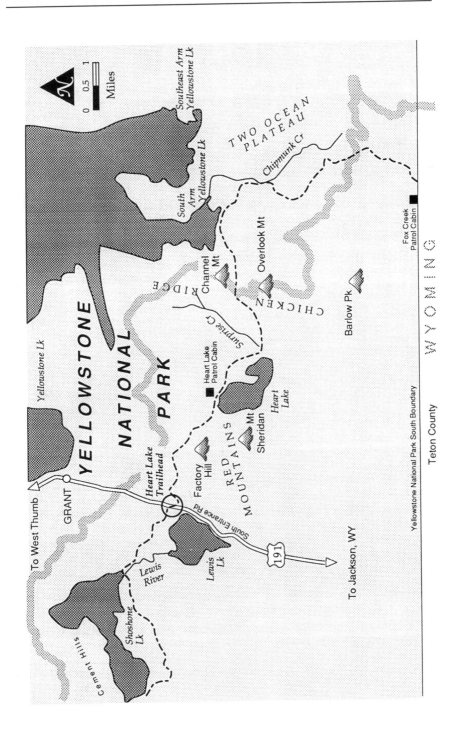

Maps: USGS (30 x 60 min.)—Yellowstone National Park. USGS (15 min. series)—Buffalo Lake, Old Faithful and West Thumb.

Supply Points: Island Park, an Idaho resort community, is 8.9 miles from the trailhead, via Forest Service roads 59 and 66. Mid-way through the hike, at 30 miles, the Old Faithful area offers a full range of services, including lodging, groceries, restaurant fare, developed camping, a post office, first aid and more. At hike's end West Thumb is seven miles to the north along the South Entrance Road, and offers groceries, camping and other amenities.

Finding the trailhead: The trailhead is west of the park in the Targhee National Forest, on Forest Service Road 066 (Black Canyon Loop Road) at Reas Pass Creek, directly southwest of Reas Pass and about eight miles northeast of Macks Inn, Idaho.

Trail description: Follow the driveable road southeast for 10.1 miles (it was blocked off to traffic after about three miles when we tried to drive it in 1989) to the point where it turns to head west. Leave the road and head southeast briefly to the West Boundary Trail, a wide, straight swath where all trees have been cut down. The trail is a utilitarian rather than scenic route where park rangers patrol the border of Yellowstone Park.

Walk south on the path to the intersection with the Summit Lake Trail, 13.6 miles. Follow this trail east on fairly flat terrain to pass a series of large hot spring pools, Smoke Jumper Hot Springs, at 20.8 miles and, at 21.3 miles, Summit Lake, a small lake where camping was not allowed in 1989 due to the burn.

From the lake swing north to head downhill for 6.7 miles, crossing the Firehole River at 28 miles amid the plethora of thermal features that is Biscuit Basin.

The trail turns south here, crossing the Firehole again and reaching the rustic Old Faithful Inn, a hotel/restaurant/general store complex starring the Old Faithful Geyser, at 30 miles. The most famous of the park's geysers, Old Faithful erupts in sparkling, violent sprays up to 160 feet high. A schedule of predicted eruptions is posted inside the hotel lobby.

From the inn, head east on the Grand Loop Road to a small parking area on the right (south). Enter forest here at the Howard Eaton trailhead, soon crossing a small creek on a bridge. The trail parallels the road for a short while, remaining level until it crosses a second creek.

Now ascend gradually for about a mile, following orange markers on trees through forest and blooming lupines and asters. At about 32 miles begin an easy, downhill trek to the intersection, at 32.5 miles, with the Lone Star Geyser trail, which forks to the left. The geyser is just a short walk off the main trail; its eruptions, once every three hours, are small, only 10 to 12 feet high, but last 25 minutes.

The main trail follows the right fork toward Shoshone Lake, passing a campsite and entering forest with occasional bluebells. At 32.9 miles cross the Firehole River in a clearing on a bridge and pass several small fumaroles in pale gray, clay-like earth. The trail becomes forested again to follow the Firehole upstream, ascending gradually.

Pass through marshes, meadows and forest, with the Continental Divide forming a low, tree-covered semi-circle from left to right ahead. At 36 miles

Black Canyon to Heart Lake Trailhead
Elevation Chart

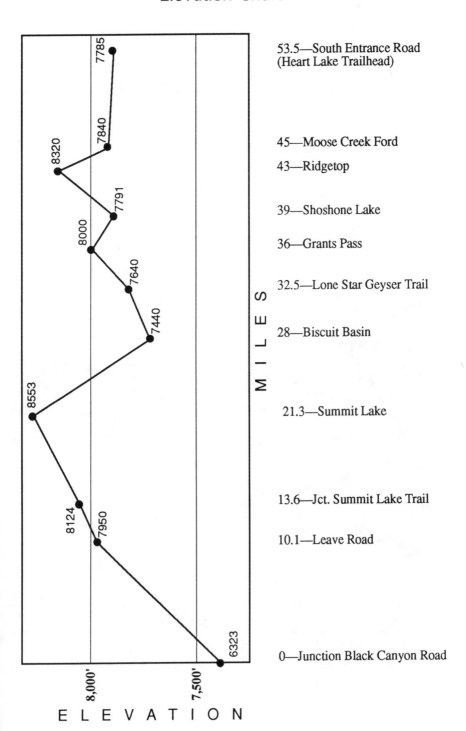

53.5—South Entrance Road
(Heart Lake Trailhead)

45—Moose Creek Ford

43—Ridgetop

39—Shoshone Lake

36—Grants Pass

32.5—Lone Star Geyser Trail

28—Biscuit Basin

21.3—Summit Lake

13.6—Jct. Summit Lake Trail

10.1—Leave Road

0—Junction Black Canyon Road

M I L E S

7785
7840
8320
7791
8000
7640
7440
8553
8124
7950
6323

8,000'
7,500'

E L E V A T I O N

cross Grants Pass on the divide with little effort; at 36.5 miles reach the intersection with the Bechler River Trail.

At the junction, take the left (southeast) fork to follow the Shoshone Lake Trail.

Soon cross small, clear-running Shoshone Creek and pass a sign pointing to the 8G1 campsite. On two subsequent crossings of the creek, note the flora growing in its shallow waters: bright yellow shrubby cinquefoil, water lilies and high grasses.

Follow the creek downstream, passing a junction with a horse trail. This trail bypasses the Shoshone Geyser Basin, which is closed to livestock.

At about 39 miles the trail climbs into the Shoshone Geyser Basin, a moon-like cauldron of steaming fumaroles, hot pots and geysers—including Union Geyser, whose three cones erupt at the same time.

Shortly after entering the basin the trail forks, leading on the left to the warm, thermally-fed shores of Shoshone Lake. The short side trip is a must, for the lake is enormous and brilliant blue. More thermal activity gurgles on its sandy shore, a lovely place for lunch.

Continuing on the main trail, pass through more thermal features as you head to the tree-covered ridge rising above the lake's south shore.

Enter forest at 39.5 miles to pick up the South Shoshone Lake Trail, then emerge briefly to skirt the edge of the lake on its sandy beach at 40 miles.

Bubbling fumaroles, hotpots and geysers lie at trailside in Shoshone Geyser Basin in Yellowstone National Park. Nearby Shoshone Lake is a mecca for wildlife.

Reenter woods to climb, sometimes gradually, sometimes steeply, to the ridge top, reached at about 43 miles.

The trail levels on top of the Moose Creek Plateau as it continues through forest toward Moose Creek, a large stream flowing through open grassy terrain. After a mile-long descent ford the creek at 45 miles, reenter forest and follow signs to the Shoshone Lake outlet.

Ascend and descend through trees, catching glimpses of Shoshone Lake below. After a final, steep plunge reach the lake's confluence with the Lewis River at 48 miles.

Ford the wide, shallow river and head south along its east bank, crossing a marshy area to pick up orange trail markers. Enter woods again, cross small, still Summit Creek on a log, and slink along the river's edge to the head of Lewis Lake, 50.5 miles.

Now the trail turns to the east to round the lake's north shore. Nice views appear of the Red Mountains across the lake to the east, the Pitchstone Plateau on the west and, between them in the distance, the rugged Grand Tetons.

The trail leaves the lake on its northeast shore, passing through meadows and forest to reach the South Entrance Road at 53.5 miles.

Heart Lake Trailhead to South Boundary — 33.1 Miles

Introduction: Large, lush meadows, nice vistas, numerous rushing streams and a geyser basin all add to the beauty of this trek through some seldom-visited areas of Yellowstone Park's south backcountry. But it is the lakes—sweet, thermally-fed Heart and the huge, crystalline South Arm of Yellowstone Lake—that highlight this section.

The South Arm, especially, may offer good fishing and a good chance to spot wildlife feeding in the grassy areas by its sandy south shore. Yellowstone Lake's "arms" actually should be called "fingers," for it was described by early explorers as resembling a hand.

Campsites are numerous around both bodies of water, as well as between them. After leaving the south arm, however, designated sites are more scarce.

Difficulty level: Moderate, with one steep climb to the divide and another steep descent near hike's end.

Scenery: Excellent as the trail passes a geyser basin, pretty Heart Lake in the shadow of rugged Mount Sheridan, and the south shore of the South Arm of huge Yellowstone Lake.

Water availability: Good, with numerous stream crossings throughout.

Maps: USGS (30x60 min. series)—Yellowstone Park, USGS (15 min. series)—West Thumb, Frank Island, Huckleberry Mountain, Mount Hancock.

Supply points: No supply points are convenient to the trail. Seven miles north from the trailhead, on the South Entrance Road, West Thumb has a store, camping facilities, water and restrooms.

Heart Lake Trailhead to South Boundary
Elevation Chart

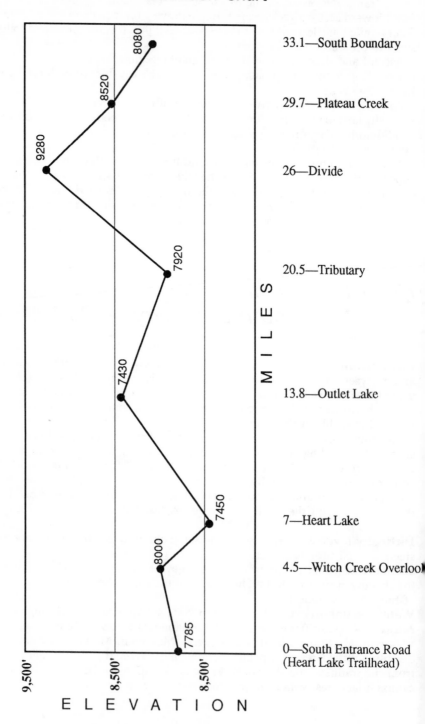

33.1—South Boundary

29.7—Plateau Creek

26—Divide

20.5—Tributary

M I L E S

13.8—Outlet Lake

7—Heart Lake

4.5—Witch Creek Overlook

0—South Entrance Road
(Heart Lake Trailhead)

9,500'   8,500'   8,500'

E L E V A T I O N

Finding the trailhead: The trailhead is on the South Entrance Road's east side, 14 miles north of Yellowstone Park's south entrance.

Trail description: Walk east through forest on fairly level ground until, at 4.5 miles, views open to the southeast of Witch Creek, Heart Lake and the roiling Heart Lake Geyser Basin, all below to the southeast. On the south rise Factory Hill, 9,607 feet, and Mount Sheridan, 10,308, both in the appropriately-named Red Mountain range.

Descend into the Witch Creek basin, dropping 400 feet in one mile to enter the Heart Lake Geyser Basin, a large meadow filled with the cauldron-like thermal features that inspired the creek's name and give its waters a delightfully warm temperature.

At seven miles reach the intersection with the Trail Creek Trail. Just south of this point, on the lake's west shore, Rustic Geyser sends plumes of steaming water shooting into the air every half-hour to 90 minutes.

The recommended route continues east on the Trail Creek Trail to pass the Heart Lake Patrol Cabin and begins rounding the lake on its sandy north shore. Campsites dot the area around the lake.

Soon enter forest and then a meadow, crossing Beaver Creek at 8.5 miles and continue through interspersed forest and parks to the junction, at 11 miles, with the Heart River Cut-Off Trail, heading south. Continue east on the Trail Creek Trail, crossing the confluence of Surprise and Outlet creeks and heading upstream along Outlet Creek's south shore through a narrow, grassy gulch.

Pass tiny Outlet Lake at 13.8 miles and step easily through a low pass on the divide between Channel Mountain, 8,745 feet, on the north, and Overlook Mountain, 9,321 feet, to the south.

From the pass drop slightly to cross Grouse Creek at 16.5 and head northeast toward the south shore of the South Arm of Yellowstone Lake, where Grouse Creek rushes in through a lovely large meadow and Peale Island makes a pretty oasis in a vast expanse of blue water.

Fishing for cutthroat trout is said to be excellent in the lake and its connecting streams.

At 19 miles the trail intersects with the Passage Creek, or Two Ocean Plateau, Trail leading south. This is the route recommended by the Park Service after July 1; before that date, possible bear activity has the recommended route continuing east on the Trail Creek Trail to bend south and join with the South Boundary Trail. Ask park rangers which route you should take.

The recommended summer route turns south at the junction to follow the Passage Creek Trail. Cross a tributary of Chipmunk Creek at 20.5 miles and the confluence of Chipmunk with Passage creeks at 21.2 miles. From here the trail begins ascending through forest toward the divide, reaching it at 26 miles after a final, steep climb to the ridge top.

In the open country this high the trail may be difficult to follow, but trail marker poles help guide the way. Look to the west, across the Snake River valley, for looming Mount Hancock, 10,214 feet and, nearer, 9,622-feet Barlow Peak.

After following the divide south for about a mile the trail drops into the Plateau Creek basin, crossing Plateau Creek at 29.7 miles. Skirt the creek's south bank for another mile to cross again, and reach the junction with the Snake River Trail at the park's south boundary at 33.1 miles.

INFORMATION

Contact the following government agencies for more information on the Continental Divide National Scenic Trail.

GLACIER NATIONAL PARK

Waterton to Swiftcurrent: Glacier National Park, West Glacier, MT, 59936, (406) 888-5441; Waterton Lakes National Park, Waterton Lake, Alberta, Canada, TOK2MO, (403) 859-2224.

Swiftcurrent to Two Medicine Camp: Glacier National Park.

Two Medicine to Marias Pass: Glacier National Park.

BOB MARSHALL WILDERNESS

Marias Pass to Benchmark: Lewis and Clark National Forest, Supervisor's Office, P.O. Box 871, Great Falls, MT, 59403, (406) 791-7700; Rocky Mountain Ranger District, P.O. Box 340, Choteau, MT, 59422, (406) 466-5341.

SCAPEGOAT WILDERNESS

Benchmark to Rogers Pass: Lolo National Forest, Supervisor's Office, Bldg. 24, Fort Missoula, Missoula, MT, 59801, (406) 329-3750; Lewis and Clark National Forest Rocky Mountain Ranger District; Helena National Forest, Supervisor's Office, 301, S. Park, Drawer 10014, Helena, MT, (406) 449-5201; Lincoln Ranger District, P.O. Box 219, Lincoln, MT, 59639, (406) 362-4265.

HELENA TO BUTTE

Roger's Pass to Flesher Pass: Helena National Forest, Lincoln Ranger District.

Flesher Pass to Stemple Pass: Helena National Forest, Lincoln Ranger District.

Stemple Pass to Dana Spring: Helena National Forest, Lincoln, Ranger District.

Dana Spring to Mullan Pass: Helena National Forest, Helena Ranger District, 2001, Poplar St., Helena, MT, 59601, (406) 449-5490.

Mullan Pass to Priest Pass: Helena National Forest, Helena Ranger District.

Priest Pass to MacDonald Pass: Helena National Forest, Helena Ranger District.

MacDonald Pass to I-15: Helena National Forest, Helena Ranger District; Deerlodge National Forest, Supervisor's Office, P.O. Box 400, Butte MT, 59703, (406) 496-3400; Deer Lodge Ranger District, 91 N. Frontage Road, Deer Lodge, MT , 59722, (406) 287-3223; Jefferson Ranger District, P.O. Box F, Whitehall, MT, 59759, (406) 287-3223.

I-15 to Homestake Pass: Deerlodge National Forest, Jefferson Ranger District; Butte Ranger District, 2201 White Blvd, Butte MT, 59701, (406) 494-2147.

Homestake Pass to Deerlodge Pass: Deerlodge National Forest, Jefferson and Butte ranger districts.

Deer Lodge Pass to Lower Seymour Lake: Deerlodge National Forest, Butte Ranger District; Beaverhead National Forest, Supervisor's Office, P.O. Box 1258, Dillon, MT 59725, (406) 683-3973; Wise River Ranger Station, Box 100, Wise River, MT, 59672, (406) 832-3178; Montana Department of Fish, Wildlife and Parks, 1420 E. 6th Ave., Helena, MT, 59620, (406) 444-3750.

ANACONDA-PINTLER WILDERNESS

Lower Seymour Lake to Chief Joseph Pass: Deerlodge National Forest; Philipsburg Ranger District, P.O. Box H, Philipsburg, MT, 59858, (406) 859-3211; Beaverhead National Forest, Wise River Ranger District and Wisdom Ranger District, P.O. Box 238, Wisdom, MT, 59671, (406) 689-3243; Bitterroot National Forest, Supervisor's Office, 316 N. Third St., Hamilton, MT, 59840, (406) 363-3131; Sula Ranger District, Sula, MT, 59871, (406) 821-3201.

THE SOUTHERN BITTERROOTS

Chief Joseph Pass to Big Hole Pass: Salmon National Forest, Supervisor's Office, P.O. Box 729, North Fork, ID, 83467, (208) 756-2215; North Fork Ranger District, P.O. Box 780, North Fork, ID, 83466, (208) 865-2383; Beaverhead National Forest, Wisdom Ranger District.

Big Hole Pass to Goldstone Pass: Salmon National Forest, North Fork Ranger District; Beaverhead National Forest, Wisdom Ranger District.

Goldstone Pass to Lemhi Pass: Salmon National Forest, Leadore Ranger District, P.O. Box 180, Leadore, ID, 83464, (208) 768-2371; Beaverhead National Forest, Dillon Ranger District, P.O. Box 1258, Dillon, MT, 59725, (406) 832-3960.

THE BEAVERHEAD RANGE

Lemhi Pass to Bannock Pass: Salmon National Forest, Leadore Ranger District; Beaverhead National Forest, Dillon Ranger District; Bureau of Land Management, Butte District Office, P.O. Box 3388, Butte, MT, 59702, (406) 494-5059; Bureau of Land Management, Salmon District Office, P.O. Box 430, Salmon, ID, 83467, (208) 756-5401.

Bannock Pass to Medicine Lodge Pass: Targhee National Forest, Supervisor's Office, P.O. Box 208, St. Anthony, ID, 83445, (208) 624-3151; Dubois Ranger District, Dubois, ID, 83423, (208) 374-5422; Beaverhead National Forest, Dillon Ranger District.

Medicine Lodge Pass to Monida Pass: Beaverhead National Forest, Dillon Ranger District; Targhee National Forest, Dubois Ranger District.

CENTENNIAL MOUNTAINS

Monida Pass to Red Rock Pass: Beaverhead National Forest, Dillon Ranger District; Bureau of Land Management, Butte District Office; Agricultural Research Service, Sheep Experiment Station, Dubois, ID, 83423, (208) 374-5306.

HENRYS LAKE MOUNTAINS

Red Rock Pass to Raynolds Pass: Targhee National Forest, Island Park Ranger District, Island Park, ID, 83429, (208) 588-7301; Beaverhead National Forest, Madison Ranger District, 5 Forest Service Road, Ennis, MT 59729, (406) 682-4253.

Raynolds Pass to Lionshead: Targhee National Forest, Island Park Ranger District; Beaverhead National Forest, Dillon Ranger Station.

Lionshead to Black Canyon Road: Targhee National Forest, Island Park Ranger District; Gallatin National Forest, Supervisor's Office, P.O. Box 130, Federal Bldg., Bozeman, MT, 59771, (406) 646-7369; Hebgen Lake Ranger District, P.O. Box 520, West Yellowstone, MT, 59758, (406) 646-7369.

YELLOWSTONE NATIONAL PARK

Black Canyon Road to Heart Lake Trailhead: Yellowstone National Park, P.O. Box 168, Yellowstone Park, WY, 82190, (307) 344-7381; Targhee National Forest, Island Park Ranger District, Gallatin National Forest, Hebgen Lake Ranger District.

Heart Lake Trailhead to South Boundary: Yellowstone National Park.

BIBLIOGRAPHY

Alt, Dave, and Curt W. Buchholtz, Bert Gildart, and Bob Frauson, *Glacier Country: Montana's Glacier National Park*. Montana Magazine Inc., Helena, Mont., 1983.

Alt, David, and Donald W. Hyndman. *Roadside Geology of Montana*. Mountain Press Publishing Co., Missoula, Mont., 1986.

Bach, Orville E. Jr. *Hiking the Yellowstone Backcountry*. Sierra Club Books, San Francisco, 1973.

Cheney, Roberta C. *Names on the Face of Montana*. Mountain Press Publishing Co., Missoula, Mont., 1983.

Craighead, John J. and Frank C. Jr., and Ray J. Davis. *Rocky Mountain Wildflowers*. Houghton Mifflin Co., Boston, 1963.

Cunningham, Bill. *Montana's Continental Divide*. Montana Magazine Inc., Helena, Mont., 1986

DeVoto, B., ed. *Journals of Lewis and Clark*. Houghton Mifflin, Boston, 1953.

Meyer, Kathleen. *How to Shit in the Woods: An Environmentally Sound Approach to a Lost Art*. Ten Speed Press, Berkeley, Calif., 1989.

Nelson, Dick and Sharon. *Hiker's Guide to Glacier National Park*. Glacier National History Assoc., West Glacier, Mont., 1978.

Schneider, Bill. *The Hiker's Guide to Montana*. Falcon Press Publishing Co., Helena, Mont., 1990.

Spellenberg, Richard. *The Audubon Society Field Guide to North American Wildflowers*. Alfred A. Knopf, New York, 1979.

Wolf, James R. *Guide to the Continental Divide Trail, Vol. 1: Northern Montana*. Mountain Press Publishing Co., Missoula, Mont., 1976.

Wolf, James R. *Guide to the Continental Divide Trail, Vol. 2: Southern Montana and Idaho*. Continental Divide Trail Society, Washington, D.C., 1979.

9375